T
ASTROLOGICAL
TAROT

THE ASTROLOGICAL TAROT

GEORGES MUCHERY

SENATE

The Astrological Tarot

First published by Rider & Company, London

This edition published in 1994 by Senate, an imprint of
Studio Editions Ltd, Princess House, 50 Eastcastle Street,
London W1N 7AP, England

ISBN 1 85958 004 1

Printed and bound in Guernsey by
The Guernsey Press Co Ltd

Summary

Foreword

"To deny the power and influence of the Stars is to deny the wisdom and providence of God."

TYCHO-BRAHE.

WE are under the influence of the stars. Many people are sure of it. If you, Reader, deny their power on each one of us, who is a microcosm in the macrocosm, we will endeavour to convince you.

Why is it that on dull days, when the Sun does not shine, you are depressed?

Will you deny the influence of the Sun upon the human body?

Does the influence of the Moon count for nought in the phenomenon of the tides? Does it count for nothing in women's menses?

How is it that in the Maternity wards in hospitals, the midwives notice that at the periods of the Moon's changes births become more numerous?

Why is it that our personalities are so different?

It is because each one of us has been influenced in a different way at the moment of birth by the state of the Heavens.

All this is mere fancy, you think, and to be born under a "lucky" or "unlucky" star makes no difference to the course of one's life.

Nevertheless, Napoleon believed in his *star*. Like him, if we draw up his horoscope, we can see it alternately clear, bright and dazzling, and then become pale and dim.

Astronomy and Astrology should go hand in hand, in spite of the astronomers, who took so long to recognise the influence of the Moon. Both are Sciences; one is mathematical, the other empirical.

The sceptical reader will say that if Astrology were a science, it ought to predict *unerringly* at birth everything that will happen afterwards, and it cannot do this!

Admittedly, *it cannot do this,*—not exactly, at any rate—for this reason:

The stars which astronomy has not yet catalogued are numerous. When these have been found, astrology, the *empirical science,* will discover their influence. When astronomy becomes as exact a science as geometry, when it no longer rests on hypotheses as is still the case at the present time, then astrology will become all-powerful. That is why we say that these two sciences must go hand in hand.

Astronomy sneers at astrology, but neither is more infallible than the other. Expert astronomers have been, and are, at variance in their conclusions. Some astrological deductions are quite as plausible as certain astronomical discourses.

You say: "The astronomer is a scientist; but the astrologer is a quack!" That is often the case, but not always. Kepler, Newton and many others were astrologers.

No, these two sciences should not be separated, any more than we separate anatomy from medicine; the one completes the other.

Again, you may say, "For two thousand years astrology has made no progress." We will go further, and say that we are less advanced.

There are some also who say that the whole system of astrology is based on a false idea—the fixity of our globe. The Earth, whether fixed or mobile, is always subject to the same influences, in the same way as a photographic plate is similarly influenced, whether we take the picture of a train on the move from a station, or the picture of a station from a train which is in motion.

The influence of the stars is not modified because the Earth is considered as fixed in the methods of astrology, inasmuch as astrologers study the angles and the aspects which the planets form between each other.

You also point out that the ancients were only acquainted with seven planets: Saturn, Jupiter, Mars, the Sun, Venus, Mercury and the Moon.

When astronomers discovered Uranus and Neptune through their telescopes they attacked astrology in order to show how false were its foundations.

These two planets certainly influence us, but very slightly. They probably form part of another system of seven planets, which astrology is waiting the pleasure of astronomy to discover.

Paracelsus has also said: "Many stars have not yet cast their influence, that is why there are many arts and sciences yet to be discovered."

Nevertheless, it may be stated emphatically that an astrologer who has studied astronomy can erect an almost perfect astrological horoscope.

According to the state of the Heavens at the moment of his birth, a child will possess certain aptitudes, a certain destiny; his luck in life (will you deny that luck exists?) will be influenced by the stars. Again, you may object: two children, born at the same moment, in the same house, will have exactly similar horoscopes, yet each will tend in very *different* directions. Astrology is therefore mythical.

No!

Any influence is received according to the condition of the person who is subjectea to it.

It is quite evident that a not over-conscientious astrologer will treat both charts in the same way.

At birth, both children possess the same mental and physical worth, in the same way that they both experience the same amount of fortunate and unfortunate events, the stars having influenced them both under the same conditions.

Twenty years later, they are different, or rather, they *appear* different.

One is wealthy, learned, well-educated.

The other is poor, ignorant, uncouth.

The birth charts could not show these differences at first sight; that is why it is necessary to know the science thoroughly before setting up a horoscope. The formula of *atavism* enters into the question. An astrologer should never form a judgment before knowing the social status of the child, and its sex. Moreover, he should work out the chart of the father and that of the mother at the hour of birth.

The destiny of a child necessarily varies according to the influences which surround him. His own will-power being almost nil, he is subject for a fairly lengthy period to the limitations imposed upon him by his parents.

In cheiromancy, atavism is shown in the hand, and without knowing the social status of a person, one sees whether he (or she) was born wealthy. (The line of Saturn and the line of Life are clearly separated at the base of the hand, and the lines of the Sun start very early.)

In order to be a good astrologer, it is necessary to know how to make an accurate judgment.

To calculate the chart of the Heavens at the hour of birth is to put the problem on an equation, and this, if carried out by twenty astrologers, should give the same result.

To study the aspects of the planets between each other is the reduction of the equation.

It only remains to find the solution, which must lead *unerringly* to the definition of the character and destiny of the subject whom the astrologer is studying. It is now no longer a question of mathematics: the Science becomes an Art: the Art of Interpretation. It is seldom treated in this way, because, unfortunately for astrology, many so-called astrologers take advantage of public credulity. To a problem set before students, the proficient ones will find the correct solution, while the novice will be wrong.

Astrology is a very difficult, but a very interesting science, which requires studying in order to make use of it in the service of mankind.

You should not deny astrology because one astrologer has talked nonsense, any more than you deny medicine because one doctor makes a mistake in diagnosis.

Both are empirical sciences which should only be studied by competent people.

The incompetent in the first case merely make one smile, in the latter, they slay!

G. M.

Introduction

THE Zodiac is the belt of the Heavens which is divided into twelve equal parts by great perpendicular circles at the ecliptic (an imaginary line crossing the Zodiac at its centre throughout its entire length, and closely followed by the Sun in its course through the twelve signs every year).

These two great parallel circles are separated by a distance of 9° and the arcs of great circles which divide this zone are 0° distant. The first crosses the equinoxial point of Spring of the current year.

While the Sun follows the ecliptic closely, the other planets deviate to the left or right of it, and this constitutes their latitude North or South.

The ecliptic is divided into 360°, the starting-point of which is at Aries.

The following is the order of the signs with their respective degrees:

0° Aries, 30° Taurus, 60° Gemini, 90° Cancer, 120° Leo, 150° Virgo, 180° Libra, 210° Scorpio, 240° Sagittarius, 270° Capricornus, 300° Aquarius, 330° Pisces.

The sphere of the Heavens is divided into two hemispheres: Northern and Southern by the horizon, and into two parts by the meridian, the one eastern or ascending, the other western or descending.

These four parts or quarters formed by the intersection of the horizon and of the meridian, are divided in turn into three equal parts. We thus obtain the twelve Houses on which the twelve signs of the Zodiac mark the commencement or cusp of each one, according to the hour, day, year and latitude of the place of birth.

There are nine planets (the Sun and Moon are reckoned as planets in astrology), and they are situated in one or the other of the signs of the Zodiac.

The Signs of the Zodiac, of the Planets and of the Aspects

Signs of the Zodiac

0°	♈	Aries	Northern Signs
30°	♉	Taurus	
60°	♊	Gemini	
90°	♋	Cancer	
120°	♌	Leo	
150°	♍	Virgo	
180°	♎	Libra	Southern Signs
210°	♏	Scorpio	
240°	♐	Sagittarius	
270°	♑	Capricornus	
300°	♒	Aquarius	
330°	♓	Pisces	

Element	Movable or Cardinal Signs		Fixed Signs		Common or Mutable Signs		Qualities
	Houses	Signs	Houses	Signs	Houses	Signs	
+ Fire	I	♈ Aries	V	♌ Leo	IX	♐ Sagittarius	Hot and Dry Diurnal
— Water	IV	♋ Cancer	VIII	♏ Scorpio	XII	♓ Pisces	Hot and Moist Nocturnal
+ Air	VII	♎ Libra	XI	♒ Aquarius	III	♊ Gemini	Cold and Dry Diurnal
— Earth	X	♑ Capricornus	II	♉ Taurus	VI	♍ Virgo	Cold and Moist Nocturnal

Fruitful Signs (Watery) (Mutable)	Cancer	♋
	Scorpio	♏
	Pisces	♓
Barren Signs (Beauty)	Gemini	♊
	Leo	♌
	Virgo	♍
Double Signs	♊ Gemini	
	♐ Sagittarius	
	♓ Pisces	
Deformed Signs	♉ Taurus	
	♋ Cancer	
	♑ Capricorn	

PLANETS

☉ The Sun is convertible, that is to say benefic or malefic according to the aspects.
☽ The Moon is convertible.
☿ Mercury is convertible.
♀ Venus is benefic, and is called the Lesser Fortune.
♂ Mars is malefic.
♃ Jupiter is benefic, and is called the Greater Fortune.
♄ Saturn is malefic.
♅ Uranus or Herschel is malefic.
♆ Neptune is convertible.
☊ The Moon's Ascending Node (Dragon's Head) is benefic.
☋ The Moon's Descending Node (Dragon's Tail) is malefic.
⊕ The Part of Fortune is convertible.

THE ASPECTS

☌	Conjunction	0°	Good or bad
⚺	Semi-sextile	30°	Fairly good
∠	Semi-square	45°	Bad
⚹	Sextile	60°	Good
□	Square	90°	Very bad
△	Trine	120°	Very good
⚼	Sesqui-quadrate	135°	Bad
⚻	Quincunx	150°	Good or bad
☍	Opposition	180°	Bad

The Parallel of declination or antisce : this occurs when two or more planets are at equal distance from the Equator. This aspect is equal to a conjunction.

DIGNITIES OF THE PLANETS

Planets	Domicile	Joy	Exaltation	Accidental Dignity
☉ Sun	♌ Leo	♌ Leo	♈ Aries	1°. Any planet situated in an angular House, viz. in I, IV, VII, IX.
☽ Moon	♋ Cancer	♋ Cancer	♉ Taurus	
♀ Venus	♎ Libra and ♉ Taurus	♉ Taurus	♓ Pisces	2°. Any planet to the East of the Sun, if the said planet be Saturn, Uranus, Jupiter, Mars or Neptune.
☿ Mercury	♊ Gemini and ♍ Virgo	♍ Virgo	♍ Virgo	
♃ Jupiter	♐ Sagittarius and ♓ Pisces	♐ Sagittarius	♋ Cancer	3°. Any planet to the West of the Sun if this planet be Mercury or Venus.
♂ Mars	♈ Aries and ♏ Scorpio	♏ Scorpio	♑ Capricorn	4°. Any planet that is not retrograde on the date of birth.
♄ Saturn	♒ Aquarius and ♑ Capricorn	♑ Capricorn	♎ Libra	
♅ Uranus	♒ Aquarius	♒ Aquarius	♏ Scorpio	5°. Any planet in reception, viz. situated in the domicile of a benefic planet, which is itself in the domicile of the planet which is being studied.
♆ Neptune	♓ Pisces	♓ Pisces	♋ Cancer	

If we establish a numerical value to mark the power of the dignities, we will give to the Domicile (five), to the Joy (four), to the Exaltation (three), and to the Accidental Dignities (two).

DEBILITIES OF THE PLANETS

Planets	Fall	Exile	Accidental Debilities
☉ Sun	♎ Libra	♒ Aquarius	1°. Any planet situated in House VI, VIII and XII.
☽ Moon	♓ Pisces	♑ Capricorn	
♀ Venus	♍ Virgo	♏ Scorpio and ♈ Aries	2°. Any planet to the West of the Sun if the said planet be Saturn, Uranus, Jupiter, Mars or Neptune.
☿ Mercury	♓ Pisces	♐ Sagittarius	3°. Any planet to the East of the Sun, if the said planet be Venus or Mercury.
♂ Mars	♋ Cancer	♎ Libra and ♉ Taurus	
♃ Jupiter	♑ Capricorn	♍ Virgo and ♊ Gemini	4°. Any planet that is retrograde on the date of birth.
♄ Saturn	♈ Aries	♋ Cancer and ♌ Leo	5°. Any planet situated in a sign in which it has no dignity.
♅ Uranus	♌ Leo	♉ Taurus	
♆ Neptune	♍ Virgo	♑ Capricorn	6°. Any planet that has no aspect.

If we set a numerical value to mark the power of the debilities, we will give to the Fall (three), to the Exile (two), and to the Accidental Debilities (one).

The Houses

First House

THIS is the eastern angle. It is the starting-point for everything that follows. It is the life, the physical constitution, as well as the moral possibilities of the subject, or of the question asked. In an interpretation, the cards which are situated in the Ascendant will always show the sense of the question, and will therefore have to be studied specially in order to ascertain whether what is being asked contains any vital possibilities. We can also see here whether the thoughts of the person pertain to sentimental, material, moral or pecuniary matters. We will be able to depict the character of the native by the Zodiacal sign which is found therein, and also by the planets situated therein, and the aspects they may receive.

Second House

This is the House of work, of personal worth, of acquired possessions, of riches. We will study it in regard to a marriage of convenience, and we will see the chances which the subject might meet in respect of material progress.

Third House

This House shows all that pertains to brothers, sisters, relatives, neighbours; in short, to all those with whom we are on terms of affection, but who do not live in our own home. We will also study this House in regard to letters to be received or sent out, as well as in regard to short journeys. This House describes the education of the native, and the outside influences which he may receive.

Fourth House

The Fourth House is very important. It is the Nocturnal Angle, the Nadir of the Heavens. We must study it in regard to the parents (the Father and the Mother), and also those who live in the home. This House represents the home, residence or place of birth. It also denotes the inheritance and all the house property of the native.

We will also consider this House in regard to the heredity bequeathed by ancestors, and especially as to what concerns material and physical matters.

Fifth House

The Fifth House deals with pleasures, love affairs, and also the lower passions. It represents places of amusement, clubs, theatres, the Stock Exchange, the bedroom; the pleasures experienced by the native, and the kind of pleasures. This House must be studied particularly for all that concerns the children.

Sixth House

This House is the Purgatory of the Zodiac, and denotes above all the health of the subject (or of the question). It concerns illnesses. We also associate it with the idea of matters relating to inferiors: servants or employees. We may also study it in regard to uncles and aunts.

Seventh House

This is the House of Love and Partnerships. It concerns women, marriage, contracts, and consequently lawsuits. We will also study it for all that concerns the Grandparents. It is a very important House, and is the Western Angle.

Eighth House

We consider this as the House of Death. In its interpretation it does not necessarily mean physical death. It also marks the end of an event, of a thing, or of a person. It is connected with inheritances and legacies.

Ninth House

This is the House of Divination. It concerns the mentality of the consultant, his moral tendencies, his religious beliefs, his philosophy. It is related to the Second House and the Eleventh House to guide us as to the position or profession of the subject. It must also be studied for all that concerns lawsuits, discussions, controversies, as well as sisters- and brothers-in-law.

It also concerns long journeys and the *imagination* of the subject.

In short, it denotes the present mental state of the native or of the question asked.

Tenth House

This is the Mid-Heaven, and is a very important House. It concerns things generally, the worldly position, employment, honours, success ; it is the zenith of the question, its apogee.

Eleventh House

This is the House of friends, protectors, associates. It denotes social relations, and we must therefore also study it in order to ascertain the social status and the position of the native. It shows the mother's position.

As in the case of the Fifth House, it also concerns all that pertains to the children.

Twelfth House

This is the Hell of the Zodiac. It concerns enemies, trials, troubles, chronic diseases, prison, hospitals, infirmities.

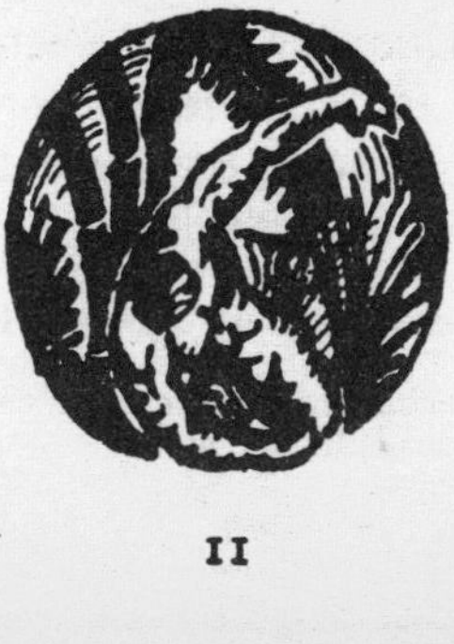

How to Work Out the Chart of the Heavens

Example

A BOY born on the 27th of July, 1927 at 3.40 p.m. *Sun-time* (that is 4.40 Summer-time by the clock) at Quimper, France.[1]

Taking Raphael's Ephemeris for 1927 for the month of July, we find that on the 27th at noon the Sidereal Time was 8 h. 16 m. 41 s.

Birth having taken place at 3.40 p.m., we must add this time, plus a *correction* of 9 seconds 86 (in practice it is sufficient to take 10 seconds) per hour, corresponding with the difference between Mean or clock time and Sidereal Time.

Thus, for 3 hours 40 minutes, 30 seconds plus, $\frac{40 \times 10}{60}$. 36 seconds 66. The Sidereal Time at birth at Greenwich will then be obtained by the addition of the Sidereal Time at Noon and that of the time elapsed between Noon and the hours of birth, plus the correction. This gives us:

8 h. 16 m. 41 s. plus 3 h. 40 m. plus 36 s., or 11 h. 57 m. 17 s. which is the time for Greenwich. For any other place the correction of the hour, according to the longitude, will have to be made.

The longitude of Quimper being 4° 15′, we convert this at the rate of 4 minutes for each degree and 4 seconds for each minute of longitude. Thus, in the present case, 0 h. 17 m. the correction of which is (9 seconds 86 per hour), about 3 seconds,

[1] (The student must never forget to calculate the *real* Sun-time at birth, and *not* the clock-time at the place of birth during the Summer months, and as the dates of beginning and ending of Summer-time vary in every country, these must be ascertained before calculating the horoscope.)

D M	Neptune. Lat.	Neptune. Dec.	Herschel. Lat.	Herschel. Dec.	Saturn. Lat.	Saturn. Dec.	Jupiter. Lat.	Jupiter. Dec.	Mars. Lat.	Mars. Declin.	Mars. Declin.
	° ′	° ′	° ′	° ′	° ′	° ′	° ′	° ′	° ′	° ′	° ′
1	0N28	13N37	0S45	0N40	2N 0	18S36	1S18	0S 7	1N14	17N27	17N16
3	0 28	13 37	0 45	0 40	2 0	18 35	1 18	0 5	1 14	17 4	16 53
5	0 28	13 36	0 45	0 40	2 0	18 34	1 19	0 2	1 13	16 41	16 30
7	0 28	13 35	0 45	0 40	1 59	18 34	1 19	0N 0	1 12	16 18	16 6
9	0 28	13 33	0 45	0 40	1 59	18 33	1 20	0 2	1 12	15 54	15 41
11	0 28	13 32	0 45	0 40	1 58	18 33	1 21	0 4	1 11	15 29	15 17
13	0 28	13 31	0 45	0 40	1 58	18 32	1 21	0 5	1 10	15 4	14 52
15	0 28	13 29	0 45	0 40	1 57	18 32	1 22	0 6	1 9	14 39	14 26
17	0 28	13 28	0 45	0 39	1 57	18 31	1 22	0 6	1 9	14 14	14 1
19	0 28	13 26	0 45	0 39	1 57	18 31	1 23	0 7	1 8	13 48	13 35
21	0 28	13 25	0 45	0 39	1 56	18 31	1 24	0 7	1 7	13 21	13 8
23	0 28	13 24	0 45	0 38	1 56	18 31	1 24	0 7	1 6	12 55	12 41
25	0 28	13 23	0 45	0 38	1 55	18 31	1 25	0 6	1 6	12 28	12 14
27	0 28	13 22	0 46	0 37	1 55	18 31	1 25	0 5	1 5	12 0	11 47
29	0 28	13 20	0 46	0 36	1 54	18 31	1 26	0 4	1 4	11 33	11 19
31	0 28	13 19	0 46	0 35	1 54	18 31	1 27	0 3	1 3	11 5	

D M	D W	Sidereal Time.	☉ Long.	☉ Dec.	☽ Long.	☽ Lat.	☽ Dec.	MIDNIGHT. ☽ Long.	MIDNIGHT. ☽ Dec.
		H. M. S.	° ′ ″	° ′	° ′ ″	° ′	° ′	° ′ ″	° ′
1	F	6 34 10	8♋38 59	23N10	6♌ 3 24	3N16	21N55	12♌28 43	20N37
2	S	6 38 7	9 36 13	23 6	18 49 37	4 6	19 4	25 6 15	17 20
3	S	6 42 3	10 33 26	23 2	1♍18 55	4 43	15 25	7♍27 56	13 21
4	M	6 46 0	11 30 38	22 57	13 33 40	5 6	11 10	19 36 33	8 54
5	Tu	6 49 57	12 27 51	22 52	25 37 5	5 15	6 34	1♎35 45	4 11
6	W	6 53 53	13 25 3	22 46	7♎33 8	5 11	1 46	13 29 46	0S40
7	Th	6 57 50	14 22 15	22 40	19 26 14	4 54	3S 5	25 23 8	5 28
8	F	7 1 46	15 19 27	22 34	1♏21 2	4 23	7 50	7♏20 32	10 7
9	S	7 5 43	16 16 39	22 27	13 22 10	3 41	12 20	19 26 28	14 27
10	S	7 9 39	17 13 51	22 20	25 33 57	2 49	16 26	1♐45 4	18 15
11	M	7 13 36	18 11 2	22 13	8♐ 0 13	1 47	19 53	14 19 45	21 18
12	Tu	7 17 32	19 8 14	22 5	20 43 56	0 39	22 28	27 12 58	23 21
13	W	7 21 29	20 5 26	21 57	3♑46 56	0S32	23 56	10♑25 53	24 11
14	Th	7 25 26	21 2 38	21 48	17 9 43	1 44	24 4	23 58 14	23 36
15	F	7 29 22	21 59 50	21 39	0♒51 11	2 51	22 46	7♒48 12	21 34
16	S	7 33 19	22 57 3	21 30	14 48 50	3 50	20 3	21 52 34	18 13
17	S	7 37 15	23 54 16	21 20	28 58 52	4 35	16 7	6♓ 7 7	13 47
18	M	7 41 12	24 51 30	21 10	13♓16 44	5 8	11 14	20 27 9	8 32
19	Tu	7 45 8	25 48 44	20 59	27 37 47	5 13	5 44	4♈48 7	2 50
20	W	7 49 5	26 45 59	20 49	11♈57 42	5 3	0N 5	19 6 8	2N59
21	Th	7 53 1	27 43 15	20 38	26 13 4	4 35	5 51	3♉18 14	8 38
22	F	7 56 58	28 40 32	20 26	10♉21 22	3 50	11 17	17 22 20	13 47
23	S	8 0 55	29 37 50	20 14	24 20 58	2 52	16 5	1♊17 9	18 10
24	S	8 4 51	0♌35 8	20 2	8♊10 46	1 44	19 58	15 1 46	21 29
25	M	8 8 48	1 32 28	19 49	21 50 1	0 32	22 40	28 35 27	23 32
26	Tu	8 12 44	2 29 48	19 37	5♋17 58	0N42	24 2	11♋57 28	24 12
27	W	8 16 41	3 27 9	19 23	18 33 52	1 52	24 0	25 7 2	23 29
28	Th	8 20 37	4 24 31	19 10	1♌36 55	2 54	22 38	8♌ 3 26	21 31
29	F	8 24 34	5 21 54	18 56	14 26 32	3 47	20 7	20 46 14	18 30
30	S	8 28 30	6 19 18	18 42	27 2 33	4 27	16 41	3♍15 33	14 42
31	S	8 32 27	7 16 42	18 28	9♍25 23	4 54	12 35	15 32 15	10 21

D M	Venus Lat. ° ′	Venus Declin. ° ′	Venus Declin. ° ′	Mercury Lat. ° ′	Mercury Declin. ° ′	Mercury Declin. ° ′	☽ Node. ° ′
1	1N17	14N43	14N19	1 S20	18N35	18N16	27♊22
3	1 8	13 55	13 32	1 50	17 58	17 40	27 16
5	0 58	13 7	12 43	2 21	17 24	17 8	27 9
7	0 48	12 19	11 54	2 51	16 54	16 41	27 3
9	0 36	11 29	11 5	3 21	16 30	16 20	26 57
11	0 24	10 40	10 15	3 48	16 11	16 4	26 50
13	0 12	9 50	9 25	4 12	15 58	15 55	26 44
15	0S 2	9 0	8 35	4 32	15 53	15 52	26 38
17	0 16	8 10	7 45	4 47	15 53	15 56	26 31
19	0 30	7 20	6 55	4 55	16 0	16 6	26 25
21	0 46	6 30	6 6	4 57	16 13	16 22	26 18
23	1 2	5 41	5 17	4 52	16 31	16 42	26 12
25	1 19	4 52	4 28	4 40	16 53	17 5	26 6
27	1 37	4 4	3 40	4 22	17 18	17 31	25 59
29	1 56	3 17	2 53	4 0	17 44	17 57	25 53
31	2 15	2 30		3 33	18 11		25 47

Mutual Aspects.

1. ☿ P ♄.
2. ☉∠♆. ♀☌♆.
3. ☉⊥♂. ☿△♄.
4. ♀P♆, ±♅ & ♃.
5. ♂⚼♃.
6. ♂⚼♅.
9. ☉⚼♄. ☿⚺♀. ♀□♄.
10. ☿△♄.
11. ♀∇♅ & ♃.
12. ☉⊥♆.
13. ☉∠♀.
14. ☿⊥♀.
15. ♃☌♅.
18. ♂☌♆.
19. ☉⚺♆, ☌☿. ☿⚺♂.
20. ☿⚺♆, ∠♀.
21. ☉⚺♂. ♂P♆, ±♅ & ♃.
24. ☿⊥♂.
25. ☉△♄.
27. ☉△♅ & ♃. ♂□♄.
30. ♂∇♅ & ♃.
31. ☉P♄.

D M	♆ Long. ° ′	♅ Long. ° ′	♄ Long. ° ′	♃ Long. ° ′	♂ Long. ° ′	♀ Long. ° ′	☿ Long. ° ′	Lunar Aspects ☉	♆	♅	♄	♃	♂	♀	☿
1	25♌ 1	3♈23	1♐59	2♈40	15♌16	24♌ 5	1♌17	⚺		△	△	△			☌
2	25 3	3 24	1℞56	2 43	15 53	25 3	1 37	∠	☌	±		⚼	☌		
3	25 5	3 24	1 53	2 49	16 30	26 0	1 53				□			☌	⚺
4	25 6	3 24	1 50	2 53	17 7	26 57	2 4	✱					⚺		∠
5	25 8	3 25	1 47	2 56	17 44	27 53	2 11		⚺					⚺	
6	25 10	3 25	1 44	3 0	18 20	28 49	2℞13		∠	☍	✱	☍	∠		✱
7	25 12	3 25	1 41	3 3	18 57	29 44	2 11	□	✱		∠		✱	∠	
8	25 13	3 25	1 39	3 6	19 34	0♍39	2 3				⚺			✱	□
9	25 15	3℞25	1 36	3 9	20 12	1 34	1 52	△		⚼		⚼			
10	25 17	3 25	1 34	3 12	20 49	2 28	1 35		□		☌		□		△
11	25 19	3 25	1 32	3 15	21 26	3 21	1 14	⚼		△		△		□	
12	25 21	3 25	1 29	3 17	22 3	4 13	0 50		△				△		⚼
13	25 23	3 24	1 27	3 19	22 40	5 5	0 21		⚼	□	⚺	□	⚼	△	
14	25 25	3 24	1 25	3 21	23 17	5 56	29♋49	☍			∠			⚼	
15	25 26	3 24	1 23	3 23	23 54	6 47	29 14			✱	✱	✱			☍
16	25 28	3 24	1 21	3 25	24 31	7 37	28 37			∠		∠			
17	25 30	3 23	1 19	3 26	25 9	8 26	27 58		☍	⚺	□	⚺	☍		
18	25 32	3 23	1 17	3 28	25 46	9 15	27 17	⚼						☍	⚼
19	25 34	3 22	1 16	3 29	26 23	10 3	26 36	△		☌	△	☌			△
20	25 36	3 22	1 14	3 30	27 0	10 50	25 56		⚼		⚼		⚼		
21	25 38	3 21	1 13	3 30	27 38	11 36	25 16	□	△				△	⚼	□
22	25 40	3 21	1 11	3 31	28 15	12 21	24 38			⚺		⚺		△	
23	25 42	3 20	1 10	3 31	28 52	13 6	24 2	✱	□	∠	☍	∠	□		✱
24	25 44	3 19	1 9	3 31	29 30	13 50	23 29			✱		✱		□	∠
25	25 46	3 19	1 7	3℞31	0♍ 7	14 32	23 0	∠	✱						⚺
26	25 48	3 18	1 6	3 31	0 45	15 14	22 35	⚺	∠	□		□	✱		
27	25 51	3 17	1 5	3 30	1 22	15 55	22 15				⚼		∠	✱	☌
28	25 53	3 16	1 5	3 30	2 0	16 34	22 0	☌	⚺	△	△	△	⚺	∠	
29	25 55	3 15	1 4	3 29	2 37	17 13	21 50			⚼		⚼		⚺	
30	25 57	3 14	1 3	3 28	3 15	17 50	21 46		☌		□				⚺
31	25 59	3 13	1 3	3 26	3 52	18 27	21D48	⚺					☌		∠

TABLE OF HOUSES FOR LATITUDES 22° TO 56°.

94 UPPER MERIDIAN, CUSP OF 10th H.

	SID. T. 11 45 19, ASC 176° 19′.8 } ♍ 26°					11 48 59, 177° 14′.8 } ♍ 27°					11 52 40, 178° 9′.9 } ♍ 28°				
H.	11	12	1	2	3	11	12	1	2	3	11	12	1	2	3
Lat.	♎	♏	♐	♑	♒	♎	♏	♐	♑	♒	♎	♏	♐	♑	♒
°	°	°	° ′	°	°	°	°	° ′	°	°	°	°	° ′	°	°
22	26.9	23.5	17 36	18.5	22.0	27.8	24.3	18 24	19.4	23.0	28.7	25.2	19 14	20.3	24.0
23	8	3	17 9	2	21.9	7	1	17 57	1	22.9	6	24.9	18 47	0	23.9
24	7	0	16 42	17.8	8	7	23.8	17 30	18.7	8	6	7	18 19	19.6	8
25	6	22.8	16 15	5	7	6	6	17 3	4	7	5	4	17 52	3	7
26	26.6	5	15 47	2	6	27.5	3	16 35	1	6	4	2	17 24	0	6
27	5	3	15 19	16.8	4	4	1	16 7	17.7	5	28.3	23.9	16 55	18.6	5
28	4	0	14 50	5	21.3	3	22.8	15 38	4	22.3	3	6	16 26	3	23.3
29	3	21.7	14 22	1	2	3	5	15 9	0	2	.2	4	15 57	17.9	2
30	26.3	5	13 53	15.8	1	27.2	3	14 40	16.7	1	1	1	15 28	6	1
31	2	2	13 23	4	0	1	0	14 10	3	0	0	22.8	14 58	2	0
32	1	20.9	12 53	0	20.8	0	21.7	13 39	15.9	21.8	27.9	5	14 27	16.8	22.8
33	0	7	12 22	14.6	7	26.9	5	13 9	5	7	8	2	13 56	4	7
34	25.9	4	11 51	2	5	8	2	12 38	1	5	7	0	13 24	0	6
35	8	1	11 19	13.8	4	7	20.9	12 6	14.7	4	6	21.7	12 52	15.6	4
36	7	19.8	10 47	3	2	6	6	11 33	2	2	5	4	12 19	1	3
37	6	5	10 14	12.9	1	5	3	11 0	13.8	1	27.4	1	11 46	14.7	1
38	25.6	2	9 40	4	19.9	26.4	0	10 26	3	20.9	3	20.8	11 12	2	21.9
39	5	0	9 6	11.9	7	3	19.7	9 52	12.8	7	2	5	10 37	13.7	8
40	4	18.7	8 31	4	5	2	4	9 16	3	6	1	1	10 1	2	6
41	3	4	7 56	10.9	.3	1	0	8 40	11.8	4	0	19.8	9 25	12.7	4
42	25.2	0	7 19	4	1	0	18.7	8 4	3	2	26.9	5	8 48	2	2
43	1	17.7	6 42	9.8	18.9	25.9	4	7 26	10.7	0	8	1	8 10	11.6	1
44	0	3	6 4	2	7	8	0	6 47	1	19.9	7	18.8	7 31	0	20.9
45	24.9	0	5 25	8.6	6	7	17.7	6 8	9.5	7	6	5	6 51	10.4	7
46	8	16.6	4 44	0	4	6	4	5 27	8.9	5	5	2	6 10	9.7	5
47	7	3	4 3	7.3	2	5	1	4 46	2	3	26.4	17.8	5 28	1	3
48	.6	15.9	3 21	6.6	0	25.4	16.7	4 3	7.5	1	3	4	4 45	8.4	1
49	24.4	5	2 38	0	17.7	3	3	3 19	6.8	18.8	1	0	4 1	7.7	19.8
50	3	1	1 54	5.3	4	1	15.9	2 34	1	5	0	16.6	3 15	0	5
51	2	14.7	1 8	4.5	1	0	5	1 48	5.3	2	25.8	2	2 29	6.2	2
52	1	3	0 21	3.7	16.8	24.9	1	1 1	4.5	17.9	7	15.8	1 40	5.4	18.9
53	23.9	13.9	♏ 29 33	2.8	5	8	14.6	0 12	3.6	6	6	3	0 51	4.5	6
54	8	5	28 43	1.8	1	6	1	♏ 29 21	2.6	2	5	14.8	0 0	3.5	3
55	6	0	27 51	0.7	15.7	4	13.6	28 29	1.6	16.8	3	3	♏ 29 7	2.5	0
56	5	12.5	26 58	♐ 29.6	3	3	1	27 35	0.5	4	2	13.8	28 13	1.4	17.6

	11 56 20, 179° 5′.0 } ♍ 29°					12 0 0, 180° 0′.0 } ♎ 0°					12 3 40, 180° 55′.0 } ♎ 1°				
H.	11	12	1	2	3	11	12	1	2	3	11	12	1	2	3
Lat.	♎	♏	♐	♑	♒	♏	♏	♐	♑	♒	♏	♏	♐	♑	♒
°	°	°	° ′	°	°	°	°	° ′	°	°	°	°	° ′	°	°
22	29.7	26.0	20 3	21.2	25.0	0.6	26.8	20 52	22.1	26.0	1.5	27.7	21 41	23.0	27.0
23	6	25.8	19 36	20.9	24.9	5	6	20 25	21.8	25.9	4	4	21 14	22.7	26.9
24	5	5	19 8	5	8	4	3	19 57	4	8	3	2	20 46	4	8
25	4	2	18 40	2	7	3	1	19 29	1	7	2	26.9	20 18	0	7
26	3	0	18 12	19.9	6	0.2	25.8	19 1	20.8	6	1.1	6	19 50	21.7	6
27	29.3	24.7	17 44	5	5	2	5	18 33	4	5	0	4	19 21	4	5
28	2	4	17 15	2	24.4	1	3	18 4	1	25.4	0	1	18 51	0	26.4
29	1	2	16 45	18.9	3	0	0	17 34	19.8	3	0.9	25.8	18 22	20.7	3
30	0	23.9	16 16	5	2	♎ 29.9	24.7	17 4	4	2	8	5	17 52	3	2
31	28.9	6	15 45	1	0	8	4	16 34	0	1	7	2	17 21	0	0
32	8	3	15 15	17.8	23.9	7	2	16 3	18.7	0	6	0	16 50	19.6	25.9
33	7	1	14 43	4	8	6	23.9	15 31	3	24.8	5	24.7	16 18	2	8
34	6	22.8	14 11	0	6	5	6	14 59	17.9	7	0.4	4	15 45	18.8	6
35	5	5	13 39	16.6	5	29.4	3	14 26	5	6	3	1	15 13	4	5
36	28.4	2	13 6	1	23.3	3	0	13 52	0	4	2	23.8	14 39	17.9	25.3
37	3	21.9	12 32	15.7	2	2	22.7	13 18	16.6	3	1	4	14 5	5	2
38	2	6	11 58	2	0	1	3	12 44	1	1	♎ 29.9	1	13 30	0	0
39	1	3	11 23	14.7	22.9	0	0	12 8	15.6	23.9	8	22.8	12 54	16.5	24.9
40	0	0	10 47	2	7	28.9	21.7	11 32	1	7	7	5	12 17	0	8
41	27.9	20.7	10 10	13.7	6	8	3	10 55	14.6	6	6	1	11 40	15.5	6
42	8	3	9 32	1	4	6	0	10 17	1	4	5	21.7	11 2	0	4
43	6	0	8 54	12.6	2	5	20.7	9 38	13.5	2	29.4	4	10 22	14.4	2
44	5	19.6	8 15	0	0	28.4	4	8 59	12.9	0	2	0	9 42	13.8	0
45	4	2	7 34	11.4	21.8	3	0	8 18	3	22.8	1	20.6	9 1	2	23.8
46	27.3	18.9	6 53	10.7	6	2	19.6	7 36	11.7	5	0	3	8 19	12.6	6
47	2	5	6 10	1	4	1	2	6 53	0	3	28.9	19.9	7 36	11.9	5
48	1	1	5 27	9.4	2	27.9	18.8	6 9	10.3	1	8	5	6 52	2	3
49	0	17.7	4 42	8.7	20.9	8	4	5 24	9.6	21.9	6	1	6 6	10.5	1
50	26.8	3	3 56	7.9	6	7	0	4 38	8.8	7	5	18.7	5 19	9.7	22.9
51	6	16.9	3 9	1	4	6	17.6	3 50	0	4	28.3	3	4 30	8.9	6
52	5	5	2 20	6.3	1	27.4	2	3 1	7.1	1	1	17.9	3 40	0	3
53	4	0	1 30	5.4	19.8	2	16.7	2 10	6.2	20.8	0	4	2 49	7.1	0
54	3	15.5	0 38	4.4	4	0	2	1 17	5.2	5	27.9	16.9	1 56	6.1	21.7
55	1	0	♏ 29 45	3.3	1	26.9	15.7	0 23	4.2	2	7	4	1 1	5.1	4
56	25.9	14.5	28 50	2.2	18.7	7	2	♏ 29 28	3.0	19.9	5	15.9	0 5	4.0	1

Extract from Dalton's Table of Houses

which must be *added* because the longitude is *West* of Greenwich, this being the point crossed by the Meridian 0.

The Sidereal Time at birth at Quimper is therefore 11 h. 57 m. 20 s. We now take a Table of Houses and find the hour nearest approximating that of the Sidereal Time at the place of birth. We find 11 h. 56 m. 20 s., which corresponds to 29° of Virgo as the Cusp of the Tenth House.

We then look for the latitude of Quimper, which is 48° North, and we find that the Eleventh House is at 27° 1′ of Libra; the Twelfth House at 18° 1′ of Scorpio; the First House (ascendant) at 5° 27′ of Sagittarius; the Second House at 9° 4′ of Capricornus; the Third House at 21° 2′ of Aquarius.

The Fourth, Fifth, Sixth, Seventh, Eighth and Ninth Houses will be at the corresponding degree of the Sign opposite to that of the Tenth, Eleventh, Twelfth, First, Second and Third Houses, and we thus obtain:

First House at 5° 27′ of Sagittarius; Seventh House at 5° 27′ of Gemini;

Second House at 9° 4′ of Capricornus; Eighth House at 9° 4′ of Cancer;

Third House at 21° 2′ of Aquarius; Ninth House at 21° 2′ of Leo;

Tenth House at 29° of Virgo; Fourth House at 29° of Pisces;

Eleventh House at 27° 1′ of Libra; Fifth House at 27° 1′ of Aries;

Twelfth House at 18° 1′ of Scorpio; Sixth House at 18° 1′ of Taurus.

We now have to calculate the positions of the planets, these being given for Greenwich time at noon for each day (Raphael's Ephemeris). As birth took place at Quimper, we must obtain the corresponding hour of birth at Greenwich.

The longitude of Quimper is 4° 15′, which corresponds in time to 17 minutes. These 17 minutes must be added to the time of birth, as the longitude is West of Greenwich.

We will therefore calculate the position of the planets for 3 h. 57 m. p.m. on 27th July, 1927.

The longitude of the Sun at noon is 3° 27′ 9″ of Leo; the Sun's motion in 24 hours is 0° 57′ 22″, or, in round figures, 0° 57′. (See Table, page 18).

At the end of Raphael's Ephemeris we find a Table of daily proportional logarithms (P.D.) which makes it easy to calculate

PROPORTIONAL LOGARITHMS FOR FINDING THE PLANETS' PLACES.

Min.	0	1	2	3	4	5	6	7	8	9	10	11	12	13	14	15	Min.
	DEGREES OR HOURS.																
0	3.1584	1.3802	1.0792	9031	7781	6812	6021	5351	4771	4260	3802	3388	3010	2663	2341	2041	0
1	3.1584	1.3730	1.0756	9007	7763	6798	6009	5341	4762	4252	3795	3382	3004	2657	2336	2036	1
2	2.8573	1.3660	1.0720	8983	7745	6784	5997	5330	4753	4244	3788	3375	2998	2652	2330	2032	2
3	2.6812	1.3590	1.0685	8959	7728	6769	5985	5320	4744	4236	3780	3368	2992	2646	2325	2027	3
4	2.5563	1.3522	1.0649	8935	7710	6755	5973	5310	4735	4228	3773	3362	2986	2640	2320	2022	4
5	2.4594	1.3454	1.0614	8912	7692	6741	5961	5300	4726	4220	3766	3355	2980	2635	2315	2017	5
6	2.3802	1.3388	1.0580	8888	7674	6726	5949	5289	4717	4212	3759	3349	2974	2629	2310	2012	6
7	2 3133	1.3323	1.0546	8865	7657	6712	5937	5279	4708	4204	3752	3342	2968	2624	2305	2008	7
8	2.2553	1.3258	1.0511	8842	7639	6698	5925	5269	4699	4196	3745	3336	2062	2618	2300	2003	8
9	2.2041	1.3195	1.0478	8819	7622	6684	5913	5259	4690	4188	3737	3329	2956	2613	2295	1998	9
10	2.1584	1.3133	1.0444	8796	7604	6670	5902	5249	4682	4180	3730	3323	2950	2607	2289	1993	10
11	2.1170	1.3071	1.0411	8773	7587	6656	5890	5239	4673	4172	3723	3316	2944	2602	2284	1988	11
12	2.0792	1.3010	1.0378	8751	7570	6642	5878	5229	4664	4164	3716	3310	2938	2596	2279	1984	12
13	2.0444	1.2950	1.0345	8728	7552	6628	5866	5219	4655	4156	3709	3303	2933	2591	2274	1979	13
14	2.0122	1.2891	1.0313	8706	7535	6614	5855	5209	4646	4148	3702	3297	2927	2585	2269	1974	14
15	1.9823	1.2833	1.0280	8683	7518	6600	5843	5199	4638	4141	3695	3291	2921	2580	2264	1969	15
16	1.9542	1.2775	1.0248	8661	7501	6587	5832	5189	4629	4133	3688	3284	2915	2574	2259	1965	16
17	1.9279	1.2719	1.0216	8639	7484	6573	5820	5179	4620	4125	3681	3278	2909	2569	2254	1960	17
18	1.9031	1.2663	1.0185	8617	7467	6559	5809	5169	4611	4117	3674	3271	2903	2564	2249	1955	18
19	1.8796	1.2607	1.0153	8595	7451	6546	5797	5159	4603	4109	3667	3265	2897	2558	2244	1950	19
20	1.8573	1.2553	1.0122	8573	7434	6532	5786	5149	4594	4102	3660	3258	2891	2553	2239	1946	20
21	1.8361	1.2499	1.0091	8552	7417	6519	5774	5139	4585	4094	3653	3252	2885	2547	2234	1941	21
22	1.8159	1.2445	1.0061	8530	7401	6505	5763	5129	4577	4086	3646	3246	2880	2542	2229	1936	22
23	1.7966	1.2393	1.0030	8509	7384	6492	5752	5120	4568	4079	3639	3239	2874	2536	2223	1932	23
24	1.7781	1.2341	1.0000	8487	7368	6478	5740	5110	4559	4071	3632	3233	2868	2531	2218	1927	24
25	1.7604	1.2289	0.9970	8466	7351	6465	5729	5100	4551	4063	3625	3227	2862	2526	2213	1922	25
26	1.7434	1.2239	0.9940	8445	7335	6451	5718	5090	4542	4055	3618	3220	2856	2520	2208	1917	26
27	1.7270	1.2188	0.9910	8424	7318	6438	5706	5081	4534	4048	3611	3214	2850	2515	2203	1913	27
28	1.7112	1.2139	0.9881	8403	7302	6425	5695	5071	4525	4040	3604	3208	2845	2509	2198	1908	28
29	1.6960	1.2090	0.9852	8382	7286	6412	5684	5061	4516	4032	3597	3201	2839	2504	2193	1903	29
30	1.6812	1.2041	0.9823	8361	7270	6398	5673	5051	4508	4025	3590	3195	2833	2499	2188	1899	30
31	1.6670	1.1993	0.9794	8341	7254	6385	5662	5042	4499	4017	3583	3189	2827	2493	2183	1894	31
32	1.6532	1.1946	0.9765	8327	7238	6372	5651	5032	4491	4010	3576	3183	2821	2488	2178	1889	32
33	1.6398	1.1899	0.9737	8300	7222	6359	5640	5023	4482	4002	3570	3176	2816	2483	2173	1885	33
34	1.6269	1.1852	0.9708	8279	7206	6346	5629	5013	4474	3994	3563	3170	2810	2477	2168	1880	34
35	1.6143	1.1806	0.9680	8259	7190	6333	5618	5003	4466	3987	3556	3164	2804	2472	2164	1875	35
36	1.6021	1.1761	0.9652	8239	7174	6320	5607	4994	4457	3979	3549	3157	2798	2467	2159	1871	36
37	1.5902	1.1716	0.9625	8219	7159	6307	5596	4984	4449	3972	3542	3151	2793	2461	2154	1866	37
38	1.5786	1.1671	0.9597	8199	7143	6294	5585	4975	4440	3964	3535	3145	2787	2456	2140	1862	38
39	1.5673	1.1627	0.9570	8179	7128	6282	5574	4965	4432	3957	3529	3139	2781	2451	2144	1857	39
40	1.5563	1.1584	0.9542	8159	7112	6269	5563	4956	4424	3949	3522	3133	2775	2445	2139	1852	40
41	1.5456	1.1540	0.9515	8140	7097	6256	5552	4947	4415	3942	3515	3126	2770	2440	2134	1848	41
42	1.5351	1.1498	0.9488	8120	7081	6243	5541	4937	4407	3934	3508	3120	2764	2435	2129	1843	42
43	1.5249	1.1455	0.9462	8101	7066	6231	5531	4928	4399	3927	3501	3114	2758	2430	2124	1838	43
44	1.5149	1.1413	0.9435	8081	7050	6218	5520	4918	4390	3919	3495	3108	2753	2424	2119	1834	44
45	1.5051	1.1372	0.9409	8062	7035	6205	5509	4909	4382	3912	3488	3102	2747	2419	2114	1829	45
46	1.4956	1.1331	0.9383	8043	7020	6193	5498	4900	4374	3905	3481	3096	2741	2414	2109	1825	46
47	1.4863	1.1290	0.9356	8023	7005	6180	5488	4890	4365	3897	3475	3089	2736	2409	2104	1820	47
48	1.4771	1.1249	0.9330	8004	6990	6168	5477	4881	4357	3890	3468	3083	2730	2403	2099	1816	48
49	1.4682	1.1209	0.9305	7985	6975	6155	5466	4872	4349	3882	3461	3077	2724	2398	2095	1811	49
50	1.4594	1.1170	0.9279	7966	6960	6143	5456	4863	4341	3875	3454	3071	2719	2393	2090	1806	50
51	1.4508	1.1130	0.9254	7947	6945	6131	5445	4853	4333	3868	3448	3065	2713	2388	2085	1802	51
52	1.4424	1.1091	0.9228	7929	6930	6118	5435	4844	4324	3860	3441	3059	2707	2382	2080	1797	52
53	1.4341	1.1053	0.9203	7910	6915	6106	5424	4835	4316	3853	3434	3053	2702	2377	2075	1793	53
54	1.4260	1.1015	0.9178	7891	6900	6094	5414	4826	4308	3846	3428	3047	2696	2372	2070	1788	54
55	1.4180	1.0977	0.9153	7873	6885	6081	5403	4817	4300	3838	3421	3041	2691	2367	2065	1784	55
56	1.4102	1.0939	0.9128	7854	6871	6069	5393	4808	4292	3831	3415	3034	2685	2362	2061	1779	56
57	1.4025	1.0902	0.9104	7836	6856	6057	5382	4798	4284	3824	3408	3028	2679	2356	2056	1774	57
58	1.3949	1.0865	0.9079	7818	6841	6045	5372	4789	4276	3817	3401	3022	2674	2351	2051	1770	58
59	1.3875	1.0828	0.9055	7800	6827	6033	5361	4780	4268	3809	3395	3016	2668	2346	2046	1765	59
	0	1	2	3	4	5	6	7	8	9	10	11	12	13	14	15	

the motion of the planets for the required hour. (See Table, page 17).

Log. P.D. 3 h. 57 m.	. . . .	.7836
— 0° 57′	. . . . .	1.4025
	Total . .	2.1861

The logarithm nearest approaching to this number in the table is 2.2041, which corresponds to 9′.

The position of the Sun at 3 h. 57 m. will therefore be at 3° 27′ 9″ of Leo, plus 9′, or 3° 36′ 9″ of Leo.

The longitude of the Moon at noon is at 18° 35′ 52″ of Cancer. Its motion in 24 hours is 13° 3′ 3″, or in round figures 13° 3′.

Log. P.D. 3 h. 57 m.	. . . .	.7836
— 13° 3′	. . . . .	.2646
	Total . .	1.0482

JULY.

D	☉ ° ′ ″	☽ ° ′ ″	♂ ′	♀ ° ′	☿ ° ′	☽ dec ° ′
1	0 57 14	12 46 13	37	0 58	0 20	2 51
2	0 57 13	12 29 18	37	0 57	0 16	3 39
3	0 57 12	12 14 45	37	0 57	0 11	4 15
4	0 57 13	12 3 25	37	0 56	0 7	4 36
5	0 57 12	11 56 3	36	0 56	0 2	4 48
6	0 57 12	11 53 6	37	0 55	0 2	4 51
7	0 57 12	11 54 48	37	0 55	0 8	4 45
8	0 57 12	12 1 8	38	0 55	0 11	4 30
9	0 57 12	12 11 47	37	0 54	0 17	4 6
10	0 57 11	12 26 16	37	0 53	0 21	3 27
11	0 57 12	12 43 43	37	0 52	0 24	2 35
12	0 57 12	13 3 0	37	0 52	0 29	1 28
13	0 57 12	13 22 47	37	0 51	0 32	0 8
14	0 57 12	13 41 28	37	0 51	0 35	1 18
15	0 57 13	13 57 39	37	0 50	0 37	2 43
16	0 57 13	14 10 2	38	0 49	0 39	3 56
17	0 57 14	14 17 52	37	0 49	0 41	4 53
18	0 57 14	14 21 3	37	0 48	0 41	5 30
19	0 57 15	14 19 55	37	0 47	0 40	5 49
20	0 57 16	14 15 22	38	0 46	0 40	5 46
21	0 57 17	14 8 18	37	0 45	0 38	5 26
22	0 57 18	13 59 36	37	0 45	0 36	4 48
23	0 57 18	13 49 48	38	0 44	0 33	3 53
24	0 57 20	13 39 15	37	0 42	0 29	2 42
25	0 57 20	13 27 57	38	0 42	0 25	1 22
26	0 57 21	13 15 54	37	0 41	0 20	0 2
27	0 57 22	13 3 3	38	0 39	0 15	1 22
28	0 57 23	12 49 37	37	0 39	0 10	2 31
29	0 57 23	12 36 1	38	0 37	0 4	3 26
30	0 57 25	12 22 50	37	0 37	0 2	4 6
31	0 57 24	12 0 58	38	0 36	0 8	4 33

AUGUST.

D	☉ ° ′ ″	☽ ° ′ ″	♂ ′	♀ ° ′	☿ ° ′	☽ dec ° ′
1	0 57 26	12 1 13	37	0 33	0 15	4 47
2	0 57 26	11 54 31	38	0 33	0 21	4 52
3	0 57 27	11 51 37	38	0 31	0 28	4 47
4	0 57 28	11 53 10	37	0 29	0 34	4 35
5	0 57 28	11 59 34	38	0 28	0 41	4 12
6	0 57 29	12 10 59	38	0 27	0 47	3 39
7	0 57 30	12 27 16	38	0 25	0 53	2 53
8	0 57 31	12 47 47	37	0 23	0 59	1 53
9	0 57 31	13 11 27	38	0 22	1 6	0 38
10	0 57 33	13 36 34	38	0 19	1 11	0 46
11	0 57 33	14 0 54	38	0 18	1 17	2 15
12	0 57 35	14 21 53	38	0 16	1 22	3 37
13	0 57 36	14 37 10	38	0 14	1 27	4 44
14	0 57 37	14 45 2	38	0 12	1 32	5 32
15	0 57 39	14 45 0	38	0 10	1 37	5 50
16	0 57 40	14 37 47	38	0 8	1 40	5 9
17	0 57 42	14 25 12	38	0 5	1 45	5 39
18	0 57 44	14 9 25	38	0 4	1 47	5 1
19	0 57 45	13 52 28	38	0 1	1 50	4 6
20	0 57 46	13 35 53	38	0 1	1 53	2 58
21	0 57 49	13 20 35	38	0 4	1 55	1 39
22	0 57 50	13 6 50	39	0 6	1 56	0 16
23	0 57 52	12 54 28	38	0 8	1 58	1 2
24	0 57 53	12 43 12	38	0 11	1 58	2 14
25	0 57 55	12 32 38	38	0 13	1 59	3 12
26	0 57 57	12 22 33	39	0 15	2 0	3 57
27	0 57 58	12 13 1	38	0 18	1 59	4 27
28	0 58 0	12 4 18	39	0 19	1 59	4 46
29	0 58 1	11 56 58	38	0 23	1 58	4 53
30	0 58 3	11 51 46	39	0 24	1 58	4 51
31	0 58 4	11 49 28	39	0 26	1 57	4 40

The logarithm nearest approaching to this number is 10.478, which corresponds to 2° 9′. The position of the Moon will therefore be at 20° 42′ 52″ of Cancer.

The motion of Mars is 38′ in 24 hours.

The motion of Venus is 39′ in 24 hours.

— 1926 —

DATES	T.S	☉	☽	☿	♀	♂	♃	♄	♅	♆
	h m	°	°	°	°	°	°	°	°	°
6 janvier	19.3	285.26,7	186,3	263,7	323,6	246,5	300,1	233,3	352,1	144,4
16 —	19.42	295.37,7	327,1	277,5	326	253,5	302,4	234,1	352,4	144,1
26 —	20.22	305.48,6	99,8	292,2	324,5	260,4	304,8	234,8	352,8	143,9
5 fév.	21.1	315.57,6	220,3	308,3	319,4	267,4	307,2	235,3	353,3	143,6
15 —	21.41	326. 4,7	5,1	325,7	313,4	274,5	309,5	235,7	353,8	143,3
25 —	22.20	336. 9,2	132,3	343,3	310,5	281,6	311.8	236	354,3	143,1
7 mars	22.59	346.10,8	256,3	2,2	311,3	288,6	314	236,1	354,8	142,8
17 —	23.39	356 9,5	41,7	13,6	315,6	295,9	316,1	236	355,4	142,6
27 —	0.18	6. 4,8	164,7	12,6	322,1	303,1	318,2	235,7	356	142,3
6 avril	0,58	15.56.5	294,2	4,9	330,3	310,3	320	235,3	356,6	142,2
16 —	1.37	25.45.2	76.3	2,9	339,5	317,5	321,7	234,7	357	142,1
26 —	2.17	35.30	197,7	8,7	349,4	324,8	323,2	234,1	357,6	142
6 mai	2.56	45.12,4	333,3	19,9	359,8	332,1	324,6	233,4	358	142
16 —	3.35	54.52	109,3	35	10.7	339,2	325,6	232,6	358,5	142
26 —	4.15	64.29	232,1	53,6	21,7	346,4	326.4	231,9	358,8	142,1
5 juin	4.54	74. 3.8	12,5	75,1	33	353.4	327	231,2	359,1	142,3
15 —	5.34	83.27,6	141,3	95,3	44,4	0,3	327,1	230,6	359,3	142,5
25 —	6.13	93.10	268,1	114,3	56,1	7,1	327	230,1	359,4	142,7
5 juil	6.53	102.42	50,2	128,4	67,7	13,7	326,5	229,7	359,4	143
15 —	7.32	112.14,8	173,2	137,9	79,5	20	325,9	229,5	359,4	143,3
25 —	8.11	121.46,9	305,8	141,2	91,4	26,1	824,9	229,4	359,3	143,6
4 août	8.51	131.20,6	85,9	136,7	103,5	31,7	323,7	229,5	359,1	144
14 —	9.30	140.56,2	205,9	130	115,5	36,8	322,4	229,7	358,8	144,3
24 —	10.10	150.33,6	344,6	131,4	127,7	41,3	321	230,1	358,5	144,7
3 sept.	10.49	160.13,5	119,6	145,8	139,9	44,3	319,8	230,7	358,2	145,1
13 —	11.29	169.56,4	239,9	164,4	152,2	47,7	318,9	231,4	357,8	145,5
23 —	12 8	179.42,1	23,2	182,9	164,6	49,2	317,9	232,4	357,4	145,8
3 oct.	12.47	189.31,2	152,1	199,9	177	49,3	317,5	233,1	356,9	146,1
13 —	13.27	199.23,9	275,7	215,5	189,5	47,9	317,3	234,1	356,6	146,3
23 —	14. 6	209.19,7	60,2	229,7	202	45,3	317,4	235,2	356,2	146,6
2 nov	14.46	219.18,9	184,4	212,3	214,5	41,9	317,9	236,3	356	146,7
12 —	15.25	229.21,4	313,5	250,7	227,1	38,5	318,7	237,5	355,7	146,9
22 —	16. 5	239.26,2	95,1	247,4	239,7	36	319,7	238,7	355,6	147
2 déc.	16.44	249.33,7	217	236,1	252,2	34,7	321,1	239,9	355,6	147
12 —	17.23	259.53,1	352,7	238,7	264,8	34,8	322,6	241,1	355,5	147
22 —	18. 3	269.53,6	128,2	250,4	277,4	36,4	324,4	242,2	355,7	146,9

Extract from Paul Flambert's Table of Planetary Positions

We may therefore take the same motion for these two planets, and we thus obtain:

Log. P.D. 0° 38′	. . . .	1.5786
— 3 h. 57 m.	. . . .	.7836
	Total . .	2.3622

The nearest approaching number being 2.3802, which corresponds to 6′, this places Mars at 1° 28′ of Virgo, and Venus at 16° 1′ of Virgo.

The motion of Mercury is 15′ in 24 hours, its longitude at noon being at 22° 15′ of Cancer.

Log. P.D. 0° 15′	. . . .	1.9823
— 3 h. 57 m.	. . . .	.7836
	Total . .	2.7659

The nearest number is 2.6812, corresponding to 3′, which places Mercury at 22° 12′ of Cancer (the motion of Mercury on this day being retrograde).

We need not trouble about the motion of Jupiter, Saturn, Uranus and Neptune, as this is very slight for 3 h. 57 m. We find that: Jupiter is at 3° 30′ of Aries, Saturn at 1° 5′ of Sagittarius, Uranus at 3° 17′ of Aries; these three planets being retrograde; Neptune is at 25° 51′ of Leo. The Moon's Nodes are: Ascending Node (Dragon's Head) at 25° 59′ of Gemini; Descending Node (Dragon's Tail) at 25° 59′ of Sagittarius, while the Part of Fortune will be found at 22° 33′ of Scorpio.

Rules :

A. Take the Ephemeris for the year required. To the Sidereal Time at noon add the time elapsed between noon and the hour of birth, and then add the correction of this time at the rate of 10 seconds per hour.

B. Calculate in time the longitude of the place of birth. The longitude will be given in certain tables, or can be found on a good atlas. The time will be obtained at the rate of 4 minutes for each degree, and 4 seconds for each minute of longitude.

C. Make the correction of the time thus obtained at the rate of 10 seconds per hour, the new time obtained will then be added to the sum given by A when the longitude is West, and subtracted when the longitude is East Greenwich.

The sum of A and of C is the Sidereal Time at birth, or the Right Ascension of the Mid-Heaven.

Next, take a Table of Houses for the Latitude of the place and find the Sidereal Time approximating nearest that of birth.

Draw a circle of, say, 6 inches diameter and divide it into 12 sections, each of these sections representing 30 degrees.

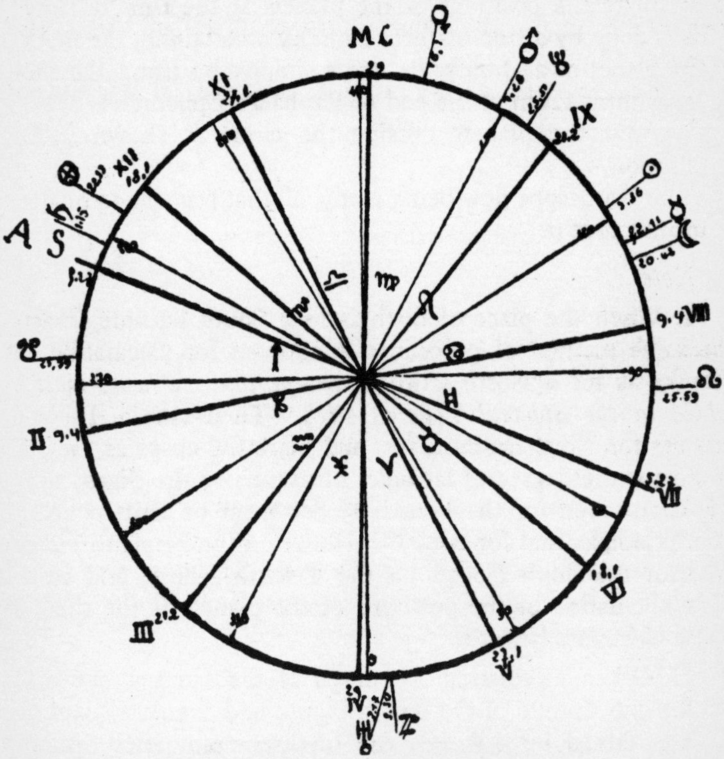

On the topmost portion of the circle facing yourself mark on the circumference the degree of the Tenth House, and in the angle corresponding to the arc, write the Sign. Carry out the same procedure for each of the angles, working in the *opposite* direction to that of the hands of a watch, putting in the Signs of the Zodiac in their proper order, starting from that which indicates the Mid-Heaven.

Proceed by marking on the arc the degree of the Eleventh House, then that of the Twelfth, First, Second and Third Houses, drawing diametrical lines from these points in order to obtain the chart of the twelve Houses.

Next, calculate the time of birth at Greenwich by adding B if the longitude is West, or by subtracting it if the longitude is East of Greenwich.

The Ephemeris gives the position at noon, so we will have to calculate the positions of the planets at the time obtained. This is done by a rule-of-three sum, by ascertaining the motion of the planet in 24 hours, or, more simply, by using the table of logarithms given at the end of Raphael's Ephemeris.

We put the planets outside the circle as shown in the illustration.

The Horoscope now being ready, all that remains to be done is to interpret it.

Notes :

I. When the place of birth is in a South latitude, exactly the same method of procedure is adopted for calculating the Houses as for a North latitude, *except that 12 hours must be added to the Sidereal Time at birth.* Then take a Table of Houses for Northern latitudes, and mark the cusps as they are given for the degree of latitude, but *reversing* the Signs, thus : the Sign given for the Fourth House must be written on the Tenth House, that for the Fifth House on the Eleventh House, that for the Sixth House, on the Twelfth House, and so on. The calculation of the positions of the planets is the same as for a Northern latitude.

II. When calculating the cusps of the Houses, the exact degree and minute of the Tenth House and the Ascendant can be ascertained by a simple rule-of-three sum. For ordinary purposes the nearest degree for the Tenth House is sufficient, the Tables of Houses giving it degree by degree, while the *orb* of a House is slightly more than 4 degrees.

In order to make an exact calculation, proceed as follows :

If, on looking at the Table of Houses, we cannot find the exact number as given by the Sidereal Time, we take one that is a little greater and one that is a little less and work out the difference. We subtract the less from the greater and call it *a* ; we then subtract the lesser number from the Sidereal Time at birth and call this second result *b*. In order to obtain the exact cusp of the Tenth House, we multiply *b* by 60 and divide by *a*; the result will be minutes of longitude which must be added to the *less* Sidereal Time.

Take the example we have chosen:

The greater number is 12 h. or	11 h. 59 m. 60 s.
The less number is . .	11 h. 56 m. 20 s.
The difference is	3 m. 40 s. (*a*)

The Sidereal Time is .	11 h. 57 m. 20 s.
The less number is . .	11 h. 56 m. 20 s.
The difference is	1 m. (*b*)

We multiply *b* by 60, which gives 60, and we divide this by 3.40 *a*, which gives 17′, which we add to the degree corresponding to the less number, that is to 29° of Virgo, so that the exact cusp of the Tenth House will be 29° 17′ of Virgo.

For the Ascendant, we subtract the degrees and minutes given in the First House column that correspond to the less Sidereal Time, from those that correspond to the greater Sidereal Time. Multiply by *b* and divide by *a*. Add the result obtained to the degrees and minutes of the Ascendant which correspond to the less Sidereal Time.

For latitude 48 we find for 11 h. 56 m. 20 s. the ascendant at 6° 9′ of Sagittarius or 5° 69′, the difference being 42′ which we multiphy by *b* and divide by *a*, 3.40 thus, $\frac{42}{3.4}$ which gives 12′, and we add this to the less Sidereal Time for the Ascendant, so that the exact Ascendant will be 5° 27′ plus 12′, or 5° 39′ of Sagittarius.

III. To calculate the Horoscope we require Raphael's Ephemeris for the year of birth.

We also require a Table of Houses, Dalton's being the best, as it gives, degree by degree, the cusps of the Houses for the latitudes included between 22° and 56°.

[illegible] the example we have chosen [illegible]

The sidereal time [illegible]

The difference is [illegible]

The difference is [illegible]

We multiply 5 by the number given [illegible] and we divide [illegible] which gives 1', which we add to the degree corresponding [illegible] the first example, that is to 29° of Virgo [illegible] at the [illegible] will be 29° [illegible] of the degree [illegible] [illegible]

[illegible]

THE PLANETS

IN THE HOUSES AND IN THE SIGNS

The Sun

THIS planet is dry, warm, positive; colour orange; domicile in Leo, exile in Virgo, fall in Libra, exaltation at 19° of Aries. Its element is partly Air and partly Fire. It represents the husband, the Chief, the father, the political ruler. It is somewhat barren, but is favourable to commercial undertakings and money matters. It procures the support of influential people. In a lay-out of the cards it is taken for the day, as it brings light, success, stability and fixity in all things.

It governs the metal Gold, and Sunday.

It exerts a special influence on the heart, and must be considered in a horoscope as the Lord of Life (hyleg) unless it is very weak. It should be more closely studied in regard to health, its position being of great importance, both from the standpoint of its place in the House and that of the Sign it occupies, as it represents the Ruler of the Nativity.

The Sun in the Houses

The Sun in the First House

This position, providing the Sun is not weak, is the indication of a long and successful life in accordance with the Consultant's social condition. It makes him ambitious and lofty in his aims, and also kind and just.

The native's life will be a centre of attraction for those who come into contact with him, so that he will often be the head, the one in authority, the one who is admired or feared. He may have many enemies, and, without being conscious of it, arouse envy and jealousy in those whom he thwarts.

He is of average height, of noble appearance and endowed with much nervous energy. Often of a delicate outward appearance, he is nevertheless possessed of remarkable strength, and while his muscles are not so marked as with Mars, they are more resistant owing to their flexibility.

Balance and harmony pervade his whole person, morally and physically. The skin is fair and smooth, eyes large, bright and piercing, often flecked with gold. Under a Lunar influence the eyes are weak, and necessitate the wearing of glasses early in life.

The Sun in the Ascendant is always a good influence from every point of view.

The Sun in the Second House

This position is very favourable from the financial standpoint. It gives unusual personal worth, self-confidence, physical attributes rather than real courage; marked taste for beautiful things, but also strong tendencies to extravagance and display. If the Sun is in a weak Sign (Aquarius or Libra) the native is a spendthrift, he is misunderstood; if an artist or a Bohemian, he may sink into poverty.

Under a good influence or a benefic aspect of Venus, it denotes a wealthy marriage, far above the native's social status.

If the Sun is in a domicile of Mercury—Gemini or Virgo—the marriage will be for pecuniary motives rather than for love.

The Sun in this House often makes heads of business houses, company directors, bankers, politicians.

The Sun in the Third House

This position is good for the education of the native. It gives good chances for success through his mental faculties. He has a good all-round education with a taste for all that is beautiful and true, and which may be useful, but he will possess above everything else a polish that will enable him to hold his own in any social sphere.

It also indicates the support of those who surround the native, as they will, under every circumstance, give him their moral and material help. The Sun in this position will make the native the most powerful member of his family.

In a watery sign (Cancer, Scorpio or Pisces) it denotes numerous journeys, chiefly for pleasure.

The Sun in the Fourth House

This gives the family instinct. It is a sure sign of increased wealth derived through the native's own virtues.

It means great success for the father or through the father. This position will therefore show in a horoscope (provided the Sun is powerful) that the child is born of a father who is in affluent circumstances, or who is able to attain to such a position in the future.

It is also the sign of great success for the native towards the fortieth year, often consisting of honours rather than riches.

From the moral point of view the Sun in this House makes the native taciturn, reserved and cautious.

This position being at the Nadir is not so favourable for the health. It causes constitutional disorders the; native may be delicate, and suffer from some chronic ailment of the nature of the Sign which occupies the Fourth House.

The Sun in the Fifth House

This position in the Fifth House is not very favourable for children, the Sun being barren, even in the fruitful signs (Cancer, Scorpio or Pisces), and gives few children. Such children, moreover, will be delicate in health and likely to die young if the Moon does not help by a good aspect.

In this position the Sun gives a love of pleasure, or compels the native to become connected with matters relating to pleasure, as he has a refined nature. There will be much unnecessary expenditure during the course of his life, but this will in no way affect his position, since the Sun in this House and in a favourable sign always denotes riches and a good position.

Badly aspected, it often leads to immoral, but financially profitable undertakings.

The Sun in the Sixth House

This is certainly one of the worst positions for the Sun unless it is powerful in the sign it occupies, and in any case it is always very unfavourable for the health of the native. He will suffer from a chronic ailment which will endanger his life, and will often prevent him from undertaking things which his horoscope in general, if it is a good one, might have enabled him to do.

The Sun in this House gives great organising powers. Unless well aspected, this position never indicates a chief, but one who succeeds through others.

The Sun in the Sixth House always signifies providential help in difficult periods, apart from health.

It also indicates a native who possesses healing powers.

The Sun in the Seventh House

As in the case of the Second House, the Sun in the Seventh House indicates the possibility of a marriage far above the native's social status. It also often denotes considerable moral help from the marriage-partner, so that fortune, riches and honours come after marriage.

It is the ideal position for those who wish to enter into politics, as it is a sure sign of popularity. It always procures an uplift at some period in life, and stability is certain if the Sun is powerful and well aspected.

It is also an indication of a long life, and is favourable for lawsuits.

In a Martial sign, in the Seventh House, the Sun does not bring domestic harmony, and is an almost sure sign of divorce or separation.

The Sun in the Eighth House

Here it is a sign of sudden or violent death towards the fiftieth year through heart trouble, provided, of course, aspects from Mars and Saturn confirm this. In a woman's horoscope it is often a sign of widowhood. The father dies before the mother. It is favourable for associations and for marriage.

The Sun in the Ninth House

The Sun in this House brings success overseas (in one of the watery signs) or in export trade.

From the mental standpoint the Sun in a favourable sign is well situated in this House, as it gives all the qualities of mind that one can desire. The intellect is very great, the native is gifted with lofty philosophical ideas, which enable him to understand all things and see life as it really is, and makes him radiate light on mankind. It is a sure indication of success in all undertakings. In a good horoscope the Sun in the Ninth House gives a powerful position under Government, or in the native's own sphere. For the artist it is an assurance of success, and in every case bestows a moral quietude that is akin to Happiness.

The Sun in the Tenth House

This is always an assurance of success at a period more or less near to that of birth. In the Tenth House the Sun procures a position above that in which the native was born, and in accordance with his social status, his ambition and his starting-point, which corresponds to the power of the Third and Fourth Houses, his promotion to the highest responsibilities or functions becomes possible.

The support of the mother or of influential women is indicated. Moreover, the native will be the most influential member of his family, whom he will be always ready to help if Venus is well aspected.

The Sun in the Eleventh House

In this position it gives powerful friends who will help the native in his career. If the Sun is dignified it will make it possible for him to be the head of a school of artists or of a political party, which will attract a number of friends. The Sun in this House is not favourable for children : they will be few, or the native will take no interest in them.

The Sun in this position will favour all kinds of associations if it is dignified. If the contrary is the case, it will give powerful enemies, false friends and quarrels with the relatives of the marriage partner.

The Sun in the Twelfth House

The Sun in this House specially implies the idea of solitude —a retired, secluded and monotonous life. It may show the native in a nursing-home, or hospital or prison, as an inmate or as a warder. (This may apply to the father or to the guardian of the child.) If badly aspected, this position always denotes separation from relatives, and serious quarrels which necessitate living in seclusion, if not danger of imprisonment. Well aspected, it may show, on the contrary, that the native will overcome his troubles, which none the less will be very numerous.

The Sun in the Signs

Sun in Aries

THE Sun is exalted in the 19th degree of Aries. When situated in this sign it gives an ambitious and adventurous disposition, the likelihood of rash action, a chequered career, with alternate rises and falls; but, on the whole, a marked rise, since, if the native descends one rung of the ladder, he climbs two rungs afterwards.

The Sun in this position indicates a journey undertaken on behalf of a person who belongs to a higher social status than the native. In the case of an employee, it will mean a journey undertaken for his employer; for a professional man, it will mean the likelihood of a journey on account of an important matter which, unless the aspects are favourable, will not be successful, as the native will have over-estimated his strength.

The Sun in 10 of Aries may nevertheless procure success, but it is necessary to sow in order to reap, and delay in realization is certain.

In 20 of Aries it is the indication of a violent deed, possibly of scandal, which causes notoriety.

Sun in Taurus

The Sun in the sign of Venus is not very fortunate for domestic matters. If Venus is afflicted, it is a sure sign of divorce, or at any rate of serious quarrels. It gives good powers of observation, and consequently the ability to keep silent. It is also favourable for journeys.

In 10 of Taurus, the Sun is the significator of an act of jealousy, of changes in affection, and always indicates an event relating to matters connected with the House occupied by this sign. It is often the cause of unfortunate changes.

In 20 of Taurus, the position is again a token of changes in regard to matters relating to the House; it means a sorrow, or an unpleasant journey which will be undertaken in the daytime in connection with the father or the husband.

Sun in Gemini

The Sun is well situated in this sign. It denotes a progressive career which is being helped by those surrounding the native, not necessarily his relatives, but his friends. It is also the indication of a quick journey by aeroplane, or motor-car.

The mind of the native is inclined to analysis, criticism and learning in general. Success is shown from the standpoint of matters connected with mechanical arts, or even with business in general, if the Sun is well aspected and is not afflicted by the malefic planets, especially when it is in 20 of Gemini, where it gives courage, and kindness which facilitate a rise in life, the native being naturally sympathetic, and securing help from everyone.

In 10 of Gemini the position is not so good, as the native is lacking in self-confidence and his hesitation causes him to miss good opportunities. He is restless and afraid. He will nevertheless obtain results, as he is very practical, and when he undertakes anything he pursues it to its end. If the Sun is afflicted, by Venus or Mars for example, it gives, especially in a woman, a fickle and unreliable disposition.

Sun in Cancer

This is not a good position for the battle of life. The native is indolent, or at the least a dreamer, and unless he is born in affluence and possesses an income, he will not be able to do anything to benefit himself. When well aspected, this position, on the contrary, may be that of a great artist, of a thinker, of a lover of the Beautiful and the Good. It gives an inclination for travelling by water. In the Third House, with a ray from Mars, which gives activity, we may find an enthusiastic rower, whereas in the Ninth House it may mean long sea-journeys.

In 10 of Cancer, the Sun will cause many troubles, quarrels and conflicts, against which the native will not generally know how to defend himself. There will also be a constant moral unrest which will make him afraid to do anything.

In 20 of Cancer the position is more favourable. Unexpected

help will often come at the time when things look black, the Sun in this decanate bringing the Light. It is the clear, blue, sunny sky which succeeds the storm. It often means an act of violence overcoming apathy, so that the native and those matters relating to him appear to rediscover the road they must follow. The light breaks forth suddenly; evil thoughts take their flight; peace is restored.

The Sun in Cancer gives delicate health.

Sun in Leo

In its own domicile the Sun is very powerful, and enables the native to realise his desires provided the luminary is not afflicted by the malefics. He has great self-confidence, which enables him constantly to summon helpful thoughts and thereby facilitate the accomplishment of his wishes. He is always right, his natural aptitudes are always true, and love of Beauty and Truth are his customary guides. He is kind, but masterful. People must bend to his wishes if they want to remain his friends. This position often shows numerous enemies whom the native will overcome.

In 10 of Leo the Sun will give the powerful help of a faithful friend who will gather the native's other friends together, and procure for him a rapid rise, through surrounding him with devoted people who will help him in his undertakings.

In 20 of Leo the Sun enables the native to escape all the snares of life, and endows him with true power. It is through perseverance, work and confidence in himself that the native will realize his wishes, which are difficult to obtain, inasmuch as he does not desire anything mean, but is ambitious and wants a foremost place. This position of the Sun will give it to him.

Sun in Virgo

In this sign the Sun brings many ties which will hinder the native; simultaneous unions which will not be without prejudice to his peace of mind. This position denotes worries and hidden trouble in the life taken as a whole—the shadow of a mystery. Frequently, with adverse aspects, this position will be the indication of matters which it will be impossible to divulge. In some cases, especially in the Third House, it may indicate surroundings of which the native is ashamed. In the

Fourth House it will denote mean parentage. In the First House there is a mystery connected with the birth.

Well aspected by Uranus, the Sun may indicate the head of an occult religious body. It will often signify that the native secretly holds the strings of some organisation, being a sort of power-behind-the-throne in politics or finance.

In 10 of Virgo the Sun will cause serious troubles in youth. It can only bring success, if well aspected, towards the fortieth year. For current matters it is always a cause of delay.

In 20 of Virgo it gives personal benefits, which cannot always be proclaimed, especially as regards pecuniary matters. If Venus is situated in a powerful sign, it indicates a fortunate marriage, often with one who suffers from some infirmity or taint, which cannot but hinder the one who derives profit by it.

Sun in Libra

This is not a token of patience. The native does not know how to wait; he does not always pay sufficient attention to details; he may commit mistakes which he will regret when it is too late—among others, in regard to marriage, where he may leave the substance in pursuit of the shadow. This position shows a danger of separation, or divorce, and the likelihood of living apart from relatives. The Sun is in its fall in this sign, and brings moral solitude, disputes or lawsuits, numerous enmities, and danger of a short term of imprisonment. Nevertheless, if the horoscope on the whole is good, the foregoing can be avoided, as the native is always gifted with remarkable mental faculties.

In 10 of Libra, with Venus in one of the decanates of Aries, Scorpio or Virgo, it is a sure sign of separation from the marriage partner. The Sun in this sign, in good aspect with Jupiter, denotes the moral uplift of the native, success in his undertakings, but always loneliness, as the Sun in its fall in the domicile of Venus always deprives of love.

In 20 of Libra it gives abundance, the fulfilment of desires; but also anxiety in regard to the children, who will separate from the parents. Here, again, it will cause the separation from the marriage partner, an empty life far from loved ones, and if this occurs in the Ninth House it will mean death in a foreign country.

Sun in Scorpio

This is unfavourable. It indicates a consultant who is full of his own personality, vindictive, critical, selfish and vain. It is not fortunate for the health, especially in the Sixth House, which in itself is an unfavourable position for the Sun. It is a sign of numerous fevers, and often of vitiated blood. With a bad aspect of Mars, there is risk of violent death, sometimes through accident. If the Moon is in conjunction or opposition, it means impaired eyesight.

Dealings with those around the native are not harmonious, there will be many disputes with superiors, which will only be settled through cunning, in which the native excels. Apart from the Sixth, Eighth and Tenth Houses, the Sun in Scorpio may procure a momentary rise in position, and it bestows a certain amount of vitality.

In 10 of Scorpio, alternating rises and downfalls in life will occur.

The position is still worse in 20 of Scorpio, and if success is achieved at a certain period of life, it will not always be through highly praiseworthy methods. If Mercury is badly placed in the horoscope, the position of the Sun in this decanate will indicate bankruptcy, failure, or, at any rate, undertakings which will cause the native to lose his possessions.

Sun in Sagittarius

This indicates that the native is fond of good living. He loves his comfort and the enjoyment of everything that is good and beautiful. He is certainly sensuous, more especially from the artistic standpoint. He has charming manners, and knows how to live and let others live. As he is kind and obliging, he will often be the " milch-cow " for those about him, but will nevertheless derive benefit from this, as even if the Sun is badly aspected, the good he has done will not be forgotten, and he will be helped in his turn. He will, however, seldom require help, as the Sun in this sign always brings freedom from anxiety, and a continuous and natural progress, without struggle. This position is good for marriage, which occurs early, but the union is not always harmonious, constancy not being an attribute of the Sun in Sagittarius. It it also unfavourable for the children, as dissensions soon arise between the marriage partners.

In 10 of Sagittarius the Sun brings easy and rapid success' but a somewhat disturbed life brought about through pleasure and work. If the Sun is not above the horizon, it may cause death about the fiftieth year.

In 20 of Sagittarius, the mind is more austere, while retaining its spirituality. It gives more constancy, clairvoyance, a better choice of friends, less materialistic qualities, but also less kind-heartedness, less indolence, and consequently more luck in marriage.

Sun in Capricorn

This indicates great vitality, an amorous disposition. Great expenditure of the vital force may curtail the life if the Moon is not favourably placed. The mind is rather complex, cautious and reserved, and the Sun may bring success if Jupiter is well aspected.

It is specially in Capricorn that the Sun brings disappointment in love, deceit in matters connected with the affections and disagreements over matters ruled by the House in which this sign is placed.

In 10 of Capricorn it gives good powers of observation, makes the native sharp and often crafty; prevents him from being deceived, or enables him to quickly become aware of deceit, so that success may be achieved by dint of cautiousness, skill, dexterity and craftiness.

In 20 of Capricorn it gives great physical resistance, strength and power; it produces the despotic rulers who make themselves obeyed through force. It is a sure sign of rise in life if Mars is well placed in the horoscope. In this decanate, however, it indicates that the native will be lonely, principally on account of his harshness, which will cause him to be more feared than loved.

Sun in Aquarius

The Sun is in exile in this sign, and thus loses many of its good qualities from the standpoint of success, as Saturn is more potent here, and if the Sun is badly aspected it will cause many troubles connected with matters ruled by the House occupied by Aquarius.

In 10 of Aquarius the Sun brings deceit in love, unfaithfulness, violent quarrels with the marriage partner, double-dealing through motives of self-interest.

In 20 of Aquarius it gives remarkable mental powers, provided Uranus is well placed in the horoscope. Otherwise it causes peculiar ideas, and may be the cause of insanity of the father. It is invariably an indication of eccentricity if the Moon is also afflicted.

Sun in Pisces

This position is not good for the health. It is a sign of indolence, of timidity, followed by rash deeds and arrogance.

The position as a whole gives a very uneven disposition and a chequered life. The instinct of economy is carried to excess, and is followed by an impulse to spend recklessly for the gratification of the appetites, which are unlimited.

There is a good deal of ambition, but no continuity of purpose; this often causes the native's downfall just at the moment when he might have achieved his aim, unless Mars is situated in Aries.

In spite of apparent delicate health, the native has a long life, as he does not expend much physical energy.

In 10 of Pisces there is a certain amount of instability, but a happy ending to the life, with danger of death through pleurisy. It is not very favourable for marriage, or the children, who may be delicate.

In 20 of Pisces it gives more stability to the life and the health is improved. Death, which occurs rather late, will be caused through water—dropsy or kidney trouble.

The Moon

THE Moon represents material things. Its domicile is in Cancer; its exaltation at 3° of Taurus; its fall in Scorpio. It is cold, moist, changeable, nocturnal and feminine.

In the interpretation it must be taken as the Mother. It also represents Night, Luck, Hidden and Mysterious Things, Legacies, Journeys, Mobility (more from the moral than the physical aspect).

It makes the native changeable and versatile, restless and fond of travel; frequently eccentric, if aspected by Uranus.

It gives a pleasing countenance, prominent eyes, a bluey-white skin, and an indolent and lymphatic disposition.

It influences more especially the brain, eyesight and bladder.

It causes disorders of the stomach, kidneys, paralysis, and exerts great influence on child-bearing and the menses. It gives a fairly long life, and must often be taken as the Ruler of Life (hyleg) in a horoscope.

It governs the metal Silver. Its day is Monday. It must often be taken as representing the Mother or the Wife.

The Moon in the Houses

Moon in the First House

This makes the native good-tempered, inclined to magnify the slightest event in his life. He is shy, sensitive, imaginative, changeable, capable of enduring for a long time things which do not please him until the time arrives when, without a word of warning, he gives up without hope of recovery, inasmuch as though lacking in will-power his force of inertia is very great.

The Moon in this House may incline towards intemperance in drink, especially if the Ascendant is in Cancer, Pisces or Scorpio; also to mediumship or dreams if in Virgo, Sagittarius or Pisces.

When birth takes place between noon and midnight the life will usually be a long one.

Moon in the Second House

This gives unexpected gains, great strokes of luck, but with alternating ups and downs. Well aspected by Venus it conduces to a rich marriage, or at any rate to marriage with one who is above the native's pecuniary position.

Adversely aspected in this House, it is bad for money matters in general, as it brings much hesitation, often laziness or laxity, and a lack of continuity of purpose, which will cause the difficulties of life to be insurmountable. If, on the contrary, it is well aspected, the Moon in this House will prevent these things from happening, as it is a sign of Luck.

It indicates an attack of fever in early life.

Moon in the Third House

There are frequent journeys, a restless life, or, more strictly speaking, the native himself makes it restless through his changeableness, owing to his mind being rather superficial, and always influenced by the last person who has spoken to him, which does not prevent him, however, from doing what he wants to do before everything else.

The imagination is well developed and gives a bent for art or literature, but the intellectual powers are not remarkable, because the mind is lethargic.

The native will have many caprices in his life. The memory, especially the visual memory, is good. The Moon in the Third House often signifies a mystery in the family, or something hidden.

Moon in the Fourth House

This is an indication of happy domestic surroundings, but without material stability, as there is no method or system in the home. Moreover, many changes in the home surroundings are indicated.

The early period of life is not very fortunate, but improvement occurs later, and the end of life is more fortunate.

There is harmony with the close relatives, but quarrels with distant relatives are shown.

Mysterious happenings will occur in connection with inheritances or death; difficulties will arise regarding land or house property.

The Moon in the Fourth House is good for the native's mother, but may cause her to become a widow if the Sun, which represents the father, is in Aquarius or Libra.

Moon in the Fifth House

There is likelihood of many children in the fruitful signs (Cancer, Scorpio or Pisces). The Moon in this House makes the native fond of pleasures; he is fickle in love and has a tendency to sensuality and excesses.

It makes him shun solitude, and inclined to gambling and speculation.

It causes slothfulness through excess of luck in life, as it enables the native to get what he wants, especially in material matters and those relating to the senses. When well aspected it gives a taste for dramatic art, and brings success in artistic pursuits, in politics and in love affairs.

It makes the native fond of banquetting, jovial and boisterous company, and incites him to court popularity.

Moon in the Sixth House

In this House it does not make a leader; it is the position that makes a moral or material servant, no matter what his status may be. It cannot give success except in subordinate employment; it represents the employee or the person who fulfils a secret or unavowed position.

In a woman it is a sign of danger in childbirth, or of abdominal complaints. In a man there is danger of urinary disease, especially if an evil aspect occurs between Saturn and Mars in Sagittarius or Scorpio, when there will be some likelihood of an operation.

In any case the Moon in the Sixth House weakens the health of the native.

Moon in the Seventh House

From the matrimonial standpoint the influence will be the same as in the Second House, but it will be of a more lofty nature; that is to say, the marriage will be more harmonious, better balanced, but equally fortunate in every respect. The Moon, however, must not receive any adverse aspects from Uranus or Saturn.

It is very favourable for lawsuits, which will be successful. In bad aspect with Venus it sometimes causes fickleness in the affections if the cards representing unfaithfulness are drawn, but it does not break up the home. In this House, the Moon causes troubles for the wife or the Mother.

Moon in the Eighth House

In the case of a man, the Moon in this House may make him a widower. If well aspected by the Sun it may mean the death of the Mother. There is a likelihood of money through a legacy.

Grave danger is shown for the Mother, who suffers from the kidneys. If in adverse aspect with Mars, it will mean the rapid death of the Mother following upon an attack of uræmia.

There are violent quarrels with women, especially female relatives, sometimes attended with physical violence.

Moon in the Ninth House

This is always an indication of long journeys, usually across the water; these journeys are connected with money matters.

In this House the Moon gives a tendency to dreams, second-sight and mediumship. It is very similar to the position in the First House, but has more influence over the mind than the body, and therefore gives an imaginative, changeable mentality, sometimes inclined to falsehood, perhaps unconscious. It may cause abnormality of the brain (madness or genius) according to the good or evil aspects which the Moon receives. There will also be danger when travelling if the Moon is badly situated, or if it is afflicted by Mars and Saturn.

Moon in the Tenth House

There are constant changes in the worldly position. If the Moon is well aspected, these changes will be very fortunate. It brings unexpected success, often popularity, and is, in this House, the best position for men who wish to take up politics. It is likewise a good position for actors and all those who have to face the public.

It is often an indication that a woman will help the native in his career, or, at any rate, will influence his ascent, which will be a very rapid one. The Moon in this House also shows a likelihood of great gain through the sale or acquisition of house-property.

Moon in the Eleventh House

This gives many women friends, and the help and protection of influential women.

In any case the social circle is extensive; friendships are fluctuating and superficial. It is always the indication of a large family, especially girls in a woman's horoscope, and boys in a man's horoscope.

The native will obtain honours, renown or popularity in his social circle. This may often be of short duration, but it will recur in another sphere. Success is shown in large associations, the position being favourable for administrative posts. It is also an indication of journeys in the company of friends.

There is often a likelihood of a legal dispute with some one dealing with water or liquids.

Moon in the Twelfth House

This stands for peace in the domestic circle, in a calm, secluded spot. It is also an indication of great charitableness.

This position of the Moon is that of kind-hearted, helpful people; nurses, devoted women, or gentle, loving souls.

It means self-sacrifice.

If the Moon is weak or badly aspected in this House, its position causes peculiar troubles or events in life. There are nervous diseases, especially in Gemini or Virgo; convulsions in Scorpio; hysteria in Capricorn; somnambulism (sleep-walking) in Taurus; enmities in Aries, all occurring through women: the mother, the wife, or the sweetheart. It is an indication of betrayal generally, whether real or imaginary, as in this House it denotes persecution mania, if Mars or Saturn are in bad aspect with the Moon, and themselves situated in unfavourable signs.

The Moon in the Signs

Moon in Aries

In this sign the Moon gives a great deal of imagination, a quick, mobile and changeable disposition; peculiar and restless, lacking in self-confidence, with a tendency to view life from an unreal aspect. It makes poets, writers and—liars. It brings the likelihood of clairvoyance; causes unforeseen, daring voyages; gives a greater force of inertia than of true will-power.

With the Moon in this sign (especially in 20 of Aries) the native may be liable to a face-wound or head-wound.

If it is at 10 of Aries it will bring unexpected good luck at a critical moment, which will free the native from his troubles.

In 20 of Aries it is unfortunate for everything in general, as there is lack of organising power, and deficiency in courage. It is an unlucky position.

Moon in Taurus

This is lucky in the general conduct of affairs, and for love in particular. It is good for money matters. The native is gentle, somewhat weak, but on the whole sympathetic, which makes him seek peace and quietude, and go for sentimental walks near the water. The voice is pleasant, but is impaired early in life, and there are risks of throat trouble.

In 10 of Taurus the Moon shows fickleness, unfaithfulness or jealousy, which however will benefit the native.

In 20 of Taurus it always means a journey, but in connection with trouble. It is a sign of fickleness, change and alteration in the affections.

The Moon in Taurus is a sign of success for an artist, as it always gives intuition.

Moon in Gemini

There is lack of cautiousness, and indication of impulsive action; often gossip or inconsequential talk. The native is highly intelligent. He has a taste for study in general, and literature in particular (history and geography). Many short journeys will take place. The life will be a long one, but disturbed by quarrels, in spite of the native's wish for peace.

In 10 of Gemini it points to infidelity with a person in close contact with the native; often a member of his family.

In 20 of Gemini the Moon procures many and noted learned friends who will help the native to advance.

Moon in Cancer

The Moon here is in its own domicile. This gives especially great sensitiveness. There is a desire for journeys of short duration, but it always compels the native to return to his home circle, which he loves above everything else. The mental faculties are good. The great conscientiousness and straightforwardness of the native cause him to be frequently deceived. This position of the Moon always gives a healthy body and a healthy mind, unless it is afflicted by Mars or Saturn. An evil influence from these two planets causes lymphatism, or lung trouble.

With a favourable aspect from Jupiter, progress will be certain. Nevertheless, in 10 of Cancer it will be more difficult: there are unexpected set-backs from Saturn. Moreover, there is danger of accident when travelling, though not of a serious nature, but it will always point to great strain and fatigue in the course of a journey.

In 20 of Cancer an act of violence will be committed against the native. Troubled circumstances will encompass him, but help and light will come to him eventually from a woman, sometimes from the mother, or the wife.

Moon in Leo

The Moon in this sign gives the best things one can wish for. Progress is assured in a professional or intellectual career. It makes the poet, the writer, the scientist, the musician. It gives ambition, perseverance, work. The disposition is proud, self-centred, straightforward; the mind is synthetic; there is love of home and of children (especially the girls). It represents the man of good counsel who helps others.

Energy being very great, it may sometimes happen that the

native wishes to undertake more than he can accomplish, but with a good aspect of Mars, and especially with Moon in 20 of Leo, the native in spite of difficulties will succeed through industry and perseverance, and also frequently through privation.

In this sign the Moon causes weakness of sight, or compels the native to wear glasses at a premature age.

In 10 of Leo it is an indication of faithfulness, with a tendency to be too trusting.

In 10 of Leo it causes heart trouble; and in 20 of Leo blood-poisoning, if the Sun is badly placed in the horoscope.

Moon in Virgo

In this sign the Moon often gives a peculiar disposition. The mind, which is very intuitive, enables the native to succeed in the study of occult sciences. It gives a tendency to dreams and presentiments and inclines to clairvoyance and illumination. There is a notable want of experience, through which the native will make mistakes owing to lack of thought. With a bad aspect of Mars he will not be conscientious.

The evil influence of Saturn will always cause serious disorders of the digestive system. It is the position which causes the most serious abdominal disorders in women, whom it often makes childless. In spite of the diseases which it causes in this sign, the Moon gives a long life, but more sentiment than luck in marriage. In 20 of Virgo, however, if Venus is well placed, it brings a wealthy union. The union is generally harmonious, as the Moon in this sign enables the native to endure the faults or his (or her) partner.

From the standpoint of worldly position, the Moon is unfortunate in 10 of Virgo, always causing delay in the realisation of the native's plans, causing him to undertake, through lack of due thought, things which cannot succeed, as they have no real foundation.

Moon in Libra

This brings many matters connected with the law, or an occupation which necessitates dealings with magistrates, lawyers or police officials.

The mind is straightforward and conscientious, but hesitating. There is much refinement in everything, even in dress, which exhibits a taste for simplicity and subdued colours. Cheerfulness and a constant desire for enjoyment will cause the native always to seek the society of those who are younger than himself.

Reason is predominant. The native is practical and logical, and his vivid imagination makes him verbose in speech, without departing from the subject under discussion.

This position makes good politicians, especially in 10 of Libra.

In 20 of Libra the Moon is also very favourable. It gives constant progress, provided there is no evil aspect of Mars afflicting this sign, as it would then cause an unexpected, but not irretrievable downfall, as the native regains at some time or other the exalted position which belongs to him in this sign of Venus.

Moon in Scorpio

The Moon is in its fall at 3° of this sign, and is therefore very unfortunate for all matters governed by the Moon. It inclines to falsehood, and, depriving the native of any positive qualities, he cannot react against an inherent tendency towards slothfulness, intemperance or fraud. All this is naturally modified by benefic influences; but the fact remains that there will be many difficulties to overcome, misfortunes, a life of struggle, frequently of short duration, with dangers and illnesses of every kind.

This position is very unfavourable for childbirth, and is also the indication of sterility—sometimes of miscarriage if Mars is weak.

In 20 of Scorpio it denotes dishonesty to the detriment of a woman, or a dishonest action perpetrated by a woman.

The Moon in Scorpio, badly aspected by Mars or Saturn, and situated in the Eighth House is a sign of bereavement for the native.

Moon in Sagittarius

This is an indication of an unmaterial mind, much ideality and laxity in matters connected with dress. It indicates contempt for money, which will, however, never be lacking, as the Moon in this Sign often brings legacies or inheritances. Success is shown through the wife, who brings great moral support to her husband, helps him in his undertakings, and enables him to succeed in matters connected with the mind. These are often attended by difficulties and hard work, but there is always the certainty that sooner or later the desired result will be achieved.

In this sign the Moon gives a large and united family

In 10 of Sagittarius the Moon brings many changes in the native's position in life; numerous transformations take place, and whatever is undertaken always has real chances of a successful issue.

In 20 of Sagittarius it gives self-confidence, remarkable powers of divination, and an instinct of conservation which permits the native to live to a ripe age, especially if the sign occupies the Second, Third, Fifth or Eleventh House. In angular Houses, however, the life seems to be shorter.

Moon in Capricorn

This again is a malefic position, as it indicates a hypocritical, not over-scrupulous native, wanting in moral qualities, unless there are good aspects. It denotes moral and physical laziness and a lack of energy. The native is very hesitant, often finds it difficult to choose between Good and Evil, and usually inclines towards the latter, thereby tending to go from bad to worse. The disposition is unpleasant, often morose, and always spiteful.

In 10 of Capricorn the Moon sometimes brings momentary success—inevitably followed by a subsequent downfall. Numerous worries are caused through women. Marriage is usually unfortunate, and cannot be otherwise with such a position. With a malefic influence of Mercury, there is danger of fraud, swindling or bankruptcy; in any case some disreputable deed will be committed. A benefic aspect of Jupiter may entirely modify the foregoing, but the health will be unsatisfactory, and a certain lack of harmony will pervade the mind.

In 20 of Capricorn the Moon brings somewhat better health, if Mars is powerful in the horoscope, but it is a sign of violent death if Capricorn occupies the Eighth House. The danger will arise in a country other than that of birth, and often in the course of a short journey.

Moon in Aquarius

In this sign the Moon gives a somewhat sad, thoughtful and meditative disposition. The native loves solitude, is usually humane, but may become misanthropic after numerous disappointments.

It gives a tendency to utopian investigations, which cause ill-luck. The tastes and ideas of the native are peculiar, especially if Saturn is badly aspected (in Aries, for example), when the mental condition of the native may give cause for anxiety.

Favourably influenced, the Moon in Aquarius gives a morbid and wandering imagination (a sort of "Grand-Guignol"). The native's life itself will be a sad one, and this through his own fault.

Nevertheless, the Moon in this position procures the favour of women, especially in 20 of Aquarius, but the associations will be of short duration, ill-assorted and as peculiar as the native's own mentality.

In 10 of Aquarius it indicates betrayal in love, infidelity, deceit.

Moon in Pisces

This gives a great desire for comfort, indolence, often slothfulness; a fertile imagination, many plans, but few that are carried out. It is a mark of fickleness in love, with more sensuousness than vitality. In this sign the Moon makes the native over-talkative. He either slanders others, or is himself the subject of slander. He is readily inclined to allow himself to be deceived, or frequently he deceives others. It means infidelity, more than one marriage, little luck in money matters, but never indicates poverty.

In 20 of Pisces, if the horoscope is a good one, the Moon is very favourable, as it adds continuity to that which exists. The same will apply in the opposite sense in a bad horoscope.

In 10 of Pisces it often indicates a native who, unconsciously, tells falsehoods, who persuades himself that what he says has actually happened, and in consequence suffers by it. The Moon has more vitality in these degrees, but is a sure sign of infidelity in marriage.

N.B.—The position of the Moon in a horoscope is very important. It should be specially studied, both in regard to its aspects as well as its position in the House and in the Sign, in order to form an accurate judgment.

Mercury

THIS planet is mental, dry, nervous and convertible; that is to say, it is strongly modified both by the aspects which it receives, and by its position. Its day house is in Gemini, night house in Virgo; its exile is in Sagittarius and in Pisces.

It is good for things connected with knowledge, and deserves special attention in order to judge the native's mentality.

It has a special influence on commerce, medicine, speech, writings, letters. It also represents practical things, and is connected with personal property, and consequently with money. Quicksilver is the metal governed by Mercury.

Mercury also symbolises youth, liveliness, gaiety, motion, dancing, walking, and represents the child. Badly influenced, it is the ruler of falsehood, trickery and fraud.

Its colour is light grey; day, Wednesday.

It indicates a native who is witty, fond of quibbling, more analytical than synthetic. He makes many gestures, his lean, delicate hands are constantly on the move. His forehead is high, his stature usually short, nose thin and long, the whole body lithe and supple.

Nervous diseases come under the rulership of Mercury.

Mercury in the Houses

Mercury in the First House

Mercury in the First House endows the native with numerous moral attributes—vivacity, a penetrative mind, good memory, a somewhat argumentative disposition, attachment to details. This position makes it possible to succeed in smaller undertakings rather than large ones; that is to say, there is more chance of achieving success in many small enterprises than in only one large one. For a business man, retail trade will bring him more luck than wholesale. In this House, Mercury gives a practical mind, which sees things exactly as they are, which judges everything for what it is worth, and brings back people and things to reality: it is the equilibrium and harmony of the brain, unless there are evil aspects.

Mercury in the Second House

This is a fortunate position for transactions in general, and for the sale of movable property in particular. In this House it gives a flair for everything that concerns monetary matters, and enables the native, by his own merit, skill, cunning or dexterity, to acquire much money. With a good influence of Venus, a wealthy marriage is indicated with a partner in a good position, whom the native has captivated more through his cleverness than through love, so that marriage under these auspices does not always fulfil expectations. Mercury in the Second House, in square with Mars or Venus, is the sign of more than one union, separation or unfaithfulness.

Mercury in the Third House

In this House Mercury is favourable for matters connected with the native's education. This card enables him to adapt himself to the fortunate or unfortunate circumstances of life.

It makes him very adaptable, and is a token of intellectuality as well as of dexterity. It gives a taste for knowledge in general, and for literature (more for works dealing with observation than those of imagination). It gives more taste for harmony in music than for melody.

It is very favourable for brothers and sisters when well influenced. Mercury usually makes the native either the youngest or the eldest of his brothers, but never places him between them in regard to age.

Mercury is also favourable for numerous quick journeys. It gives love of motoring, aviation, walking and dancing.

Mercury in the Fourth House

When dignified, Mercury in this House gives a pleasant, cheerful home-life, surrounded by young people; plenty of money; and happy relations with the family of the marriage partner.

If the influence is unfavourable, there will be, on the contrary, much quarrelling, avarice, lack of harmony with neighbours over trivial matters.

It is very favourable for things of the mind. Mercury in the Nadir inclines to the study of the occult sciences and of mathematics. It is the position for the man who observes, who knows how to maintain silence, but who knows how to act with incredible decision and precision in his own best interests. The position of Mercury in this House is not very powerful, but it is favourable for transactions in land or house property.

It is, furthermore, the sign of instability in the home. It is the position of the officer or official who constantly changes his place of residence.

Mercury in the Fifth House

In the Fifth House, Mercury is favourable for financial speculations, provided it is not badly aspected by Mars or Saturn. In this House, which is connected with pleasures, it makes these more intellectual than sensual. It brings success in pleasures pertaining to the mind—theatres, concerts, paintings —especially if Venus or the Sun are dignified.

The position is usually unfavourable for the children. It does not incline to a large family, and causes trouble and worries in connection with offspring. This position of Mercury favours bachelorhood; it brings many short love affairs, but little constancy.

Mercury in the Sixth House

As with all planets situated in this House, Mercury will not be favourable for the health, and will cause nervous disorders, intestinal complaints, and sometimes bronchial troubles. It often necessitates journeys for the sake of health.

Nevertheless, when dignified, Mercury in this House will be favourable for servants or subordinates, who will be devoted to their master. In conjunction with an evil influence, it often means petty thefts on the part of employees.

Unless very well aspected, this position does not usually make a good employer. The native lacks initiative and he will always be more successful when working with or for others than for himself.

Mercury in the Seventh House

In this position Mercury often makes the native marry a partner who is younger than himself, or who looks very youthful. He is usually of short stature, refined, intellectual, talkative, generally dark, with aptitudes for commerce, medicine or oratory.

This influence is not very favourable for marriage. There are quarrels, discussions, and often a lawsuit which leads to the separation of the marriage partners.

On the other hand, it is a good position for business associations. Well dignified, it will make the native win many lawsuits which will benefit him.

If Mercury is badly aspected in this House, however, it will mean cheating on the part of associates, the likelihood of failure through their fault, and if Saturn is in the Twelfth House, there is risk of imprisonment or confinement caused through loss of money.

Mercury in the Eighth House

This position is favourable for marriage. It points especially to a partner who is rich and older than the native, and he will therefore inherit.

With a malefic influence, Mercury brings dissensions. Unpleasant words will be uttered in connection with a death. It often means even the embezzlement of an inheritance.

The evil influence of Mercury in this House will be the cause of numerous illnesses and it often makes the native melancholy and sad. It may happen, with an evil influence of the Moon, and with Mercury in Cancer in the Eighth House, that the native, or one of his children, will be mentally afflicted.

Dignified, Mercury procures success in writing, and in a very favourable horoscope it signifies that the native will receive recognition after his death.

Mercury in the Ninth House

This is very favourable for matters pertaining to the mind. Mercury, dignified in this House, indicates a superior intellect, and the sure promise of success in all pursuits followed by the native, in consequence of his powerful mentality. He is highly intuitive, and will interest himself in philosophic or religious subjects. This position in trine (120°) with the Ascendant is favourable to the native, who absorbs the qualities of Mercury.

Mercury in the Ninth House causes numerous long journeys. It is also a good position for those who have dealings with foreigners, and gives aptitude for foreign languages.

In a lay-out of cards, it will also indicate the departure of one or more of the children to a foreign land, where they will readily make their fortune.

Mercury in the Tenth House

In this House, Mercury signifies a native of an intellectual or commercial occupation, and indicates that the children should be guided on similar lines, provided the Fifth House is in good aspect with the Tenth. This position is favourable for acquaintances, who will be numerous and clever, and also for the worldly position, as it enables the native to gain money through his own merit. If the planet is badly aspected, it is often a sign of incompetence. The native undertakes too many things, and will not be able to bring them to a successful issue, his mobility of mind being too great. It is the position which gives great inventive possibilities, but when Mercury is weak we find ourselves in the presence of the inventor who does not derive any benefit from his work, but benefits others.

Mercury in the Eleventh House

Mercury in this position brings numerous acquaintances. The friends or associates are learned, hard-working and alert. The native seeks his own interests. He is calculating and always succeeds through his own merit.

It is a favourable House for the children, who will also be very clever, and who will, at some time, become the associates of their father.

This position is not good for love affairs; it makes the native fickle, but does not break up the home. The native mixes freely in the world; he loves dancing, social life and theatres.

In bad aspect, especially with Mars, Mercury causes disagreements with associates, discussions, spiteful words; quarrels with the children; all this through motives of self-interest.

Mercury in the Twelfth House

This House, which is always unfortunate, can hardly be favourable to Mercury, especially in Taurus, Scorpio or Capricorn, in which it causes disappointments corresponding with the sign. When dignified it may, on account of its close proximity to the Ascendant, and its mobility, justify the prophecy of good fortune pertaining to matters within its domain: eloquence, commercial gain, intellect, money. It must, however, be very powerful in the horoscope, and be free from bad aspects from the malefics, as it would otherwise be a token of incompetence, and everything undertaken would fail at the very moment when success seemed assured.

Badly aspected, it is also unfavourable for the child, who cannot be reared except under strange or peculiar conditions. With a malefic aspect from Venus, it will not be favourable for the emotions, and indicates a liability to cerebral trouble through sensual excess.

Mercury in the Signs

Mercury in Aries

ARIES adds still greater nervousness to Mercury. It does not always enable the native to act with the necessary poise. He does not like to be contradicted, and lacks the necessary flexibility for undertaking commercial transactions. It is the position of those who are at war with the world, who do not think like other people, and who are always inclined to side with the minority. Well influenced, this position is good for writers and lawyers, but with an evil aspect of the Moon it incites to falsehood. With good aspect, the native possesses good mental qualities, a cunning mind, or at any rate sufficient skill to enable him to extricate himself from his difficulties, which may be numerous, as he will be surrounded with many enemies

In 10 of Aries, Mercury points to the likelihood of many journeys, often attended with difficulties. Nevertheless, a good aspect of the Sun will make them favourable, and frequently at the moment when matters seem at their worst the native will obtain what he wants.

Mercury in 20 of Aries causes serious danger in regard to worldly matters. Moreover, it is often a sign of nervous depression due to a destiny which the native finds it difficult to escape. There is also the possibility of typhoid fever in early life, or nervous disorders.

Mercury in Taurus

Mercury in Taurus has a fortunate influence on the native, to whom he gives a prepossessing appearance and a cheerful disposition. He is well liked by those around him, and has an opportunity of contracting a lucky marriage, at any rate from the pecuniary point of view.

This position is good for matters connected with the

affections. It is a token of marked selfishness, the native seeking his own pleasure before that of his mate. It is favourable for artistic pursuits, but these will profit the native, as he does nothing without benefit to himself, and if he is an artist, he expects that Art shall provide him with material returns. He prefers money now to honour after death.

In this sign Mercury procures the likelihood of earning money easily.

In 10 of Taurus, Mercury indicates a great deal of jealousy which occurs through the native's own fault. Difficulties will frequently arise, and there are possibilities of a setback in progress. This position also denotes a complete change in the position or vocation at a certain period of life.

In 20 of Taurus, unless very well aspected, the life is unsettled; it is again the sign of journeys undertaken without preparation, and which are costly. In the Seventh House this position of Mercury causes worries or sorrow in regard to matrimony.

Mercury in Gemini

This is a fortunate position from the mental standpoint. Mercury is here in his own domicile, and being very powerful it confers great benefits in regard to matters connected with the House it occupies. If in Tenth House, it is proof of success in life. The native is naturally sympathetic; he will be able to make many friends, who will help him according to the aspects received by Mercury from the benefic planets and the Houses in which they are situated.

In 10 of Gemini this position is favourable for the mind, but the temperament is inclined to be weak. There is also the likelihood of the native worrying needlessly, and creating imaginary troubles for himself. He is hyper-sensitive and emotional. He feels things of which others are unaware, and suffers accordingly. His strong intuition enables him to see a long way ahead, and anticipate events. He has a studious mind, and according to the education received (study the Third House in this respect) he will make his mark in life.

In 20 of Gemini, Mercury is also well placed. It enables the native to succeed in life through his acumen. The general kindness of his disposition partakes of the nature of Jupiter, and a good aspect from Mars will help him to progress rapidly.

Mercury in Cancer

In Cancer, Mercury does not give faithfulness in love. The mind is fickle, inconsiderate and changeable. For life in general it is a good position, giving acumen and success. It is one of the most powerful promises of long journeys, especially if Mercury is in the Ninth House. In the Third House it means many journeys of short duration. This is also a fortunate position for business, especially in the Second House. Unless well aspected by Venus, marriage will be hindered; the native will live long with his mother, and according to the longevity of the latter, he may not marry at all, or marry very late. This position of Mercury often denotes a secret union with a woman older than the native, or, in the case of a woman's horoscope, with a lover younger than herself.

If Venus is dignified in the horoscope, and casts a good aspect to the Ruler of the Seventh House, Mercury in Cancer will cause the native to marry early, or the marriage partner will be younger than himself.

In 10 of Cancer, Mercury causes serious danger while travelling. There is likelihood of a railway accident, especially if Mars casts a malefic aspect. It is a sign of disputes regarding matters connected with the House in which Cancer is situated In the Third House, with the family; in the Fourth House, with the father or in the home; in the Fifth House, with the children; in the Sixth House, trouble on account of the health (danger of illness); in the Seventh House, disagreement with the marriage partner; in the Eighth House, disputes over legacies or with the grandparents; in the Ninth House, discontent with oneself; in the Tenth House, inharmonious relations with the Mother; in the Eleventh House, with friends and acquaintances; in the Twelfth, with the law; in the First House, it causes physical deformity; in the Second House, difficulties with creditors, debtors or customers.

In 20 of Cancer, Mercury makes it possible for the native to succeed through his own intelligence. He is very practical, knows what he wants, and will show it in difficulties. This will be very helpful to him, and his good management will enable him to extricate himself from his troubles. This position in the Second House is favourable for business connected with foreign produce, especially if the Ruler of the Ninth House casts a benefic aspect and is well placed.

Mercury in Leo

In this sign Mercury gives influential friends, and if the Ninth House is well disposed the native may become an ambassador, a diplomat, or simply a successful business man. It is a very good influence: the character is ambitious and firm; the native is gifted, noble-minded, trusting and benevolent; he has fine aptitude for art, and if education shows it, he may succeed along these lines. This position also brings success in any business or undertaking connected with luxuries. The native is gifted with fine powers of oratory, and, with the help of good aspects from the benefic planets, he will succeed in any branch. In the Fifth House, in Leo, Mercury may make him a theatre or entertainment manager, or a great artist or musician.

In 10 of Leo, if this sign occupies the Tenth House, Mercury makes the native an orator, or a mere chatterer, according to the aspects. It gives a good memory, an investigating mind in search of knowledge; not usually that of a leader, but of a good and faithful employee, who will render many services to his employer, provided the latter lets him exercise his own initiative.

In 20 of Leo, Mercury causes many petty difficulties which will cause trouble in life, connected with matters ruled by the House occupied by the sign: in the Sixth House there will be bowel trouble, and the danger of auto-toxæmia if Mars casts an evil aspect; in the Second House, especially, it is the position of unfortunate inventors or misunderstood people.

Mercury in Virgo

In his own domicile Mercury is very favourable for matters connected with the mind, which it renders idealistic, but somewhat over-analytical, causing the native to attach undue importance to the petty details of life. The mind is argumentative, especially with an aspect from Mars, but is none the less of a superior order, although not productive. It inclines to matters pertaining to philosophy, occultism or religion, which do not bring material success, so that the native's position will not be brilliant. He may be esteemed and honoured, but he will never be wealthy. It is a good position for the scientist or the professor, but not for the banker or business man, unless other positions and good aspects indicate the contrary, in which case such a banker or business-man will become a magnate.

In the 10 of Virgo, Mercury causes many delays in progress. It makes the scientist or inventor whom everyone admires, but whom no capitalist helps. It may also mean plans that benefit others—too much trust in others and a lack of practical common-sense.

In 20 of Virgo, and well aspected, Mercury may bring success through the help of a woman, the native's superior nature appealing to a wealthy woman who may become his wife, or, at any rate, will provide him with the monetary facilities necessary for the realization and success of his lofty aspirations. But for this to happen Venus and the Moon must be dignified in the horoscope, and Mercury must not be afflicted by either Saturn or Uranus.

Mercury in Libra

The position of Mercury in Libra indicates great likelihood of lawsuits or disputes with lawyers. If Mercury is dignified and well aspected, it will procure gains through lawsuits; if afflicted, it will cause losses, troubles and disputes, especially in the Twelfth House.

Well aspected, Mercury in Libra will give love for the children, helpful associations, profitable contracts and investments. This position is also favourable for those who interest themselves in politics, as it procures rapid progress and popularity.

Badly placed, and afflicted by the malefic planets, Mercury causes disappointments in connection with matters governed by the House occupied by this sign.

In 10 of Libra, Mercury is very favourable for the mind. It is a sure sign of good mental faculties, and of success, provided there are no evil aspects. This position is good for study, and in the Ninth House it should incline the native to learn foreign languages, which will benefit his position in life.

In 20 of Libra, Mercury procures an exalted position, but is not favourable for the children, who will cause grave anxiety. If Mars casts an evil aspect to Mercury in 20 of Libra, and this sign occupies the Fifth House, there is danger of premature death of the offspring.

Mercury in Scorpio

In Scorpio, Mercury often brings dangerous dealings with violent people, or very grave quarrels over matters connected with the House occupied by the sign. An evil aspect of Venus will cause infidelity or deceit in love, with danger of separation from the marriage partner. The native's character is impetuous, though crafty when necessary. The Martial influence is manifested here as in Aries, but with less straightforwardness and more diplomacy, which will tend to make the life more successful.

This planet in Scorpio is not very favourable for the health; in the Sixth House it causes danger of intestinal trouble, or affections of the generative system.

In 10 of Scorpio the health is improved, and there is even likelihood of a ripe old age if the luminaries are well placed.

Mercury in 20 of Scorpio is detrimental to the native's position in life; bad company, or the society of those with whom he is compelled to mix, may harm him. There is grave danger of theft, robbery or fraud, and even of violent death, if 20 of Scorpio is situated in the Eighth House.

Mercury in Sagittarius

This position favours the progress of the native, who has good chances of success in an administrative capacity. He is well fitted to be a Government official, and if the Third House indicates it, he may succeed in a diplomatic or consular career. Mercury in Sagittarius is also well placed for trade with foreign countries, or with foreigners, or for the sale of foreign produce. Fortune will be gained with some difficulty through exertion, as luck will not help the native. (Though Sagittarius is one of Jupiter's signs, the fixed stars in this sign are not favourable to Mercury; moreover, this sign cannot be considered lucky, as it should not be overlooked that the Moon's Descending Node [Dragon's Tail] receives its fall therein.)

Mercury in 10 of Sagittarius is more favourable. With prudence it may bring worldly success. Reflection is very helpful here, and it will be necessary to think well before doing anything, setbacks being likely over matters connected with the House occupied by the sign.

In 20 of Sagittarius, Mercury makes the native careful and far-seeing, slow to act, desirous of retaining what he already possesses, and with the ability to do so; but in order to achieve this he must never forsake his cautiousness, as the least deviation may cause his downfall, should Mars, Uranus or Saturn cast an evil aspect.

Mercury in Capricorn

This position in the domicile of Saturn is not favourable to Mercury—youth does not go well with old age, and if Saturn is in bad aspect with Mercury, it is invariably a sign of grave trouble bearing upon matters ruled by the House occupied by this sign. Apart from the Angular Houses, this position is very bad for the native's health, and causes nervous disorders. He is nevertheless well endowed, or, more strictly speaking, possesses great ability for the study of abstract subjects. As this does not conduce to practical sense, the material position in life is thereby often handicapped.

In 10 of Capricorn it is even more unfortunate for legitimate affairs; but the native, being more cunning, may achieve success in questionable undertakings. If Mercury is well aspected by the benefics, it is an assurance of success, but the native will live in retirement.

In 20 of Capricorn the position is improved as regards health, and the native may live to a very advanced age. It is not a good position for marriage; it is that of the recluse, living far from kith and kin, and having few friends, or friends who do not care for him.

Mercury in Aquarius

In Aquarius, Mercury gives great pleasure through friendships. The native's friends will be learned, and he will enjoy being in their company, and they also will seek his companionship, as his synthetic mind will captivate them. In this sign Mercury will also be a token of fidelity and benevolence; it is favourable for associations, and also for the mother and children.

In 10 of Aquarius, Mercury makes th native less straightforward, less benevolent, but also more capable. It is good for a wealthy union, which the native should seek, but this, occurring somewhat late in life, may at a later period be the cause of matrimonial disagreements.

In 20 of Aquarius, Mercury is also beneficial for matters connected with the mind, pointing to a man of refined taste, a lover of the Beautiful and the Good. Dealing in antiques is clearly shown, and the native may succeed in this direction.

Mercury in Pisces

This position is not a signal one for faithfulness in marriage: it is a sign of infidelity or deceit in love, usually on the part of the native himself. It also means words spoken against the native, gossip which will harm him and which may at a certain period seriously jeopardise his position, especially in matters connected with the affections.

In 10 of Pisces this planet gives many acquaintances, but few lasting friendships. The native's friends are as transitory as his ideas and wishes, and caprice is often the master of his Destiny. Life is usually wasted with Mercury in this decanate.

In 20 of Pisces the position is very favourable. The native is highly esteemed, Mercury therein being a token of the intelligence that compels success; he will benefit as an exporter.

Mars

MARS is dry, hot, masculine. Its day domicile is in Aries, and its night domicile in Scorpio. It is in exile in the domiciles of Venus (Taurus and Libra); its exaltation is in Capricorn, its fall in the opposite sign, Cancer, and it receives joy in Scorpio.

It is furthest distant from the Earth when situated in Virgo, and is, on the contrary, nearest when in Pisces.

This planet gives impetuosity, passion, energy, expansion, and produces the active temperaments, over whom it rules.

In a laying-out of cards Mars will indicate anger, vitality. It is the triumph of Force; it gives straightforwardness and represents the Man, while Venus (as we will show) represents the Woman.

The stature is average, but it gives a robust constitution, and strong muscles, which is the part of the body ruled by Mars. The powers of resistance are considerable. The hair is usually russet-brown and wiry, either straight or curly (frizzled), but dry and coarse. The whole aspect of the face as well as of the body gives an impression of ruggedness, with a daring, masterful manner, which is not displeasing, especially in a man.

Mars depicts a man who may appeal to women on account of his physical strength. On the contrary, he will not usually appeal to men, with whom he often seeks quarrels, being combative and vindictive. Favourably influenced, the native will be a fine and noble character, ever defending the weak, even when the latter are in the wrong.

Mars inclines to sports: with aspects from Mercury it makes an aviator; it always makes a good soldier in time of war; but a strong head in times of peace.

Its colour is bright red; metal, iron; day, Tuesday. Its diseases are: fevers, inflammatory complaints, and it often causes wounds or accidents.

Mars in the Houses

Mars in the First House

This position signifies an instinct of domination, more especially over others than over oneself. It also means moral and physical courage, if Mars is well aspected; otherwise it may indicate cowardice, and cause the native to attack those who are weaker than himself. It is often a sign of quarrels and disputes. In an ordinary laying-out of cards Mars, coming out near the Ascendant, always prophesies an event of a sentimental or passionate nature. In this House it gives energy, vitality and great expenditure of the Life Force.

Mars in the Second House

With Mars situated in this House, the native will have uncontrollable inclinations to extravagance. His appetites being considerable, it will be necessary, if the balance is to be maintained, that he should be endowed with a corresponding amount of wealth. This will induce him to earn money through his own efforts and exertions. With Mars well aspected, he will have many and potent ideas, which will never allow him to see anything from a narrow standpoint. His activity will be overflowing, but often muddling. There will be a lack of system, but this will be compensated by a good memory and an inborn sense of organisation. Moreover, Mars in this House makes a leader, and his usual subordinates will be influenced by Mercury or Jupiter, which will mitigate the mistakes of their Chief. It is a fortunate position when Mars is well aspected and placed in one of his own signs. If Jupiter sends a good aspect to the Second House, the native will contract a wealthy marriage which, while it may not fulfil his emotional desires, will give him complete satisfaction from the monetary standpoint.

Mars badly placed in this House, with bad aspects from

Uranus or Saturn, will cause many troubles, and unavoidable pecuniary losses.

Mars in the Third House

Mars in this House will be the cause of quarrels with those surrounding the native: violent disputes will arise, and there is danger of blows or wounds. Harmony between brothers and sisters is far from perfect, the native being impetuous and desiring to have the upper-hand at all costs. As there is the probability of the parents being similarly inclined (through heredity), peace is impossible. The native's mind being critical, he may, education permitting, become a first-class controversialist or politician—a leader. This position is not good for travelling. It causes accidents of locomotion—railway, tramway or motor accidents, or even through beasts of burden, if Saturn sends a bad aspect, and these will be due to the native's own recklessness.

Mars in the Fourth House

Mars in this position causes the premature death of the marriage partner. It is always a sign of approaching danger in an ordinary laying-out of cards. In the horoscope it implies disorders of the circulation, and a domineering and despotic character, which interferes with domestic harmony. This position also presages a risk of destruction of house property by fire, especially if the Sun is in bad aspect with Mars. This planet in the Nadir of the Heavens is usually a sign of the sudden death of the father, following upon a heart attack, or an accident. If well aspected, Mars may increase the inheritance through work and exertion. If afflicted, it shows continual troubles in life.

Mars in the Fifth House

This indicates a life disordered and lacking in organisation. The native lives from hand-to-mouth, and it often shows that one is dealing with an unfortunate gambler or speculator, whose fortune rapidly dwindles. It is an indication of activity in the pursuit of pleasure, with little zest for serious matters. There is danger for the children, who will suffer from diseases of the nature of the sign in which Mars is situated. In the case of a woman, an evil aspect will point to trouble connected with child-birth, and if it comes from Neptune, there is danger of miscarriage. If Mars is dignified, it gives activity to the children, who will be turbulent and difficult to train; they will be haughty and independent, but will have every chance of success in life.

Mars in the Sixth House

Mars badly aspected in this House and situated in a bad sign, gives fevers and inflammation of that part of the body ruled by the sign in which this planet is placed. If, on the contrary, it is well aspected, Mars denotes considerable physical resistance, which will render the native immune from disease.

This position favours the acquisition of money, and the constant improvement of the home surroundings from the material point of view. Badly placed or aspected, it causes numerous disputes with servants and employees.

Mars in the Sixth House often indicates robbery with violence on the part of some one employed in the home, to the detriment of the consultant, or his uncles and aunts. In Scorpio in the Fifth House, Mars influences more especially those who are fitted for taking care of their fellow-creatures.

Mars in the Seventh House

In this House Mars confers a great amount of sex passion, thus causing an early love affair or marriage. Well aspected, this planet inclines to a wealthy marriage with a woman who will want to rule in the home, and who will be of the Martial type, with all its virtues and vices. In the absence of good aspects to Mars, the couple have not much chance of remaining united, especially if the Ascendant contains a feminine planet, as this causes friction in the home, due to the indolence of one of the marriage partners, and the excessive activity of the other. This position also denotes loss of the marriage partner, and is bad for contracts and partnerships.

Well placed, and receiving a good aspect from Mercury, Mars in this House is a sure token that the native will undertake big things, which will bring, along with appreciable gains, a trail of envy and jealousy, as well as endless lawsuits.

Mars in the Eighth House

When Mars falls in this House, it indicates the violent death of the consultant, or, if it is in aspect with the Sun or the Moon, the death of the father or mother. If the aspect is a good one, the native will benefit by it. An aspect with Venus may also mean the sudden death of the marriage partner, who is of a domineering and violent disposition.

In a horoscope in which Saturn, Uranus or the Moon are afflicted, Mars in the Eighth House shows the possibility of suicide.

Mars in the Ninth House

In the Ninth House, Mars, if it is dignified, gives good chances of success for the native, as it makes him enterprising and energetic, from the physical as well as the mental standpoint.

He is gifted with a fine synthetic mind, which enables him to take a broad view of things, exactly as they are. While this position is often the sign of struggles, it also promises success if the sign occupied by Mars in the Ninth House is powerful. If the contrary is the case, and if Mars is afflicted, it gives a tendency to neurasthenia, depression, lack of self-confidence, and often misunderstandings with the parents. In this House Mars inclines to travelling.

Mars in the Tenth House

The power of Mars in the Mid-Heaven is very great, if it is dignified. It favours the most hazardous enterprises, and these can be carried to a successful issue. This position may be that of a political leader, or a Dictator; it enables the native to overcome his enemies, and all kinds of snares. Difficult times will often occur, numerous struggles will be his lot, but he will be able to defend himself, and if the horoscope generally is good, he will obtain power and authority through strife. This position does not go well with a subordinate post. The native will be an undisciplined soldier, or an employee who cannot submit to his employer's authority, unless he is given a great deal of latitude. When Mars is dignified in the Tenth House, it gives success with women, but may cause misunderstandings on the part of the Mother.

If Saturn is situated in the Fourth House it will mean

premature death of the Father, and may also indicate a relatively untimely death for the native. Mars in the Tenth House always makes the native violent and self-willed.

If the position and aspects of Mars are unfavourable, this position in the Tenth House may cause the worst catastrophes, from imprisonment to accidental death.

Mars in the Eleventh House

This is usually an evil position. It indicates numerous disputes and even physical violence with friends or social acquaintances. It means disagreements between the parents and their children, and will cause their loss if Saturn occupies the Fifth House, and casts an evil aspect.

Dignified in the Eleventh, Mars will give power, and will make a leader who is more feared than loved ; but for this to happen, the Sun, Venus or Jupiter must be in good aspect. Mars is the planet of ambition, and it will thus attain its high aims, but not always without causing sorrow to others.

Mars in the Twelfth House

In this House Mars often exhibits a credulity approaching stupidity, so that this position causes great difficulty and strife. There will be scandals, or unfaithfulness, if Venus is afflicted in the Seventh House. If Mercury occupies the Seventh, it means trouble with the Law, and may cause imprisonment for the native. If the Moon is afflicted in the Ninth House, the native may end his days in a lunatic asylum. In this House Mars cannot be fortunate, and the least harm it can do is to cause danger through an accident or operation.

Good aspects from Jupiter, Venus or the Sun may mitigate the difficulties, which will be constant and numerous, but without which the consultant would consider life to be drab and purposeless.

Mars in the Signs

Mars in Aries

IN his own domicile Mars is strong and has a good measure of affective power, by which we mean that Mars has more influence over the heart than the brain; that it is more emotional than mental.

This position gives stubbornness and independence, daring and masterfulness.

It may also cause anger and hot-headedness. It readily inclines to hasty deeds, rashness, and causes numerous quarrels which, if it is afflicted, will entail an accident or a head-wound.

With a good influence from Mercury or Saturn, Mars always indicates mental activity in the chart of an intellectual worker or a professional man. Mars should always be studied in regard to its aspects and its position.

In 10 of Aries, Mars gives a desire to render service, but also to meddle with other people's affairs, to take the part of the weakest, and thereby to get into difficulties. The position enables the native to undertake things which are beyond his apparent capacities, and to bring them to a successful issue.

An evil aspect from Saturn to Mars when the latter is in 20 of Aries, signifies the imminent danger of accident, or of grave misfortune in matters ruled by the House.

Mars in Taurus

Mars in Taurus always indicates a passionate, emotional, and often sensual temperament, with little constancy. This position is dangerous for a woman, in whom it causes great emotional excitement, especially when Mars occupies the Seventh House. According to whether Venus is well or ill aspected, this position causes the marriage partner to suffer, or to cause suffering. This planet in this sign may signify a wealthy union, but it never gives complete harmony in the home, either the husband or wife being unfaithful.

Apart from sentimental matters, Mars gives vitality, moral and physical courage which helps the native to succeed, if Mercury is well situated in the chart.

The position of Mars in 10 of Taurus is evil: it is the cause of violence, jealousy, frequent blows or wounds, and separation from the marriage partner.

In 20 of Taurus, Mars entails innumerable difficulties in the affections, causing domestic sorrows and disturbances, especially in the Fourth House. In the Ninth or Third House, it shows a journey connected with a love affair, and this will be the result of ill-considered action which can only cause sorrow.

Mars in Gemini

In this sign, and well aspected by Mercury, Mars is a clear token of the native being a good talker, quick and nimble-witted, intelligent, one who knows how to steer his course in life, and who is bound to succeed.

This position often inclines to make easily formed friendships, but the affections are somewhat superficial. The native is kind, but his benevolence is scattered; his warm and attractive tone of voice brings him many friends, and enables him to succeed in a political or business career, or as a barrister. From the educational standpoint, this position is favourable in the Third House, the native possessing great capacity for acquiring knowledge.

In the Twelfth and in the Sixth House, Mars in Gemini causes danger of accident to a limb.

In 10 of Gemini, Mars gives great sensitiveness, a tendency to anger, and heart trouble; if in the Eighth House, there is risk of sudden death, especially through angina pectoris. The native is more inclined to worry than to face real obstacles, and his pessimistic tendencies will be directed to matters ruled by the House occupied by Mars in this decanate.

In 20 of Gemini, Mars gives manliness and physical endurance; if Jupiter is well aspected in the chart, this position is very favourable for the House occupied by this sign.

Mars in Cancer

Mars is not well placed in Cancer. It denotes a native who has more ideas than ability to carry them into effect. This position makes a "bluffer," a boaster and a coward, unless the evil influence is modified by good aspects from other planets.

With good aspects, Mars in Cancer gives periods of foolhardiness rather than real courage. The native does not perceive danger. There is much ambition, and if Jupiter is well situated it may procure rapid progress, and unexpected and easily acquired gains.

In 10 of Cancer, Mars often gives secret enemies, who will cause much harm to the native, either physically or morally. When Mars is in square aspect to Saturn, this decanate is the sign of a serious accident in life, and will indicate death if the aspect occurs in the Eighth House, with a badly situated Sun.

In 20 of Cancer, Mars gives fits of violence that are difficult to conquer; but the native is a lover of Truth and of straightforward things. If in an unfavourable House, this position causes serious stomach complaints, with spitting of blood, due to an ulcer or wound in the stomach.

Mars in Leo

Mars in Leo is favourable. It enables the native to have authority over others and to control himself. It is always a sign of successful combat. The logical powers are pronounced in this sign, and Mars also confers a fine synthetic intellect, sometimes slightly blunder-headed, like the energy which is over-brimming and unruly. It is an indication of enemies who are often powerful, and of unsuccessful competitors who will endeavour to injure the native, but only with partial success. In the Eighth House it is again the sign of sudden death through heart disease; in the First House it will cause an accident to the eyes, or a wound near the eyes of the native during his childhood.

Mars in Leo gives leniency and benevolence, but little patience; the native wishes to be obeyed immediately.

In 10 of Leo the native is frank and has an instinctive desire to confide in others and disclose his plans. This lack of concentration and want of caution will prove detrimental. He likes to help others, but he also meddles with what does not concern him, which may benefit others, but not always himself.

In 20 of Leo, Mars brings success after many struggles and disputes over matters ruled by the House occupied by Leo. There is risk of wounds or obstacles, in spite of which success will be achieved; the native is not averse to strife.

Mars in Virgo

Mars in Virgo gives a marked pessimistic tendency. The native is not satisfied with his lot, and criticises everything, even himself. He is an incorrigible contradictor, and will not know how to create lasting friendships. His life will be a lonely one, and marriage will be difficult, unless Venus is well placed in the chart.

When Mars is badly placed it always causes general inability to achieve anything. The native will be unfortunate in love, usually through his own fault, and his life will be lonely, without children and without affectionate ties.

Mars in 10 of Virgo is still more unfavourable: everything goes wrong with the native, unless Jupiter is well aspected.

In 20 of Virgo, if Venus is powerful, he will marry, and this will benefit him pecuniarily if Mercury is in an angular House.

Mars in Libra

In this sign Mars brings great mental activity, which is favourable for artistic pursuits, and if the native is not a professional artist, he will at any rate be a man of artistic tastes. This position gives the necessary courage and perseverance for conquering adversity and overcoming difficulties.

From the sentimental standpoint the native is capable of much feeling, which will not always be responded to. If Mars occupies the Seventh House, and Jupiter is afflicted, divorce will be inevitable.

In 10 of Libra, Mars gives a fine synthetic mind, and a ready understanding, which enables the native never to be at a loss for words in the course of a conversation. This position gives success in a career in which the native is his own master.

In 20 of Libra, Mars may confer riches, even if the native start in modest circumstances, as this position gives abundance in material things. In the Fifth House, Mars may cause the loss of a child when Saturn is in evil aspect.

Mars in Scorpio

This indicates numerous struggles and difficulties, which can only be conquered if Mercury is powerful in the chart. It will be necessary to act with more cunning than violence, more dexterity than force. The native's character is over-quarrelsome and aggressive, and he easily forgets that flies are not caught with vinegar. He will have many and vindictive enemies, and there is a danger of wounds. In the Sixth House this position often causes chest trouble, or bronchitis, if the Moon is afflicted, or tuberculosis if Venus and Saturn are in bad aspect.

As we have already said, Mars in this House enables the native to conquer with the help of a good influence of Mercury, In this case, Mars in Scorpio will favour commercial or industrial undertakings connected with poisons or chemical products.

In 10 of Scorpio, Mars gives good health and vitality. It will help the native to live to an advanced age if the Sun is well placed. In the Tenth House it makes him follow several occupations at the same time.

In 20 of Scorpio it is a sign of deceit in love, and infidelity unless Venus is well placed. Otherwise it may even cause a violent and reprehensible act to be committed.

Mars in Sagittarius

This is a very benefic position for Mars, which enables the consultant to attain an enviable position through his own exertions and intelligence. He is kind, loyal and generous.

In the Sixth House, if Jupiter is not powerful in the horoscope, the health is precarious, and Mars may signify an operation before the fortieth year, after which period the health improves.

In 10 of Sagittarius, Mars enables the native to succeed in his enterprises, and to overcome difficulties with ease, as he will know how to take the bull by the horns.

In 20 of Sagittarius it brings gains, but only if Mercury is well placed in the chart, as an evil aspect of the latter can only cause loss of money, in spite of all precautions, there being a danger of robbery or loss of valuable things.

Mars in Capricorn

With Mars in Capricorn the life will be a troubled one. Many journeys and changes of position will be the lot of the native, who is lacking in continuity of thought, and is moreover very capricious, inasmuch as if Saturn is well placed he will be spoiled by Fortune.

With Saturn weak, and Capricorn situated in an unfavourable House, Mars in this sign will cause serious injuries to the legs.

With good aspects the native is sympathetic and knows how to gain the good-will of those around him. He will come into contact with influential people, and is himself endowed with a fine personality.

In 10 of Capricorn, Mars makes the native more cunning, more supple. His personality is not so charming, but his chances of success remain the same, provided Jupiter and the Moon are well situated in the horoscope.

If the Sun or the Moon is weak and in bad aspect with Mars in the Eighth House, it indicates grave danger, or death.

In 20 of Capricorn the native will undertake many journeys, especially if this occurs in one of the Houses of Travel—the Third or Ninth House. It is also a sign of health and endurance. In the Eighth House (House of Death) it may signify a fatal accident away from home.

Mars in Aquarius

This position inclines to anger, but the native is kind and benevolent, daring and stubborn. He loves weird things and is fond of change, is interested in occultism, philosophy and controversy.

In the Sixth House, in this Sign, Mars brings danger of suffocation, often asthma. The native will suffer from rheumatism, complaints affecting the legs, or varicose veins.

In 10 of Aquarius there is danger of being deceived, the fraud arising from matters ruled by the House occupied by Aquarius.

In 20 of Aquarius the position is good for the mind, and, if Uranus is well placed in the horoscope, it may enable the native to evolve some original idea which will help him to extricate himself from trouble at the most critical periods of his life.

Mars in Pisces

This position denotes a Government official, an employee or a business man in a small way, the position never being very exalted, nor yet very lowly. The native will seek the company of those who are in better circumstances than himself, and this may be useful to him in difficulties. He is cautious, and steady; there is more poise than in the other signs, and intelligent economy may sanction the prophecy that he will have a comfortable income, at any rate, if not riches.

In 10 of Pisces, Mars gives vitality, and a long life, free from serious illness. This position is not very favourable for love, as it denotes unfaithfulness and deceit of the marriage partner, or of some one described by the House occupied by this decanate.

In 20 of Pisces, Mars gives slow but very sure progress in life, the patience and exertion of the native securing for him, if not an exalted post, at any rate a well-established, steady position, free from anxiety.

Venus

THIS planet is temperate, moist, fruitful, benefic, magnetic and negative. Its day domicile is in Libra, its night domicile in Taurus; its places of exile are in Aries and Scorpio; its joy is in Taurus, and its fall in Virgo.

It is a strengthening influence, and is called the Lesser Fortune. Its metal is copper; day, Friday. It is the planet of Love, Beauty, Form.

It represents Affection, Friendship, Unions, Pleasures, the Arts, Love.

In a laying-out of cards, it will be taken to represent Woman.

It makes the native kind and benevolent, affectionate and cheerful, inclined to pleasure. In appearance he is rounded and well formed, with refined features. It is Venus who, in certain circumstances, makes the native selfish, as she cannot be better compared than to a cat who strokes and rubs herself against you, because it affords pleasure to herself first and foremost.

Venus thus causes a sensuousness which, in the absence of evil influences, remains refined and artistic.

It often causes affections of the generative system and of the chest, due to excesses of pleasure.

Venus in the Houses

Venus in the First House

In this House, Venus, if not afflicted, exerts a favourable influence over the whole life of the native, on whom it confers many attributes: a kind and loving disposition, pleasing manners, a sense of form and harmony, and the love of Beauty.

The health is good at birth, and life will be long, unless Mars casts an evil aspect, which would cause serious bodily disease, due to excesses in pleasure.

With an evil influence, this Key in the First House may cause profligacy, infidelity, and innumerable love affairs; weakness of the bronchial apparatus, or of the spinal fluid.

Venus in the Second House

Unless situated in an unfavourable sign, this is a good position for financial enterprises. The native may contract a wealthy and happy marriage, and succeed in anything and everything. In this House, which is the House of personal worth, it gives marked artistic tastes, which, if the Third House is well situated, can be developed and will lead to renown.

It gives, however, a love of spending money on oneself and on others. The native desires expensive clothes, especially of light colours. He likes to help others. He only associates with wealthy, gay and refined people, and his friends, who will be numerous, will only belong to a high station in life.

In a woman's horoscope, this position is less favourable for marriage, as the husband is a flirt, a gambler and a spendthrift.

Venus in the Third House

This always brings harmony in the family circle and amongst those around the native, and favours journeys for pleasure.

Unless there are bad aspects, the native's education will be cultured. He will love everything that is beautiful, this position belonging to writers of literature, or those who take pleasure in writing (especially with the Moon in the Ninth House). This position inclines the native to prefer strangers to the members of his own family, with whom he will nevertheless be on good terms, as Venus is never on bad terms with anyone, and its friendship or affection is scattered broadcast even if it is never very deep.

In a feminine horoscope, Venus in the Third House is often the sign of a meeting with a refined man in the course of a journey. The union will be socially eminent, but will not bring great financial advantage.

Venus in the Fourth House

This helps to procure undisturbed domestic happiness and a peaceful, cheerful and pleasant home life. The home will be furnished in good taste.

It also promises money coming from the Mother or the Wife; a legacy or settlement of property from women, more especially in the country.

Life will be long, undisturbed and free from material cares. Mars or Saturn in bad aspect with Venus in the Nadir of the Heavens portends the premature death of the Mother or Wife.

Venus in the Fifth House

In this House, which is its true position, Venus rules over pleasure and the emotions. It gives a love of social life and gaiety; affection, cheerfulness, benevolence and sensibility. It is lucky for speculations and games of chance; also for a large family (girls especially). This latter indication is confirmed if there are no evil aspects of Saturn, which is inimical as regards children.

Venus dignified in the Fifth House may bring financial success in an artistic career, or it may cause the native to interest himself in matters connected with places of entertainment.

For a woman this position often means early love affairs. With an evil influence, or weakly placed, Venus in this House may cause disappointment in love.

Venus in the Sixth House

Venus in this House loses its significance in regard to health, for which it is decidedly unfavourable, especially in the watery signs (Pisces, Scorpio or Cancer).

Dignified, it remains favourable for domestic life, which will be harmonious. It also gives honest and faithful employees. It is good for the uncles and aunts, and, if the position justifies it, may signify inheritance from kinsmen.

Venus in the Seventh House

The position is very favourable in the House of Unions, Marriage and Partnerships, Venus being the Ruler of Love. If well dignified, it will help marriage, which will occur early in life and be happy.

It gives many friends and social acquaintances; honest and thrifty associates in business, who will contribute to the fortune of the native. It also enables him to make profitable contracts, brings success in commercial ventures, and always promises a rise to a good position in life.

A bad aspect of Mars in this House will cause great danger of adultery, but in spite of this malefic influence the partners will remain together.

Venus in the Eighth House

Venus in Eighth House promises a peaceful and natural death at an advanced age. It is also very favourable for legacies from women. Marriage will be fairly advantageous, and the position brings gain in all things. A bad aspect of Mars entails the possibility of loss of the marriage partner. An aspect of Saturn may indicate the likelihood of union with a widower or a widow.

Venus in the Ninth House

This is very favourable for matters relating to the mind, and also for long journeys. It may also indicate union with a foreigner, but always a wealthy union that also procures intellectual advantages.

It gives a taste for philosophical subjects, and religious tendencies, especially in a woman.

Venus in the Tenth House

Well dignified in this Angular House, Venus brings the assurance of success in the native's chosen career. It always gives an honourable position, with honours or material rewards.

Things in general are favourably influenced by this position in the Mid-Heaven; money, pleasure and renown are harmoniously distributed to the native, if Venus is powerfully situated therein.

If the contrary is the case, it will cause trouble over worldly matters, due to women or on their account.

Venus in the Eleventh House

Numerous and influential friends who will help the native to progress in life are indicated. The friends will be helpful and well-born. Venus in this House is also favourable for the children, who will be healthy and good-looking.

It may also give popularity. For a man it procures great success with women, and they will help him to secure his position in life.

Venus in the Twelfth House

Venus is not very well placed in this unfortunate House, as it attracts the native towards those who are of an inferior social status; it often signifies obscure and disreputable occupations, or illicit love affairs.

It often brings about separation from the marriage partner in consequence of scandal, especially if Venus receives an evil aspect from Mars in this ill-omened House.

Neither is it good for the health, as it causes contagious diseases of the nature of Venus.

Venus in the Signs

Venus in Aries

VENUS in Aries does not confer much will power. The native is changeable and too much inclined to listen to what others tell him. He is also too ready to trust others, which will cause him constant anxiety and trouble. He will be disappointed in love early in life, although this position inclines to an early marriage.

In 10 of Aries, Venus conduces to a marriage that does not fulfil the native's expectations and causes him to suffer in silence, while caressing the hope of freedom. This may occur at some time and, if the Moon is in bad aspect with Mars, it may be due to death of the marriage partner, and lead to a second union. If Venus is well aspected by the Sun, it often means, on the contrary, a difficulty in gaining the affection of the loved one, with the certainty of the desired result being achieved.

In 20 of Aries, Venus usually causes separation of the couple, the marriage partner not being in sympathy with the tastes of the native, especially in a feminine horoscope, in which this position often denotes a coarse and brutal husband, especially if Mars casts an evil aspect.

Venus in Taurus

Venus in its own domicile, if well aspected, is very favourable for marriage, as it brings harmony between the heart and senses. Badly aspected, it indicates a fickle and inconstant, but kind partner. Venus in conjunction or square with Mars in this sign denotes vexations in love affairs. Well aspected, this planet assures success in all things. It is the Lesser Fortune, and brings pleasures in matters ruled by the House which it occupies.

In 10 of Taurus it is often a sign of unfaithfulness in

marriage. It entails jealousy and causes a change in the affections.

In 20 of Taurus, Venus is indicative of insensate passion. The native is in love with some one who does not respond to his advances, which makes him unsettled. If Saturn afflicts Venus, it means innumerable sorrows. With an aspect of Mercury or the Moon, especially in the Third House, it denotes a journey connected with the affections, which, however, does not usually procure the pleasure expected from it.

Venus in Gemini

In this sign Venus gives many friends. The native is universally loved. He, on the other hand, although loving everyone, is not deeply affectionate, this being a source of sorrow to his friends. It is sometimes an indication of unfaithfulness in marriage, or it may mean that the native is loved by two people simultaneously. In this double sign the children will be good-looking, and if the Fifth House is favourable, and the Moon well placed and aspected, the native will have twins.

In 10 of Gemini, Venus is again a sign of fickleness in love. Sometimes it signifies anxiety on account of the loved one, and consequent jealousy.

In 20 of Gemini the position of Venus is improved. It gives the possibility of success in matters ruled by the House occupied by this planet: it is a mark of progress, friendship, fidelity and good repute.

Venus in Cancer

This is not a good position. It gives fickleness, secret love affairs, and is a clear indication of infidelity. An evil aspect of Mars will cause separation of the marriage partners. It may signify marriage with some one who has already been married, either a widow (or widower) or a divorced person. It does not promote harmony in marriage, and causes numerous disagreements in the home, especially in the Fourth House and if the Moon is in evil aspect. The disagreement between the couple may come from the mother or mother-in-law. If Venus is well aspected in Cancer it brings success in life, though not from the standpoint of the emotions. More strictly speaking, Venus does not cause unhappiness in love, but makes the native soon grow tired, whereby he makes others suffer more than he does himself.

In 10 of Cancer it shows, even in the absence of evil aspects from the malefic planets, separation in marriage and disputes. It often means danger of accident or wound in connection with a love affair, especially if Mars sends an evil aspect to Venus.

In 20 of Cancer it enables the native to overcome his troubles over love affairs, and to be happy in spite of everything, even by resorting to violence, which is successful in certain unions, if the marriage partner is of a strongly Venusian temperament.

Venus in Leo

Unless afflicted by evil aspects, Venus in Leo is favourable for marriage, which will take place early in life. The marriage will bring honour, happiness and satisfaction to the native. The same applies even with evil aspects, but in that case the union does not last long, weariness soon comes. The native or his partner is ignorant of life and wants to make its acquaintance (especially in 20 of Leo), hence this will cause numerous annoyances and disputes which will be difficult to mitigate.

In 10 of Leo it is a token of fidelity and of marriage that only ends with the death of one of the partners. Nevertheless if Mars sends an evil aspect, there will be disputes, although these will be short-lived, as great physical attraction will exist between the couple.

Venus in Virgo

Venus in Virgo is not very favourable for marriage. It often causes peculiar ideas regarding love, which is more physical than sentimental. An evil aspect of Mars, Saturn or the Moon sometimes indicates sexual perversion.

This position often makes bachelors, spinsters, monks or nuns. An aspect of Saturn to Venus causes serious sexual disorders.

In 20 of Virgo, Venus is not favourable for love; it often conduces to a wealthy marriage with some one older than the native, who thereby suffers later in life, as Venus in this decanate always entails moral loneliness.

Venus in Libra

In her most favourable domicile Venus in Libra gives an idealistic love nature and a superior character, appreciative of everything that is Great, Beautiful and Noble. It is an ideal position for artists and men of refinement. The native will contract a noble and wealthy marriage which will bring him happiness, unless the Sun is in conjunction with Venus, which may signify separation after a short time.

As occurs with many happy marriages, this will not be without causing a great deal of jealousy and enmity from those around the couple, but with a good aspect from the benefics they will remain content in their wealthy and harmonious home, letting others say and do what they like.

This position, especially in 10 of Libra, is very lucky for a man; it should make him rise to an exalted position in life, through his own intelligence and good-fortune. In this decanate, Venus permits the native to dare and undertake everything, for Love guides and leads him to success.

In 20 of Libra, Venus is a token of stability and abundance, but an evil aspect of Mars to Venus in this decanate will cause anxiety regarding the children, especially if this occurs in the Fifth or Eleventh House.

Venus in Scorpio

In this sign, which is one of the domiciles of Mars, Venus is not favourably placed, causing many troubles, and even danger over matters connected with the affections, the danger referring to matters ruled by the House. In the Sixth House it means disorders of the generative system; in the Fifth, it may cause the death of the children; in the Eighth, it indicates the premature loss of the wife. In a feminine horoscope, this position is disastrous; it causes grave disappointments in love and is often the sign of betrayal of a young girl. If the Moon casts an aspect to Venus in this sign, and this occurs in the Fourth House, it often shows an illegitimate child.

In 10 of Scorpio, Venus denotes disagreements between husband and wife, separation and a second marriage, which does not usually turn out more successful than the first. In a man's horoscope it is the indication of many illicit unions with women, whom he will deceive, and, if Mars casts an aspect to Venus, this may entail an accident to himself.

In 20 of Scorpio it is a sign of infidelity in marriage, and numerous disputes and unpleasantness in married life. In the Seventh House it causes scandal, followed by separation and lawsuits, and the risk of being defrauded by the marriage partner. If the aspect occurs in the First House, the native himself may try to defraud the community.

Venus in Sagittarius

This position is very fortunate for great artists, on whom it will confer riches, honours and eminence.

It is not, however, good for marriage, which it delays (although there may be more than one illicit union, which will materially benefit men or women equally). Such unions may often occur even in the absence of great love (especially in a feminine horoscope), and with an evil aspect of Mars they may cause scandal.

In 10 of Sagittarius, Venus causes a deep affection to count for more than passionate love in the native's life, and the end of his life will be harmonious from the standpoint of the affections, while he will also be fortunate from the material aspect, if Venus is not afflicted.

Venus in 20 of Sagittarius denotes a marriage of convenience in which love is rarely taken into consideration, money counting first and foremost. An aspect of Mars to Venus in this decanate of the sign and in the Eighth House is a token of widowhood, or marriage with a widower (or widow).

Venus in Capricorn

Venus in Capricorn is not favourable for love or marriage. It gives fickleness, peculiarity, and abnormality in love matters. If Venus is well aspected, especially in the Seventh House, the native will marry some one older than himself (or herself) of a Saturnian disposition, and this will not conduce to cheerfulness in the home, which will be dreary and childless. The children die young if Mars casts an evil aspect and Venus occupies the Fifth House.

This position also causes disagreements between the married couple.

In 10 of Capricorn, Venus causes danger in regard to women, or on their account. An evil aspect of Saturn may cause death through grief (especially in a feminine horoscope), or it may be, if the chart on the whole indicates it, that death occurs through suicide, with Mars, Venus and Saturn in square aspect, and Venus being situated in this decanate in the Eighth House.

In 20 of Capricorn the position is improved. The danger through matters regarding the affections remains, however, and the loneliness persists, but there is no risk of death as the will power of the native regains the ascendant after the disappointment in love.

Venus in Aquarius

From the standpoint of character, the position of Venus in this sign is not favourable for the native's battle in life, as it gives an indolent and effeminate disposition, much benevolence, or, more strictly speaking, weakness which often closely resembles flabbiness. If the horoscope is fortunate, the position of Venus in this part of the Zodiac will not be so unfavourable, and indicates, on the contrary, that the native will have a very peaceful life. If the sign is situated in the Fourth House, the home life will be restful, quiet, monotonous, but harmonious, and this is what the native desires.

If, however, the horoscope shows struggle, Venus is not favourable in this sign, as it will cause early separation of the married couple, the native not being stout-hearted, and possibly not too straightforward in matters relating to love. Infidelity is shown, and illicit ties will occur which may either cause loss of money, or bring wealth, according to the aspects and position of Mercury.

In 10 of Aquarius, Venus is very badly placed in regard to the affections; it indicates profligacy, double-dealing and fraud in love affairs, and this will benefit the native materially.

In 20 of Aquarius, Venus is more benefic, and unless afflicted may permit and bring lasting benefits, which, however, will be slow in coming. These will occur through the help of someone of the opposite sex.

Venus in Pisces

In Pisces, Venus brings about an early marriage and indicates that two marriages will occur in life. For a woman, it will be the indication of marriage with a man much older than herself, of good position, and who will spoil her. For a man, this position will make him a widower early in life, if the sign is in the Eighth House. The worldly position is good, as Venus in this domicile of Jupiter and free from affliction brings luck, and enables the native to succeed easily in his undertakings, especially in Angular Houses.

In 10 of Pisces it loses some of its virtues, as it is the sign of deceit in love, and of disagreements due to untruthful words. It causes infidelity and separation, and also loss of position if Uranus afflicts Venus, which misfortunes will be correspondingly grievous in accordance with the House involved.

In 20 of Pisces, Venus gives great happiness in the family life. It conduces to harmonious relations between the parents; there will be many fine, healthy children; and the worldly position, if not extraordinarily brilliant, will be comfortable, and the life will end happily. All this, of course, providing there are no evil aspects from the malefics.

Jupiter

THIS is a benefic and favourable Planet, which must be taken to represent Protection. It is called the Greater Fortune, and strengthens the fortunate indications in a Horoscope, while it mitigates the unfortunate ones.

Jupiter is temperate, dry and fruitful; its colour is light or purplish-blue; its metal, copper; its day, Thursday.

Its day domicile is in Sagittarius; its night domicile in Pisces; its place of exaltation is in Cancer; its fall in Capricorn; it is in exile in Gemini and Virgo; its Joy is in Sagittarius.

Jupiter is closest to the Earth in Aries, and furthest away in Libra.

This planet makes diplomats; Church dignitaries; gives Government posts, and specially influences business men and all who occupy eminent positions.

It gives a lively, cheerful, benevolent, though somewhat selfish disposition. It gives a love of display and of feasting and of friendly reunions. The native has a great sense of organisation and administration; has much love for his family, and regard for respectability and esteem, but he also has a certain amount of vanity and a desire to patronise, with a view to self-advertisement.

Jupiter inclines to troubles arising from plethora (over-richness of the blood), more especially to gout and apoplexy, which are the natural consequences of a life lived to the utmost in regard to work as well as pleasure.

It usually denotes a native who is fairly tall, strong, with somewhat stooping shoulders, oval face, a high forehead with a tendency to premature baldness, and an inclination to profuse perspiration at the slightest exertion. It inclines to excess of adipose tissue at a premature age. Jupiter is a friend of the Moon and the enemy of Mars.

Jupiter in the Houses

Jupiter in the First House

In this House it brings fine chances of a rise in life, in accordance with the social environment of the native. It also gives ambition and the desire to progress rapidly by honest, legitimate and recognised methods.

In the absence of evil aspects from Mars, the life will be a long one, with much luck, esteem, protection and many powerful friends.

Jupiter in the Second House

Jupiter is very fortunate in this House, as it promises assured gains in a profession ruled by Jupiter, such as business on a large scale. It also favours the acquisition of land and house property, the accumulation of money, corresponding to the dignity of the Luminaries.

When this position occurs in a fortunate sign, it promises a wealthy marriage with a member of a good family. This position occupied by Jupiter may cause the native to be deprived of affection in his childhood, or may indicate lack of domestic harmony, as the parents may be divorced or separated, especially if Jupiter is in one of the Fiery signs.

Jupiter in the Third House

In this House, Jupiter is favourable for education and things relating to the mind. It often shows that the native has been brought up religiously. This position often belongs to those who are holders of several University diplomas. It also brings harmonious relations between brothers and sisters, parents, friends and neighbours. In this House, which rules over short journeys, Jupiter favours travelling, which will always occur under comfortable circumstances. It gives the possibility of business partnership with the parents, and if there is no evil aspect of Mars, this cannot be otherwise than fortunate. According to the native's aptitudes, Jupiter in the Third House will make him the representative of an important enterprise, which may be either a business firm or a Government Department. In the latter case, we meet an official, especially a member of the Consular or Diplomatic corps.

Jupiter in the Fourth House

Jupiter in this House indicates a good and often a noble heredity. It is also a token of good health and physical resistance. It gives a specially great love of the home and domestic ties, an appreciation of comfortable surroundings, and denotes a systematic and methodical personality.

It implies the idea of a landowner, and often denotes gain through house or land property, wealth coming through the Father. If the Sun is well situated, it is a token of inherited and increased wealth.

The life will be fairly long and fortunate, especially from the fortieth year.

This position, if the Tenth House is powerful, may promise power and renown towards the end of life.

Jupiter in the Fifth House

In this House, Jupiter usually gives a large family of comely children, and much happiness through them. The position sometimes makes the native fickle, especially with an evil aspect of Mars and Venus in the horoscope. There will be many illicit friendships. The love of pleasure, gambling and feasting predominates.

This position implies the idea of a banker, theatre or entertainment manager.

When dignified, Jupiter in the Fifth House will always bring progress in the worldly position, and honours. The native will love feasting and pleasure, and will enjoy great good fortune.

He is unquestionably selfish, but this is allied with benevolence and a desire to help others in an ostentatious manner. Jupiter in the Fifth House always realises the desired attainment. If Mars sends an evil aspect, or is weak, and Ruler of the Fifth House, the native will experience reverses in his worldly position, but he will make several fortunes.

In this House Jupiter again gives the possibility of a wealthy marriage, in which money or worldly position will count for more than love.

Jupiter in the Sixth House

If Jupiter is dignified, it gives good health in this House, but towards the fiftieth year disorders of the digestion and circulation will arise, but these, however, will be temporary.

Jupiter is not so favourable here in regard to worldly position; it points to a subordinate official or an employee with a steady position, but never a chief. It gives a peaceful, and often monotonous domestic life.

Jupiter in the Seventh House

In this House, Jupiter is very favourable for business partnerships, or unions; in fact, for everything that pertains to co-operation, whether this be material, mental or emotional.

The position inclines to widowhood and to a second marriage if in Gemini, Virgo or Pisces.

It gives success in public affairs, makes the native triumph over his enemies, procures happiness in old age, but often deprives it of feminine affection, especially in Sagittarius.

If the aspects are evil, Jupiter gives many troubles, especially those relating to the affections.

Jupiter in the Eighth House

Jupiter in this House, and well aspected in Sagittarius, Pisces or Cancer, brings money through legacies, inheritance, or marriage with some one much above the native's social status. Jupiter in Capricorn in the Eighth House is very evil; it means first of all pecuniary loss, and this sign becomes the significator of the disease which will cause death.

If Jupiter is dignified the native will have the assurance of a peaceful and natural end.

Jupiter in the Ninth House

In this House Jupiter exerts a very beneficial influence on the moral and mental development of the native. It makes him prudent, well-balanced, calm, industrious, and gives him lofty philosophic conceptions. He will interest himself in religious subjects or in matters relating thereto, and will be attracted towards occultism.

This position is good for travelling, and may signify commercial relations with foreign countries. It also makes leaders of philosophic or religious thought. Journeys will be fortunate. It gives intuition and may cause veridical dreams.

Jupiter in the Tenth House

This position is one of the most fortunate in a horoscope as regards worldly affairs. In this House of business in general, if Jupiter is well influenced, the possibility of rising to, and maintaining an exalted position is indicated. This planet in the Tenth House is a sure sign of wealth and happiness.

Jupiter in the Eleventh House

In this House Jupiter is very favourable for political matters, as it gives many friends who will follow the lead indicated by the native. The social circle is pleasant and helpful, the native loves company, boisterousness, music, singing and feasting.

Popularity and progress will come through the friends which the native will have gained through his ready helpfulness, his jovial manners and his good humour, which are always employed for the furthering of a great ambition and the display of an intellect which dominates the masses.

Marriage will occur early in life, and if the Fifth House is dignified, there will be many children who will bring happiness to their parents. Boys will be in the majority in a man's horoscope if the Moon is well aspected, while in a woman's horoscope the girls will predominate.

In a feminine horoscope, Jupiter in the Eleventh House is very fortunate for marriage, and this occurs with a man holding an exalted position under Government, or the head of some enterprise.

Jupiter in the Twelfth House

In this evil House, Jupiter will afford help and protection, so that the native will be able to defend himself in life, overcome his trials, and turn enmities into friendships.

The native is kind and generous, likes to give pleasure, and realises that he will not always help people who are ungrateful.

In an unfortunate sign this position is bad for marriage, and with an evil influence of Saturn causes loss of position or disgrace, which always happens with Jupiter, who very often only owes his position to helpful friends. Mars, especially, will bring about sudden changes in the opinion of the native's superiors, or of the masses. They will cast him from his place of honour, but through these very revolutions, and with the help of favourable aspects, he may regain his lost status.

Jupiter in the Signs

Jupiter in Aries

JUPITER in Aries gives much ambition and will power. In this sign it is a protection against fire and sword. The position makes domineering, but kind and just leaders. With good aspects, Jupiter raises the native to prominence through his own merit.

In 10 of Aries, Jupiter usually makes it possible, especially for a woman, to contract a marriage somewhat late in life, but which will fulfil her ideals. It often happens that difficulties arise with the marriage partner's family, who are against the union, but it takes place notwithstanding.

In 20 of Aries, Jupiter enables the native to escape from snares, gives Faith, and in times of stress the native should remember that Jupiter will protect him and bring him safely out of his troubles. The physical resistance is good. Illnesses may occur, but these will be short, and in spite of their severity the native will recover.

Jupiter in Taurus

In Taurus, Jupiter brings marriage far above the native's worldly position, especially from the pecuniary standpoint. The union will be stable, even if it is not a love-match, the husband or wife doing everything possible that the home may be well established.

In a masculine horoscope the native gains the approbation of women. His numerous good fortunes may help his worldly progress, for he is a skilful lover, and if he deserts a sweetheart, he will manage to retain her as a friend. An evil aspect of Mars will upset all this, especially in 10 of Taurus. There will be jealousy, and serious disagreements will occur with men concerning women, or with women concerning men. It is a sign of infidelity and of disputes in the home. This position also prevents progress in the worldly position, which a good aspect of the Moon will nevertheless cause to be very fortunate.

In 20 of Taurus, Jupiter is a sign of difficult progress in the worldly position, especially in the early portion of life. This position is always an indication that from the thirtieth year onwards the native will occupy an enviable position, which will procure advancement for him. This may compel him to travel, so that he will not be able to make a home until late in life, and he will not wish to have a family until he is well-established.

Jupiter in Gemini

In this sign of Mercury, in which Jupiter is in exile, its position is not favourable for the emotions, which it upsets on account of pecuniary interests taking precedence over love, so that the native, in his youth, will sacrifice the joys of love for the sake of material gain, with the result that in old age, or, more strictly speaking, in middle-age, towards the forty-fifth year, at the period when he will have attained a good position (Jupiter in Gemini procures success towards this period), he will experience disappointment in sentimental matters, and may suffer through his emotions. Having nothing further to wish for from the material standpoint, he will nevertheless be unhappy, wishing for a family which he will probably not have, unless Venus and the Moon help Jupiter, which is very badly placed in 20 of Gemini.

In 10 of Gemini, Jupiter makes directors of banking concerns, or of large business undertakings. It gives great aptitude for figures, and a love of system and method, which promote success.

This position makes the native the wealthiest or the most notable member of his family. Here again it is not fortunate for marriage, often entailing divorce and a second marriage.

Jupiter in Cancer

Jupiter brings great luck in this sign, which is the domicile of the Moon, with which Jupiter is sympathetic. It procures unexpected gains, and enables the native to benefit by lotteries or speculations. Success is due far more to lucky influences than to personal merit, and as results only count in life, the native will be perfectly happy. His worldly position will be as easily established in his own country as in foreign lands.

In 10 of Cancer travelling is shown, as Jupiter is in the sign of its Exaltation.

In 20 of Cancer the position is equally fortunate; there is luck, but more personal merit, so that results, while more slowly obtained, will be more beneficial for the native, who will have to exert himself to achieve his aspirations.

Jupiter in this sign, and especially in the Ninth House, may make a Colonial Administrator, or the head of a foreign enterprise. If Jupiter, at birth, is situated exactly on 15° of Cancer, a very notable rise in life can be prophesied.

Jupiter in Leo

In this sign, which is the domicile of the Sun, Jupiter gives a noble ambition, intellect and benevolence. Wisdom is well developed, the native's ideals are of the loftiest, Destiny favours him, and he may undertake anything, for the results will prove satisfactory, provided Mars and Saturn do not disturb this good influence.

In 10 of Leo, Jupiter grants many friends. A host of people help the native and facilitate his work; a circle gathers round him, which will not fail to cause gossip or slander, so that it will be necessary for him to abstain from divulging his plans, and not allow himself to be influenced by those around him, as some people bring ill-luck.

In 20 of Leo, Jupiter helps to overcome the difficulties which will inevitably confront the native, owing to the fact that he will seek an exalted position in life.

In the Sixth House, Jupiter in Leo, if afflicted by Mars, causes disease of the heart or blood.

Jupiter in Virgo

In Virgo, Jupiter does not give a prominent social position. It pertains to the commercial traveller. The native's disposition is kindly, but cautious; cunning, as well as boastful. It promises many love affairs, but not of a permanent nature. The native is fundamentally independent, and as he is industrious, success may come as a result of his own exertions.

In 10 of Virgo it causes difficulties in establishing a position in the world, and this would seem to occur only towards the forty-fifth year, changes of occupation being indicated, and delays in making headway. It signifies an arduous life, but the native is able to face ill-luck cheerfully, and assume the appearance of being a lucky man, which may help him to become so in reality, since good thoughts attract good things.

In 20 of Virgo, Jupiter brings luck in love, or, more strictly, enables the native to contract a wealthy union. It is a good position for the native to marry the son or daughter of his (or her) employer, whom he (or she) will succeed in business, to the material development of which he will contribute.

Jupiter in Libra

This position influences more especially matters pertaining to Law, Politics, Medicine, and also Art.

With good aspects, Jupiter will be beneficial in all directions, after an initial period of difficulty. The thirtieth and fortieth years will mark two notable stages of worldly progress.

It is also the sign of numerous and helpful friends.

In 10 of Libra, Jupiter gives a synthetic mind which enables the native to understand all things, and to make himself understood by everyone. The position gives great logical powers. It will make a notable professor or magistrate. There is great love of Form, and it is therefore a good position for artists and sculptors. If the Sun sends an evil aspect to the Seventh House, or is situated therein, Jupiter in Libra will cause unhappiness in wedlock, and perhaps divorce.

In 20 of Libra, Jupiter is the sign of a notable rise in worldly position from the fortieth year onwards. Progress from this period will be rapid, material gains and honours being obtained simultaneously, along with the well-being he desires for those around him. With this position it will be necessary for him to be careful in regard to money, towards his fiftieth year, if Mars, which is in Exile in Libra, sends an evil aspect to Jupiter. In this case the native should invest part of his money in sound concerns, and rigorously avoid speculations.

Jupiter in Scorpio

In this sign Jupiter gives a domineering and quarrelsome disposition. The native endeavours to subjugate those around him, and generally succeds, more through underhand and persuasive methods, which are inborn, than through the forcibility of Mars. If Jupiter is well aspected by the luminaries in this sign, it brings rapid success.

In 10 of Scorpio, Jupiter gives excellent health, stamina, and physical strength. It often causes (especially in an Angular House) sudden reverses of fortune, and the native may often have to start again in life.

In 20 of Scorpio, Jupiter brings trouble through the Wife or Mother in a masculine horoscope, and through the Father or the Husband in a feminine horoscope, the trouble always being due to gossip.

This position is, however, a safeguard against fraud and deceit, the native knowing how to defend himself against lying and cunning.

Jupiter in Sagittarius

Jupiter in Sagittarius, which is one of its domiciles, gives a love of sport, hunting, athletic games, and horse-riding. The native loves the country-side and a free and easy life. This position is very favourable for agriculture and cattle-rearing, in which the native should succeed. He will lead a healthy, simple life, which will benefit him physically. This position thus promises a long life, but a solitary old-age, caused through loss of the marriage partner.

In 10 Sagittarius, Jupiter brings success, but through manual labour; the native is not afraid to put his hand to the plough. Difficulties may arise, but if Jupiter receives no evil aspect from Saturn, success will be achieved towards the thirty-eighth year.

In 20 of Sagittarius, Jupiter enables the native to know exactly what he desires and to do what is required to obtain it. This position there is a sign of continuity of ideas, perseverance, industry, and a slow, but certain rise in life.

Jupiter in Capricorn

Jupiter is unfortunately placed in this sign. It indicates enemies in every direction, often through a lack of firmness, and a constitutional indolence which prevent the native from reacting against people and events. These would not be so unfortunate if he would take the trouble to face them as he should, and strenuously react against them. The heredity is not good, and Jupiter in this sign also gives delicate children. There is a lack of ambition, and the life is barren and dreary.

In 10 of Capricorn the influence is also very unfortunate, but there is more energy, and success may be attained with a good influence from the Moon.

In 20 of Capricorn the health and also the heredity are improved. Nevertheless the native is threatened with danger towards the forty-third year; there may be an accident or an illness which will affect more especially the circulation of the blood in the legs.

Jupiter in Aquarius

Jupiter in this sign gives a pronounced liking for the exact sciences. The mind is analytical, and the native loves a life far from bustle and noise. It is the position of the laboratory investigator or the student, and gives good possibilities for invention, and for mechanical or marine engineering. Jupiter in this sign does not give a love of riches as it does in the majority of other signs in which it is situated, so that the life will be laborious on account of a contempt for material gains. This position often makes the native either very peaceable or very quarrelsome, according to the aspects of Mars.

It gives the possibility of marriage with some one older than the native, for the sake of peace, and this will be more or less successful according to the aspects. Any disagreements or troubles which occur will usually arise from the native's indolence.

In 10 of Aquarius, Jupiter brings deceit or theft of documents, the fruit of the native's labour or study, and this will cause him losses.

In 20 of Aquarius, Jupiter gives great protection. The native's lofty character may enable him to attain to a position of honour, and he may gain renown in his own country, according to the aspects of the Third and Ninth Houses.

Jupiter in Pisces

The position of Jupiter in Pisces enables the native to succeed through his own merit, through industry, study, or his numerous achievements. He will have the support of influential friends, but this may disturb the domestic life, especially in 10 of Pisces, as rivalry may occur with a superior, which may entail the possibility of divorce or loss of position. An evil aspect of Mars to Jupiter in this decanate indicates two marriages, with the possibility of premature death of the husband or wife.

In 20 of Pisces, Jupiter gives a steady and fairly good position but never an independent one. It also gives a long and peaceful life, free from care, provided this decanate occupies a fortunate House.

Saturn

THIS is a cold, dry, barren planet; its day domicile is in Aquarius; its nocturnal domicile in Capricorn. It is exiled in Leo and in Cancer. Its exaltation is at 21° of Libra; its Joy is in Capricorn; its Fall in Aries. It is furthest distant from the Earth in Sagittarius, and closest to it in Gemini.

It influences more especially the bony structure, the digestive and nutritive system, the liver, bowels and stomach. It usually gives a tall stature, brown hair and a sallow skin.

Its metal is lead; colour, very dark green; day, Saturday.

From the moral standpoint it makes the subject suspicious, sceptical, lacking in self-confidence, but very proud, cautious, melancholy, patient, industrious and laborious.

It is an intellectual planet, and gives an over-analytical mind which does not always permit the native to take a broadminded view of things. It makes specialists, scientists, engineers; in a lower social scale, labourers, miners, gardeners.

It is called the Great Misfortune, and its evil aspects to the Houses or to the other planets are dangerous when it is badly situated in the horoscope. In spite of its title of Great Misfortune it may, if it occupies a powerful position, bring great success in every aspect of life.

It causes delay in all things. Saturn is slow, but wise, and it therefore denotes stability, provided it is well aspected.

In material things it influences especially land and house property.

The native who comes under the influence of Saturn usually lives long, but is afflicted with numerous and chronic illnesses.

In an ordinary lay-out of cards, it indicates Old Age, Patience, Pride and Good Counsel.

Saturn in the Houses

Saturn in the First House

In this House, Saturn puts obstacles in early youth. It gives depth of mind and an inclination to solitude and independence, which will pursue the native throughout his life. This planet makes him studious, wishing always to know and to learn something new. It often denotes a child who is not very gifted, but who is plodding; and this, in conjunction with his innate pride, will enable him to win the highest marks in examinations or competitions. If Saturn is dignified or in good aspect with the benefics, it may enable the native, after difficulties, to attain to an eminent position.

Saturn in the Second House

In this House, Saturn gives a hesitation which does not help money matters. It is bad for personal merit, as well as for finance. The native must not engage in business; he is not fitted for it. This position may cause ruin, downfall and poverty.

It is evident that good aspects of Venus, Jupiter and the Sun will greatly mitigate all this, but nevertheless success will only come slowly through industry, perseverance and economy. Moreover, Saturn does not incline to extravagance.

A good aspect of Mercury favours the safe investment of money.

Saturn in the Third House

The native's personality develops late in life. As a child, he is very shy; he does not know how to play, and lives alone, away from his little playmates. If Saturn is badly placed, and afflicted by Mercury, he will be liable to contract bad habits, which later on, if the Sixth House is also afflicted, may seriously endanger the health. In later years the native does not make many friends; he will confine himself to his family, and a few friends whom he will not retain for long. This position causes disagreements with those around him, and is not favourable for travelling, Saturn being an indication of fixity. A good aspect of Mercury gives an aptitude for the study of abstract sciences.

Saturn in the Fourth House

In the Nadir of the Heavens, Saturn, when well aspected, gives stability to the family, which is of good ancestry. Respect for heredity is shown. This planet indicates land and house property. The native's inheritance will considerably increase, and he will never live up to his income. When Saturn is weak or badly aspected, the fortunate things just indicated will be replaced by disagreements with, or between, the parents. It gives a mean home life, and shows that the native will make an unhappy marriage, or, in many cases, may not marry at all. The native will live in seclusion, without ties of affection, and will not be more unhappy on that account, his misanthropic inclinations urging him to solitude. This position makes the native what is colloquially called "a bear."

Saturn in the Fifth House

This Planet in this House of Pleasures is not in its right place. There is a marked absence of harmony, and it can only cause disappointments, even if it is dignified. It indicates a childless marriage, or else is unfortunate for the children, who will die young. It often makes the native fond of gambling, but he is an unlucky gambler. Saturn constantly tries its luck in life, and is ever unsuccessful, especially if Mars sends an evil aspect.

This position often gives peculiar tastes regarding pleasure; the native likes morbid things. In a watery sign such as Cancer or Pisces, it inclines to neglect of one's person and may conduce to slovenly habits.

Saturn in the Sixth House

In the Purgatory of the Zodiac, Saturn increases the ills which afflict mankind. It causes troubles and difficulties of every sort. There is no lasting domestic harmony; the health is often in danger (the part of the body affected will be indicated by the sign occupied by Saturn), and it often causes serious disease resulting in decomposition of the body tissues.

If Saturn is dignified in this House, it may give material

security, but always in a subordinate position. A bad aspect of Mercury will cause theft on the part of servants or employees. An evil aspect of the Moon will bring serious disagreements with an uncle or aunt in connection with an inheritance.

Saturn in the Seventh House

This position, which is that of bachelors and spinsters, causes unhappiness in marriage, especially in a feminine horoscope, as it points to a jealous and selfish husband.

It also predicts that the native will marry late in life, if at all, and that he will marry some one older than himself, or else he may marry a widow.

If Saturn is dignified and well aspected, it gives a peaceful married life, but the native may be widowed prematurely.

In this House, which influences commercial associations, Saturn is not well placed. If there is a partnership—which rarely happens—Saturn is too independent to submit to its tutelage, and the association is quickly dissolved, often through a sensational lawsuit, if the Sun sends an evil aspect.

Saturn in the Eighth House

This is a good position for living to a ripe old age, if the Sun is powerful in the horoscope. It causes trouble in connection with inheritance following upon the death of the marriage partner, or one of his (or her) parents.

This planet in the Eighth House often causes a chronic illness, and an evil aspect of Mars may cause the premature death of the Father.

With a bad aspect, it is a sign of marriage with some one who is poor, or it may mean pecuniary difficulties after marriage.

Saturn in the Ninth House

This Planet in the Ninth House does not give practical sense. It makes the native indulge in utopian dreams which will never be realised. A good influence will, however, give depth of mind, and an idealistic and philosophical bent. This position may be good for a politician. It also inclines to fixed occupations; a disinclination to travel, and sedentary tastes. The native is wise and of good counsel, and according to the indications of the Third House he may be a clever barrister, or professor, or sometimes a Churchman.

Saturn in the Tenth House

Well placed in this House, Saturn gives ambition, and denotes a native of superior character, who is sure to succeed, but who will nevertheless be liable to ups-and-downs in his fortune. Saturn may give him the topmost position in his native country, but a sudden turn of fortune often brings him down to the lowest. Saturn in this House should be very carefully studied, especially in regard to the aspects which it receives, as it is a critical position, and may either cause the loss of everything that has been gained, or else stabilise the native's worldly position.

Saturn in the Eleventh House

Saturn in the Eleventh House restricts the social circle. The native does not make many friends, and does not readily give his friendship, so that the steadfastness of his affection may be relied upon. His friends will be few but faithful; they will be older than the native, and will occupy good positions, which will help him. He may link his fortune with theirs.

This position does not give many children. They will be delicate in health, but if they survive, their father's name and social circle will enable them to progress rapidly in life.

If Saturn is adversely aspected, it is bad for the children. It may also cause deceit on the part of a friend, the deception being connected with the native's affections and bearing upon matters ruled by the planetary aspects.

Saturn in the Twelfth House

In this most unfortunate House, Saturn, if afflicted, will be most evil. Everything is jeopardised through this position. It causes reverses of fortune, prison, exile, estrangement from the family, loss of friends, deaths, failure in business, insanity, and death in poverty, or in a hospital.

If Saturn is well aspected, or dignified in the sign which occupies the Twelfth House, nothing very evil will happen. Progress, however, will not be very notable, but the native will have a steady and comfortable position, and his life may be a happy one through his own cautiousness and industry. The end of life will be lonely, but in no way unfortunate.

Saturn in the Signs

Saturn in Aries

THE Planet in this sign is not favourable for domestic harmony. The native is obstinate, determined, hyper-critical, sometimes boastful; he is gifted with good reasoning powers, but there is a marked tendency to anger, and he is often vindictive.

Progress will be difficult, and there will be many ups-and-downs in life, and a tendency to gambling and speculation, so that according to the planetary positions success or strife will be indicated. This position always brings delay in establishing the position in life.

In 10 of Aries, Saturn is again the cause of delay in marriage. It is a sign of disappointment in the affections, or of a separation, which may be only temporary if the aspects are favourable. If the Sun is well situated it gives success and a firm and well-established position.

In 20 of Aries, Saturn is very unfortunate. It brings countless disasters, which the native magnifies in his own mind, thereby causing continual worries. This position is also unfavourable for the health, especially in the Sixth and Twelfth House.

Saturn in Taurus

In Taurus, Saturn does not bring equilibrium of the senses. It is a sign of inclination to vice on the part of the native or those around him, according to the House occupied by Taurus. The affections are more cerebral than sentimental. This position gives the possibility of success through women.

Here again there is a desire for solitude; also prudence and economy. The native will be able to maintain his position in life through his own exertions, if the nature of his profession calls for the exercise of his mental faculties.

This Planet in the Sixth or the Twelfth House is a sign of

liability to contagious diseases. In the Eighth House it may indicate the premature death of the Father.

In 10 of Taurus, Saturn causes sensual disorders which may rapidly bring about a decline in the health of the native. Moreover, he is of a jealous disposition, and will suffer on this account. He is very ill-balanced, to the detriment of his health.

In 20 of Taurus, Saturn gives a melancholy, meditative, morbid and unstable disposition, and the position in life on the whole is likewise.

Saturn in Gemini

In this Mercurial sign Saturn gives an inventive mind, with indication of mechanical aptitude, especially if the planet is well aspected by Mars. In this sign envy or jealousy on the part of others is indicated.

In 10 of Gemini the mind is very restless. There is a total lack of self-confidence, pessimism, and a tendency to magnify the slightest unpleasant incidents of life, which will be numerous if Saturn is powerful in the horoscope.

In 20 of Gemini there is great resignation. The native is calm and kind, he takes things as they come, but he does not react sufficiently against them to be able to achieve success and happiness.

Saturn in Cancer

This again is not a good position for Saturn, as this planet, when situated in the Moon's domicile, brings a certain want of balance, or, at any rate, it makes the native hesitant and lacking in steadiness from the mental point of view.

In the Sixth House, especially, there is danger from water or liquids. Disease of the stomach (dilatation), pleurisy, kidney or affections of the bladder are indicated.

Saturn in Cancer does not favour success; it hinders plans and causes reverses of fortune.

In 10 of Cancer there is risk of accident or grave danger while travelling. If the position occurs in the Seventh or the Fourth House, it will mean danger of disagreement with separation from the marriage partner, or acute trouble with the family. An evil aspect of Mars will cause a violent or accidental death while travelling, especially if this aspect occurs in the Eighth House.

In 20 of Cancer the position, although not so unfortunate, does not give greater security. If there are occasional periods of brightness on account of the more fortunate tendency of the decanate, Saturn nevertheless retains its evil influence, causing violent deeds connected with matters ruled by the House occupied by the sign.

Saturn in Leo

Saturn in Leo, especially in the Seventh House, will not be very fortunate for marriage, as this planet causes the separation of the marriage partners, and sometimes divorce, according to the position of the Fourth House. It is also the indication of two unions.

The disposition is alternately too reserved or else too talkative; the mind is quick and intelligent, but not always kindly. There may even be a tendency to spitefulness, especially in a feminine horoscope, and this does not tend to attract sympathy.

The disposition is especially spiteful when evil aspects occur in 10 of Leo, and there may also be meanness or servility.

In 20 of Leo the position of Saturn is even more evil, for it never relents. Nothing succeeds in life, there is continual strife, disappointment and vexation. It is a position which causes its native to be constantly buffeted by Fate.

The malefic influence is specially noticeable in matters signified by the House occupied by Leo, but it will also have a good deal of repercussion on the House which receives the evil aspects of Saturn in a weak position.

Saturn in Virgo

In Virgo, Saturn gives a melancholy and resigned disposition. Life is a burden to the native, who cannot see anything worth while in it. He is not afraid of death. There is a suggestion of moral loneliness, and with evil aspects it may conduce to suicide. This position is not good for marriage, and in any case the union is childless. There is much intuition, the ideals are lofty, and thoughts of the Beyond haunt the native, who is interested in occultism.

In 10 of Virgo, Saturn causes physical and moral weakness. The native encounters a Destiny against which he can do nothing except wait for better days to come. Even with good aspects, the position of Saturn in this decanate will nevertheless cause delays.

In 20 of Virgo, Saturn brings to a woman a wealthy marriage with a man older than herself, but they will not have any children. For a man this position is more favourable than 10 of Virgo, as it brings gratifications, which though long delayed, will prove satisfying, especially from the moral standpoint.

Saturn in Libra

The native's mind is very argumentative. He is intellectual, but does not like to be contradicted. On the other hand, he is a devotee of the law, and he will have much litigation, the result of which will correspond to the good or evil aspects. This position is not good for marriage, which will occur late in life, or else will be with a person older than the native, or in delicate health.

It is also a sign of deceit or falsehood directed towards the native, or enacted by himself towards others.

In this sign, and in an unfavourable House, especially the Twelfth, Saturn may cause loss of position or failure in business.

In 10 of Libra, Saturn gives good mental faculties, and a taste for knowledge. The mind develops, but unfortunately the worldly position does not do likewise, and it remains precarious.

In 20 of Libra, Saturn is very powerful, and is not malefic. If the Luminaries and the benefic planets are well situated in the horoscope, this position may procure a steady and eminent position in life, but it is none the less unfortunate for marriage, as there are no children, or else the children are delicate; in any case, there is always some trouble connected with them.

Saturn in Scorpio

As in the case of Aries, Saturn in Scorpio, being in a domicile of Mars, implies the idea of impulsiveness and lack of thought. Anger and passion, however, are mitigated by the desire to succeed through cunning and ambition, so that benefic aspects of Mars, among others, will give a daring which may bring success if the Luminaries and benefics are well situated.

In 10 of Scorpio, Saturn gives a long life, good health, and the possibility of success through the native's skill, tactfulness, industry and intelligence. When the aspects are fortunate, the native may do something worth while, especially from the mental standpoint.

In 20 of Scorpio, little good can be expected, especially when this occurs in an unfortunate House. In the Sixth, there will be many illnesses, which will not be fatal, but which mar the native's life; in the Twelfth House, Saturn brings risk of close confinement, of dementia; in the Eighth House, it is a sign of a severe illness, or more probably of an accident which may endanger life or cause a wound which will leave painful scars.

Saturn in Sagittarius

In this sign Saturn denotes the native as being haughty and distant, but fundamentally kind and ready to help. It is the token of success through industry, and of much ambition that does not advertise itself. The native always maintains a calm attitude, without unnecessary words or gestures.

There will be many changes of position and of residence, also many illicit unions. The position in general will be established late in life.

In 10 of Sagittarius, success will be difficult to achieve. The goal aimed at is remote in consequence of the native's own ambition. Good influences will help him to obtain his desires, which are anything but modest. As he is energetic, industrious and persevering, however, as well as honest and kind, there is no reason why he should not succeed.

In 20 of Sagittarius the significance is similar. The mental qualities, however, are greater, but there is even more reserve. Aptitude for philosophical, religious or occult subjects is indicated, so that the native has a superior personality.

Saturn in Capricorn

In good Houses, Saturn in Capricorn denotes a native who is proud, but whose pride is a true moral coat-of-mail, compelling him to do what he ought to do, and to do it well. His integrity will attract to himself many influential friends, who will help him in his undertakings. In this sign, Saturn also denotes the acquisition of house property.

In the Sixth, Eighth, or Twelfth House, Saturn causes a chequered career, with many ups-and-downs to the end of life.

In 10 of Capricorn, the Exile of Jupiter and of the Moon, it is necessary, in order that something fortunate should occur, that Jupiter be well placed, in which case, with a good aspect of Mercury, success will be notable, although it is also necessary for the Moon to be well placed also.

In 20 of Capricorn, Saturn bestows a long life, and if Mars is well situated, it will be free from illness. An adverse aspect of Mars in the Eighth House, with Saturn in bad aspect with the Sun, is an indication of death by violence.

Saturn in Aquarius

In this sign, and in an Angular House, Saturn promises a notable rise in life, an exalted position, and an important and remunerative post around the fortieth year. The native is kind, quiet, reserved, prudent, industrious; his ideals are lofty, he is very magnetic. Being endowed with great powers of persuasion, he will obtain help and sympathy from everyone.

In 10 of Aquarius, when the Sun is weak in the horoscope, Saturn is not very favourable for marriage, which will be short-lived, as disagreement will occur between the couple. If, on the contrary, the Day Luminary is in good aspect, Saturn will give a long and carefree life.

In 20 of Aquarius the mind is of a superior order, especially if Uranus is well placed and aspected. The native is very original, independent, stately and kind. He is noble-minded, and his progress will be slow but steady: it will reach its zenith towards the forty-fifth year.

Saturn in Pisces

This position is far from fortunate. Saturn in Pisces gives a great tendency to melancholy and morbidity. The temper is changeable and thoughts of suicide may haunt the native. Disappointments connected with the affections and with children will be numerous, unless this position is mitigated by beneficial planetary influences.

In 10 of Pisces it is the indication of delayed marriage, which may be prevented altogether if Mercury and Venus are unfavourably situated. When marriage takes place there is not much more security, as one of the partners deceives the other, and it often happens that the native has ground for complaint on this point.

In 20 of Pisces, with good aspects, the position is less critical, as the native is able through his own industry and perseverance (which, however, is what is most lacking in this sign) to turn the current of events and thus attain to a modest position. Success will be difficult if Mars is not powerful in the horoscope.

Uranus

THIS planet (as also Neptune) is considered a transcendental planet. It appears to partake of the nature of Saturn, Mars and Jupiter. Its colour would be dark blue; its domicile in Aquarius; its Exile in Leo; its Exaltation in Scorpio; its Fall in Taurus.

It is mental, nervous, changeable, cold and barren. It exerts a marked influence on the nerves and brain.

It always brings uncommon, abnormal things, corresponding with the position which it occupies in House and Sign.

It is a sure sign of independence and insubordination, but also gives a peculiar genius, which is only recognised late in life, and which causes the native who comes under its influence to be considered by ordinary, or narrow-minded, people as a madman, or at any rate an eccentric being.

This electro-magnetic planet has a great repercussion (similarly to Neptune) on countries and agglomerations of people, and often causes unexpected and catastrophic events. Uranus partaking of the nature of Saturn and Mars, the influence of Jupiter contributes here in giving greatness and power to the event.

In a lay-out of cards this planet must be taken as representing a powerful and unexpected event corresponding to the aspects it receives, and the House and Sign it occupies; but the planet itself is a sign of selfishness, of family trouble, of originality and eccentricity.

Uranus in the Houses

Uranus in the First House

With this position the native has a curious, original, independent and obstinate mind. He is usually intelligent, and has peculiar ideas which shock those around him. He loves solitude and mental pursuits, and will be able, after much struggle and difficulty, to climb to a position of eminence, usually in some profession. As he will generally be ambitious, his station in life will be exalted, because, never satisfied with himself, the Uranian will continually endeavour to rise, so as to be master. With malefic influences it is the spirit of anarchy, the revolt against established things, which predominates, often accompanied by spitefulness and desire for vengeance. It is always a sign of selfishness and self-seeking. A native who has Uranus in the First House, whether for good or evil, is always "somebody."

Uranus in the Second House

Uranus in the Second House is not good for business affairs, as it is not flexible enough to enable the native to bend to the caprice of a customer. Nevertheless, well aspected, it will permit rapid gain in an occupation ruled by Uranus ; viz. in connection with electricity, science, metaphysics, and also in high finance.

It brings sudden alternations : great losses and unexpected gains. In bad aspect with Mercury, it will signify failure for a business man. In short, Uranus in this House must be considered as an event which will modify circumstances for good or ill according to the benefic or malefic position of this planet.

Uranus in the Third House

This position is favourable for the native's mentality, and will help him in the exercise of his profession, as it enables him to draw the attention of his associates to himself. He has "personality" which will serve him well as a writer or artist; his talent is peculiar to himself, he knows what he wants and will often say so in crude, blunt words, which will shock the weak-minded, but will cause him to be feared by the strong.

In his childhood the native is often difficult to train, and his parents wonder what to do with him. They need not worry; the child will make his mark in life, provided Uranus is well aspected. This position is also an indication of travelling, as the native cannot remain for long in the same place; he is one of those solitary travellers who work while they travel, and who travel so that they may be able to work.

Uranus in the Fourth House

In the House of the *Home*, this independent planet, which demands freedom at all costs, is very badly situated from the standpoint of domestic life. The native will be well advised not to marry, as he will either divorce, be separated, or else live apart from his family. It also indicates a lawsuit in connection with inheritance, and trouble with the family, relating to the profession or business.

This position is good for Occultism and Metaphysics.

Uranus in the Fifth House

Uranus is not well placed in this House, in which it upsets material welfare. It will cause trouble on account of the children, if there are any, but Uranus is not favourable for the offspring. For a woman, if this planet is in a fruitful sign, it is an indication of trouble connected with childbirth; the children may die young, and death may often be due to meningitis.

Uranus in this House prevents successful speculations, and may cause considerable and unexpected pecuniary losses.

Uranus in the Sixth House

This is often an indication of strange and peculiar nervous disorders. Such disorders often become chronic through want of proper care, or through a mistaken diagnosis.

As Uranus always makes a leader, this position in the House of servants and employees is not favourable, causing, as it does, serious disputes with subordinates.

Uranus in the Seventh House

In this House Uranus is not favourable for marriage, which it at least delays. It is one of the clearest tokens of an illicit union. When marriage does occur, it is still an indication of incompatibility of temperament either on the part of the native, or his partner, but more frequently the latter. It should be noted that the planet which occupies the Seventh House is a fairly accurate description of the marriage partner. In any case, home life is impossible, as either the native or his wife (or husband, as the case may be) cannot remain for long in the same place. In the generality of cases, especially if Uranus afflicts the Moon, it means separation or divorce.

Uranus in the Eighth House

In this position, and especially if it is in square aspect with Mars, Uranus will cause a violent death, usually through an accident. In any case it means loss of money for the marriage partner, and difficulties regarding inheritance. If Uranus is well aspected, it gives a possibility of gain from matters connected with funerals, or a pronounced taste for things connected with death. As with Uranus in the First House, this position in the Eighth House gives a desire for solitude.

Uranus in the Ninth House

Uranus in this House is very favourable for things relating to the mind, and gives an unconquerable attraction to metaphysical sciences and occultism. It makes the leader of a school of thought, the man who expects others to adopt his own ideas; also the man who creates new methods, whether scientific or philosophic, which run counter to official science, but which Time, which is ruled by Saturn, will prove to be correct.

In this House of long journeys, Uranus is favourable for travelling, but this will not occur without trouble, as such journeys will always be adventurous and undertaken without due preparation.

Uranus in the Tenth House

This position, if the planet is well aspected and in a favourable sign, will give the native opportunities of attaining to an exalted position, often of the highest rank, but this will be attended by numerous difficulties, antagonisms, disputes, and danger of a violent death. Serious trouble with subordinates may cause a downfall, because, although Uranus elevates, it retains, like Saturn, a capricious nature which may cause an overthrow at the most unexpected moment. It always means change of position and uncommon kinds of occupation. This position is very favourable for those who wish to take up occultism.

With bad aspects, it is most unfavourable, causing constant changes and alternations in life. It is often a sign of inability to succeed in worldly matters.

Uranus in the Eleventh House

This position gives friends or acquaintances who take an interest in mysterious things. It enables the native to become introduced into secret societies or closed circles. With bad aspects, it is unfavourable for associates, and will cause losses through friends. On the contrary, if Uranus is well aspected it indicates unexpected gains from acquaintances, or help coming at the very moment when the situation seems desperate. It also means unknown friends, or unknown enemies (according to the aspects), who will help or injure the native without his being aware of it.

In a lay-out of cards it indicates an impulsive friend with whom one should be careful of what one says, in order to avoid making an enemy of him. It always means that precautions must be taken to retain one's friends.

Uranus in the Twelfth House

In this position, if well aspected with the Luminaries, there is a likelihood of gain in secret occupations, money being acquired without trouble and with little exertion. This planet in the Twelfth House is not good for a public occupation, even if it is dignified.

If Uranus is unfortunately situated, it is a sure indication of numerous antagonisms, and enemies who will injure the native, often without his being aware of it. It sometimes means trouble with the law, misfortunes coming from those around the native, from parents, and is also an indication of nervous disorders, or brain fatigue.

A bad aspect of Mercury with Uranus means theft or unpaid debts—serious pecuniary troubles which may cause loss of position.

Uranus in the Signs

Uranus in Aries

IN this sign Uranus endows the native with excessive independence, will power, daring, firmness of opinion and fixity of ideas. From the material standpoint, however, the native, "a rolling stone," will experience a continual desire for change, which affects his position. This, however, is of little consequence, the desires and inclinations of the native being more intellectual than material. He is rather tall (especially if Uranus is on the Ascendant), with a strong constitution and a highly coloured complexion.

Ambition often urges the native not to acquire riches but honours, which is feasible if Uranus is well aspected, especially in 10 of Aries where, after a difficult period of struggle and suffering, the wheel of Fortune turns and brings the native to an envied position.

The influence of Uranus in 20 of Aries is pernicious. In this decanate the planet causes dangerous and unexpected events corresponding to the House occupied by the sign: in the Tenth House it means loss of position; in the Seventh, separation in marriage; in the Sixth, sudden illness.

Uranus in Taurus

This is a good position for taking up occultism. The native is intuitive, passionate, often stubborn, but of good faith. It often causes some abnormality of the senses, and peculiar ideas regarding love. If well aspected, Uranus in Taurus gives a well-established position, but seldom in a town, as this planet gives success in agricultural enterprises or occupations connected with the produce of the soil.

The native is reserved, and in 10 of Taurus the planet is not favourable for happy domestic life, the couple being out of sympathy with one another. There will be a lack of harmony between them, and weariness will rapidly occur if the Moon and Venus are in evil aspect.

In 20 of Taurus, Uranus causes instability, which will occur in connection with matters ruled by the House occupied by the planet. It often means troubles and worries of every kind, as Uranus is in its fall in this sign. In the Third or Ninth House it signifies accidents while travelling, and a lack of mental balance which is sometimes caused by occult practices.

Uranus in Gemini

This position is good for the study of occultism. It gives a transcendental intellect, provided Mercury, Sun and Moon are not debilitated.

The planet in this sign indicates the scientist who is fifty years ahead of official science. It is also a fortunate position for engineers who are inventors, as they will obtain pecuniary benefit through their inventions if Uranus falls in 20 of Gemini. This position gives to those who are born with it an uncommon and intellectual face; they will be considered as mad, or at any rate eccentric, by those who are backward and narrow-minded, but they are nevertheless well balanced and highly evolved.

In 10 of Gemini the position is not so powerful; the mind is not so steady, there are changes of mood and unevenness of mental productivity. In spite of the genius which may be present, the mind is not complete, there is a "vacuum" in the brain. If this position occurs in the Sixth House with a malefic aspect of the Moon, it may cause mental disorders and, with Mercury, a tendency to paralysis.

Uranus in Cancer

Unless there are very good aspects this position is not very fortunate for the native's life generally, especially during the first portion—up to thirty-five years—everything being unsettled. The native is jealous, and often embittered through an adverse fate. He will long seek his way in life, and a good aspect of the Moon may bring to him towards the fortieth year a little more stability in an uncommon occupation or business.

This position is not good for marriage, especially in a man's horoscope. It delays it or makes it unhappy, especially in 10 of Cancer. In this decanate Uranus also causes danger of wounds and accidents; often a severe stomach disorder, especially in the Sixth House.

In 20 of Cancer it is a little more fortunate and, after many failures, success will come through the help of those around the native, but will arrive rather late. If the native perseveres, good aspects of Mars and the Sun will bring him periods of luck, of which he must take advantage.

Uranus in Leo

Well aspected, Uranus in Leo should be fortunate for the native, which it renders proud, generous and handsome. It gives him a stern but noble countenance, especially in the Ascendant. The native is born to be a leader, and he often becomes one through force. He will be feared and will have many enemies, as he cannot bear to be contradicted, and expects to be obeyed forthwith. In his childhood his independent disposition does not make him liked by his family, and he will live for a long time a solitary life. His ambition will make him meditate long over the revenge he will one day take against the Fate of his youth. He will succeed therein, but with many difficulties, especially if Uranus is in 20 of Leo.

In this position, serious disputes with the family, especially with the Father, are indicated.

In 10 of Leo, Uranus does not conduce to a marriage that fulfils the native's expectations (especially in a woman's horoscope). There is a lack of harmony between the marriage partners, and an evil aspect of Mars, with the Sun in the Seventh House, promises separation within a short time.

Uranus in Virgo

In Virgo, Uranus does not give any possibility of success in business, as there is a lack of practical sense. Even if Mercury is well placed in the horoscope, denoting practical business ability, it will not give any tangible results, as at a certain period of life the native's position will suffer a reverse, especially if the planet is in 10 of Virgo. On the other hand, Uranus in this decanate may endow the native with aptitudes for success in medicine, or literature, in which latter he will produce original work. Material success will only come late.

Uranus in Virgo, especially in the First House, makes the native handsome and winning.

For a woman, if Uranus falls in 20 of Virgo, it may mean marriage far above her station in life with a man older than herself, which will bring her great happiness, especially if Venus and the Moon are well placed.

Uranus in Libra

In this sign Uranus makes the native inclined to interest himself in Art, Literature, Painting or Music, to which he will bring much originality and novelty, so that his work will be appreciated by the public and will procure for him a rapid acquisition of material comforts. If the native does not become an artist, the novelty of his ideas, his work and his merit will enable him to succeed in his chosen career.

This position is not favourable for partnerships or associations, as it entails disputes, disagreements and lawsuits. If there is a malefic influence of Mars, it is likely that legal troubles may occur, and these will often be in connection with politics.

With a good influence of the benefic planets, Uranus in 10 of Libra will enable the native, by his knowledge and skill, to rise far above his station at the time of birth, and success will be assured.

The same applies to 20 of Libra, but in this case, if the position occurs in the Fifth or Eleventh House with an evil aspect of Mars or Saturn, it will be disastrous for the children.

Uranus in Scorpio

This position is very favourable for Occultists, especially if the sign occupies the Third or Ninth House and is well situated.

The native has a studious mind, he interests himself in peculiar subjects; has a tendency to be reserved and undemonstrative; is often mischievous or teazing. Bad aspects will make him unscrupulous as to the means he adopts to achieve success.

In the Eighth House, Uranus in Scorpio presages death by violence.

In 10 of Scorpio, Uranus, if well aspected by the Sun and Moon, is the sign of a long life and good health, but it will bring many changes of occupation or position.

Uranus in 20 of Scorpio is very evil; in the Twelfth, Second, or Fifth House it leads to unlawful acts which may bring great trouble on the native.

Uranus in Sagittarius

This planet in Sagittarius gives skill and strength, and enables the native to be successful in sports, provided Mars is well placed in the horoscope. Uranus in this sign gives prudence, fine mental qualities, tenacity, moderation, good behaviour. From the general standpoint, Uranus will make the native successful, provided the Sun is not afflicted.

In 10 of Sagittarius this planet brings difficulties and many worries, but these will often be more of a moral than material nature, and success will crown the native's efforts.

In 20 of Sagittarius, Uranus gives great facility for the study of philosophic and mysterious subjects. It makes it possible for the native to come to the front in creating a new school of thought.

Uranus in Capricorn

Uranus in Capricorn is not good for marriage or friendship. It makes the native live the life of a misanthrope, far from his fellow-creatures. He only loves solitude and the study of abstract subjects. This is again a good position for occultists.

In 10 of Capricorn the native should succeed through his perseverance and subtlety; what he wants will happen. With good aspects, it is a good position for success in industry. The native is a leader by nature.

In 20 of Capricorn, Uranus may cause grave danger at some period of the life, this danger being related to matters governed by the House in which the planet is situated. It is, nevertheless, a good position for long life and health, if it is not afflicted by the Luminaries.

Uranus in Aquarius

If Uranus is free from evil aspects, and the sign occupies an Angular House, the native should attain to a good position and succeed in his adopted career, especially if this relates to metals, or to a business that necessitates travelling.

The native is benevolent, and deeply intellectual. It is

often a good position for marriage, which will occur late in life, but which will be perfectly harmonious.

In 10 of Aquarius, Uranus is not so good for the worldly position, and may cause an upheaval in the life, often due to some emotional cause.

In 20 of Aquarius it is a very favourable position, if Uranus is not afflicted. Being in its Joy in this sign, it promises great success, which is often unexpected, but none the less the result of the exertion and of the moral and intellectual qualities of the native.

Uranus in Pisces

Uranus in Pisces does not conduce to much will power or daring, but it makes the native straightforward, fond of contradiction and change, and is therefore favourable for travelling. The native is not gifted with transcendent qualities, but is lucky, and the one compensates the other. It is a good position for spiritualism, but with an evil aspect of Saturn, Uranus in this sign causes melancholy, depression, neurasthenia and pessimism.

In 10 of Pisces the native is not faithful. He will be unfaithful in a peculiar way, more in the moral than the physical sense, and this may lead to separation from his wife without any real reason.

In 20 of Pisces, Uranus is very fortunate for the native's position, and will bring him luck in matters ruled by the House occupied by this planet. If it is not afflicted, it will give the possibility of continual gains, either in lotteries or in speculations on foreign produce.

Neptune

THIS planet, according to what we have been able to observe, is distinctly related to Venus and the Moon. It is temperate and moist, and has an affinity for Pisces, in which sign it may be domiciled. Its Exile appears to be in Virgo, its Exaltation in Cancer, and its Joy in Capricorn.

In our opinion the influence of this planet affects the world in general rather than individuals ; that is to say, it exerts more influence over nations and the masses than over a particular individual, so that in a horoscope we may consider it as influencing the events which will be indicated by the other planets.

It is more especially favourable for travelling and for the study of occult or mysterious subjects. This planet makes the native emotional and changeable ; the mind is nebulous and unsettled. We may take it that it is fortunate for money and inheritance, and brings luck when it is well aspected. It is, however, not good for marriage, and causes disputes between husband and wife.

Neptune is somewhat lymphatic, and causes constitutional weakness corresponding to the part of the body influenced by the sign in which it is situated ; for instance, in Capricorn, it will signify weakness of the knees ; in Pisces, gout, rheumatism in the feet, etc.

It appears to influence the emotions rather than the mind.

Neptune in the Houses

Neptune in the First House

This position is not good for the native's health, and makes him effeminate, lacking in will power, lymphatic; it causes a chronic disease affecting the part of the body ruled by the sign in which it is placed. From the mental standpoint it is also unfavourable, making the native adopt an unreal attitude towards life. It gives a tendency to moral solitude, inability to react against events, carelessness in dress, neurasthenia and a distaste for manual work.

Neptune in the Second House

This position, when well aspected, should be fortunate for the native's position. Success is promised; the possibility of acquiring money without much difficulty; fortunate undertakings; and it should bring gains in businesses connected with liquids or foodstuffs. It inclines to a marriage based chiefly on physical attraction, but it is a fortunate union from the material standpoint, or should at all events bring the wherewithal to satisfy the native's desires. All this may be contradicted by evil aspects, when loss of position would be predicted. This would be caused through events connected with matters ruled by the planet which sends the malefic aspect.

Neptune in the Third House

The planet in this House usually inclines to sedentary tastes, but compels the native to travel on account of unexpected events. In this House it is good for the imagination, but gives an education that does not equip the native for life as it is. He is not able to defend himself, and in consequence is liable to be judged as incompetent.

If the native is wealthy, or merely in a comfortable position, he should succeed in matters calling for the exercise of imagination, among other things, writing books on travel, such writings being done quietly in his own home.

Badly situated, this planet will cause violent quarrels with those around the native, and may cause an unexpected accident in the course of a journey.

Neptune in the Fourth House

In this House, if Neptune is afflicted by the Ruler of the nativity, or by the Luminaries, it is a sign of ill-health. Moreover, there is a lack of harmony in the family, or a mystery connected with birth. It is also unfortunate for the children born of a marriage under this influence, as the domestic ties will not rest on a solid foundation. It may also mean death in some country other than the native's place of birth.

If Neptune is well aspected, luck will favour the native, and he is likely to acquire wealth in connection with land and house property, preferably situated close to the water.

Neptune in the Fifth House

This position is favourable for begetting children. It indicates a strongly emotional temperament, which often needs to be controlled, or the native's health may suffer thereby. It also indicates excessive expenditure; money will be lost through lack of organisation. It often means undesirable companions, not in keeping with the native's own education. If Neptune is afflicted, it shows unfaithfulness in marriage, and scandal which will upset the native's life.

Neptune in the Sixth House

This position of Neptune in the House of illnesses is necessarily unfavourable, but this will not prevent the native from living to a ripe old age if the Luminaries are well situated. He will, however, continually suffer from peculiar ailments against which medical science will be of little avail.

The position often gives a lonely occupation, or a mysterious position. In a woman's horoscope it indicates abdominal disorders, fibroma, and in some cases a tendency to cancer.

Neptune in the Seventh House

Neptune in this House is not very favourable for marriage, nor for partnerships. It indicates two marriages, one of which will end in divorce; it also denotes bigamy, or, at any rate, unfaithfulness. If the planet is badly aspected there is danger of loss of money which will be due to discord, and disagreement between the partners in marriage or in business.

Neptune in the Eighth House

Neptune in this House may indicate sudden, if not violent death. It is good for inheritance and also for marriage, which will be wealthy; but the native will be widowed after a short time. For the native himself, this position entails a risk of death through water (pleurisy, dropsy or drowning).

This position, with Neptune badly aspected, indicates trouble consequent upon a death; sometimes loss of inheritance through embezzlement, or worries caused through the native's children, wife, or wife's family.

Neptune in the Ninth House

In this House Neptune exerts a good influence on matters related to the mind. It enables the native to devote himself to the study of philosophy, theology or the occult sciences. It inclines to dreams and visions that come true. It is fortunate for long journeys, and may even cause the native to work out his destiny in a foreign country.

If Neptune is afflicted in this House it will cause disorders of the brain, and may produce a native who is a mystic, or a neurasthenic individual. Moreover, with a malefic aspect of Mars there is risk of death in a foreign country, while travelling, or in any case away from home.

Neptune in the Tenth House

Neptune in this House should procure a remunerative position; the native will not be his own master, but will be employed in an absolutely "safe" position, a real sinecure, which will suit his indolent temperament. He will be director of a shipping company, or manager of some association which will not require much exertion on his part. In many cases the position will be comfortable without the native himself accounting for it, and he will consider it quite natural that it should be so.

With bad aspects everything may be changed, and a reverse be suffered, again without the native knowing the reason. It will also have an unfortunate influence on his family.

Neptune in the Eleventh House

This always indicates an unfortunate choice of friends; lying and deceitful friends who will try to take advantage of the native's position, and who will desert him at a time when he may, in his turn, have need of them. If Neptune is well placed, it rather signifies disappointments in regard to friendships than pecuniary interests, but it is none the less an unfortunate position for the native's moral character, as he is hypersensitive.

Neptune in the Twelfth House

Well aspected in this House, Neptune may procure for the native real good fortune. It gives a position which, if it is not prominent, will nevertheless be remunerative. It brings success as a private-enquiry agent, or detective, or as the leader of a religious or occult sect. It makes the collector of stamps or coins, and always gives an occupation besides the one which is exercised openly.

Neptune badly aspected will cause many enmities, legal troubles, lawsuits, disputes, false friends and unpopularity. In an unfortunate horoscope it will indicate a lonely, if not unfortunate, end of life.

Neptune in the Signs

Neptune in Aries

NEPTUNE in Aries gives the force of inertia; often unconquerable stubbornness or resignation. The native is endowed with a pride that does not manifest itself outwardly. He is a long time making up his mind, but when once he does something he does it thoroughly.

This is not an unfavourable position. On the contrary, it brings a measure of luck, and procures, if in 10 of Aries, the likelihood of attaining one's wishes. The native will know how to wait for his opportunity, and act at the right moment. It is also an indication of a marriage which, though delayed, will fulfil every desire.

In 20 of Aries, Neptune is not nearly so fortunate; it may cause sudden reverses connected with matters ruled by the House occupied by this planet. It often indicates that Destiny is at war against the native or those around him.

Neptune in Taurus

This position makes the native indulgent towards others, and especially towards himself. He is kind and willing to help if it does not cause him too much trouble. He is attracted towards ancient and peculiar objects. He will usually marry an elderly woman, who may suffer from some infirmity. This position also gives a lymphatic temperament with tendencies to scrofula.

In 10 of Taurus the native is of a jealous as well as independent temperament, which causes disputes in the home. It often signifies stagnation or deadlocks in matters ruled by the House occupied by Neptune.

In 20 of Taurus, Neptune brings many sorrows, instability,

journeys for mysterious reasons, which are often connected with premature bereavements.

Neptune in Gemini

In Gemini, Neptune makes the native sympathetic, and surrounds him with helpful friends who will support him in his undertakings. These will be slow in taking shape, as the native is very punctilious. The position is good for marriage, which will be happy for the native, but not equally so for his wife, especially if Neptune is in 10 of Gemini, as it inclines to changeableness and caprice. In this decanate, and also in 20 of Gemini, Neptune is fortunate for a rise in position.

Neptune in Cancer

Neptune in Cancer also gives great power of inertia and gentleness, which nevertheless does not prevent the native from being unforgiving. His resignation being merely apparent, he only awaits the opportune moment for freeing himself from Fate or the shackles that hinder him. This position gives a tendency to take an interest in mysterious subjects, and makes the native inclined to double-dealing. Unless the planet is well aspected, his life will not be a happy one, and in any case matters ruled by the House occupied by Cancer will be adversely affected by Neptune.

In 10 of Cancer, Neptune brings grave risk of accident; stomach trouble (dilatation); troubles and disagreements over matters ruled by the House occupied by this Sign.

20 of Cancer is less unfortunate, but although Neptune is exalted in this decanate, it must be free from any evil aspect from Mars for the native to expect any pleasure or satisfaction in matters ruled by the House which Neptune occupies.

Neptune in Leo

This position is fortunate for the worldly position. It brings luck, and the native—often unknown to himself—will at some time occupy a prominent position, preferably in an administrative capacity. He may not be exactly the head, but he will have the confidence of the latter, to whom he will owe his progress, and whose right hand he will become.

In 10 of Leo, Neptune often gives tendencies to gossiping;

over-readiness to confide in others and disclose one's plans or those of other people. It is none the less a sign of faithfulness in marriage and in friendship.

In 20 of Leo it enables the native to extricate himself from difficulties without much exertion, luck always stepping in at the right moment. This position, however, is not good for the health, as it may cause blood-poisoning, or, at any rate, bad circulation of the blood, and if Venus sends an evil aspect it may entail bronchial disorders and a tendency to pleurisy.

Neptune in Virgo

In a feminine horoscope, Neptune in Virgo in the First House will permit the native to contract a wealthy marriage, as this planet usually gives beauty of face and figure.

This position does not incline to great benevolence; it may make the native vindictive and selfish, capricious and impressionable, and very difficult to please.

In regard to marriage, this position of Neptune causes marriage with some one older than the native, or else it delays marriage. In most cases there are no children, or few, and these will soon forsake the home, which they will not find warm or sympathetic, especially when Neptune is in 10 of Virgo.

In 20 of Virgo, Neptune permits a wealthy marriage, and if there are no evil aspects there is every possibility that it will be fortunate and happy, if Venus is dignified in the horoscope.

Neptune in Libra

In this sign Neptune gives an analytical mind, a carping disposition, peculiar ideas, manias. This is not a good position for marriage, which often occurs late in life, and when it takes place it is not happy, as one of the pair cannot accommodate himself (or herself) to life in common.

This planet in 10 of Libra is good for study, and may, if the education permits it, make a naval engineer, or a naval officer. If Mercury is in good aspect, it will make an aviator or help the native to make discoveries relating to naval or aerial matters.

In 20 of Libra, Neptune brings luck, and procures great material benefits. If Mars is free from affliction in the horoscope, it gives rapid gains, and should induce the native to buy or build house property. If the Fifth House is afflicted, Neptune in this decanate will cause trouble in regard to the children's health; pleurisy or kidney trouble.

Neptune in Scorpio

In this sign Neptune gives great manual dexterity, which can be applied to art or crafts, the aspects indicating the native's aptitudes. This position often enables the native to succeed in life through his own skill, cunning and luck.

In 10 of Scorpio, Neptune favours those who interest themselves in medicine or who practise it, from the ward-maid in an hospital (in the Twelfth House, for instance) up to the physician (in the Tenth or Ninth House), who will concern himself more especially with feminine disorders.

In 10 of Scorpio, Neptune brings much trouble to the native on account of his health or that of his family, according to the House occupied by the planet; but these are more due to anxiety than to real danger, inasmuch as if Neptune in this decanate is well aspected, it is a sign of good health and of a long life generally.

In 20 of Scorpio, Neptune is a sign of lymphatic and poor physical resistance. With an evil aspect of Uranus it may cause a severe illness, especially when the position occurs in the Sixth, Eighth, or Twelfth House. If Venus is weak in the horoscope, Neptune in this decanate will cause great anxiety connected with women, and is always a sign of slander.

Neptune in Sagittarius

This position is good for life taken as a whole. It gives cheerfulness, kindliness, and makes the native obliging. It favours many journeys, especially if situated in the Third or Ninth House. Neptune also gives a fine imagination, which will help the artist or writer—sometimes also the liar, as this position may tend to prolixity.

In 10 of Sagittarius the native undertakes many more things in his imagination than he accomplishes in reality. He may be a blunderer, or lack in perseverance, but with a good aspect of Mars this will be modified; luck will surely favour him, and he will be very successful.

In 20 of Sagittarius, Neptune gives occult faculties. The native takes pleasure in the study of subjects regarding the

Beyond; his tastes are modest, with leanings to economy; he is often selfish, or desires to be alone.

Neptune in Capricorn

Neptune in Capricorn gives great impressionability, so that the native will not always be very happy; he will react against insignificant trifles and suffer in silence, being of a calm, reflective and proud nature. From the physical standpoint he is not well favoured, especially if this position occurs in the First House, and he will therefore have little luck in regard to love, unless this is corrected by good aspects of Venus and the Moon.

Neptune in 10 of Capricorn is even more unfortunate and sad, and has an unlucky influence over matters ruled by the House occupied by this decanate.

If Neptune is in 20 of Capricorn, this will bring a little more luck, more energy and activity, but, unless Mars is dignified in the horoscope, it is a sure sign of injury during a journey, and this will probably affect the legs.

Neptune in Aquarius

In this sign Neptune inclines the native to a quiet life, which will be helped by favourable aspects from other planets. The native is easy-going, cheerful and sympathetic. This position is good for marriage and children, and without bringing wealth it enables the native to live a happy life in his domestic circle.

In 10 of Aquarius, unless Neptune is well aspected, the native's aspirations will not always be realised, and in spite of his desire for peace he will be continually quarrelling with people, or over matters ruled by the House which Neptune occupies. This position in an ordinary lay-out of cards indicates the receipt of a letter which is usually anonymous, and which brings trouble.

In 20 of Aquarius Neptune procures much better things. An occult protection surrounds the native, and Fate is far more kind, provided Uranus does not send an evil aspect. If, however, this planet should afflict Neptune, it would indicate that catastrophes would occur during times of the most profound quietude.

Neptune in Pisces

Neptune being here in his own domicile, this position gives great material resources and an assured income, which is necessary, as the native dislikes moral or physical exertion, desires an easy life, and is able to indulge in it.

In 10 of Pisces, Neptune inclines to unfaithfulness in marriage or double-dealing in love affairs. The native may marry twice, but he will not suffer through his affections, while he may cause suffering to others. He quickly wearies, and his fickleness is blatant.

In 20 of Pisces, Neptune influences the native to live his whole life as he began it, that is to say in a humdrum sort of way, fairly comfortably, but without anything remarkable either for good or evil. The position will be similar to that of a Government official, without anxiety about the future.

The Moon's Nodes

(*The Dragon's Head and Dragon's Tail*)

THE Nodes are the opposite points at which the Ecliptic is crossed by the Moon's orbit.

The positions occupied by the Moon's Nodes are found in Raphael's "Ephemeris." The position given is that of the Ascending Node (Dragon's Head), the position occupied by the Descending Node (Dragon's Tail) being in the same degree in the opposite sign. Thus, if the Ascending Node (Dragon's Head) is in 13° of Cancer, the Descending Node (Dragon's Tail) will be in 13° of Capricorn.

Aries is opposite to Libra;
Taurus is opposite to Scorpio;
Gemini is opposite to Sagittarius;
Cancer is opposite to Capricorn;
Leo is opposite to Aquarius;
Virgo is opposite to Pisces.

The Nodes are retrograde, and have a motion of about 6 minutes every 24 hours.

The Ascending Node (Dragon's Head) partakes of the nature of Jupiter, and is therefore benefic; the Descending Node (Dragon's Tail) partakes of the nature of Saturn or Uranus, and must therefore be considered as malefic.

For the Astrological Tarot Cards we have only made one card to represent the Nodes, so that this card will be placed on the spot occupied by the Ascending Node (Dragon's Head) while bearing in mind that the Descending Node (Dragon's Tail) is situated in the opposite sign. In order not to forget the Nodes, they should be studied at the same time as the aspects of the other planets to one another.

The Ascending Node (Dragon's Head) strengthens the good indicated by the Sign and the House, and brings help in material matters, while the Descending Node (Dragon's Tail) in the opposite position will be malefic in its influence on matters ruled by the Sign and the House it occupies. The position of the Moon in relation to its Nodes must be specially studied. If it is in conjunction with the Ascending Node (Dragon's Head), it is a token of benefit and gains; if, on the contrary, it is in conjunction with the Decending Node (Dragon's Tail), it always indicates losses and trouble.

The Nodes in the Houses

First House

The Ascending Node (Dragon's Head) in the First House is good for the native; it brings him a measure of support which will enable him to succeed in life. It is also a sign of wealth from the intellectual standpoint: a practical imagination, an inventive and fruitful mind. This position is good for the health.

The Descending Node (Dragon's Tail), being in the Seventh House, signifies worries and troubles regarding partners. It often indicates a very material union, so that if the planets are well placed in the Horoscope this position will be fortunate for money and material things, but where marriage is concerned, not for the emotions.

Second House

The Ascending Node (Dragon's Head) in the Second House is fortunate for the native's personal worth; his business will prosper, he will accumulate wealth fairly rapidly, and many strokes of luck will urge him onward. It also favours a rich marriage for love, with an intellectual partner, of tall stature, gentle disposition and clear complexion.

The Descending Node (Dragon's Tail) in the Eighth House will bring trouble connected with the senses; abuse of the animal passions. It is also a sign of a peculiar death, often connected with a relative, or the marriage partner, or his (or her) parents who may suffer from heart trouble. This position also implies trouble in connection with inheritance.

Third House

The Ascending Node (Dragon's Head) in the Third House is a sure sign of the native's good education and of his being able to live on good terms with those around him; it means harmonious relations with brothers and sisters. It procures the means of success in an intellectual occupation, especially in literature, history or geography. The native has an observant, studious and imaginative mind; ideas flow in abundance, and they are usually good and help him to progress rapidly, as much on account of his skilful management as on account of the help given by those around him. This position is also favourable for travelling for educational purposes.

The Descending Node (Dragon's Tail) in the Ninth House denotes a practical, and often materialistic mind, which either scoffs at religion or else is very superstitious. In this House it indicates danger while travelling, trouble in connection with a journey regarding mysterious matters, or matters of which the native alone has any knowledge.

Fourth House

The Ascending Node (Dragon's Head) in the Fourth House gives a cheerful and happy home life, and harmonious relations with the family. The Father, or the marriage partner, occupies a prominent post. The Dragon's Head in the Nadir of the Heavens is favourable for marriage, and will be a sign of happiness if the Moon is well placed in the horoscope. It is also a sign of good heredity from the physical as well as the mental standpoint.

The Descending Node (Dragon's Tail) in the Tenth House may be fortunate for material things if the horoscope on the whole is good. It may, however, bring at some period in life serious worries and troubles affecting things in general—losses and damage if the Moon is afflicted.

Fifth House

The Ascending Node (Dragon's Head) in the Fifth House indicates pleasure in regard to the children, who will be intelligent and have a generous measure of luck in life. This position is also fortunate for an artist, or anyone who is connected with matters that appeal to the mind. It is good for theatrical managers, musicians, and for all engaged in artistic occupations. For everyone it is a sign of luck in games and speculation, but prudence must be exercised in this direction, as an evil aspect of Mars to this House would upset everything. It is especially at the period of the annual revolution that this position of the Ascending Node is fortunate for speculating, if the horoscope at birth on the whole shows that the native is lucky.

The Descending Node (Dragon's Tail) in the Eleventh House does not always bring friends and acquaintances of a specially high social status. It causes the native to come into contact with people who may do him harm. Some of his associates will not be disinterested, and will try to cause him pecuniary losses. This position may also indicate a heavy monetary loss to the Mother, or Wife, if the Moon is in bad aspect.

Sixth House

The Ascending Node (Dragon's Head) in the Sixth House is good for the native's health, and even when he is ailing, or seriously ill at some time of his life, the Dragon's Head will help him to get over his illness, so that if his life should be despaired of he will have a chance of recovery. It also implies good fortune derived from employees, and if the horoscope on the whole predicts it, it confirms gain through an inheritance from an uncle or aunt.

The Descending Node (Dragon's Tail) in the Twelfth House is one of its most unfortunate positions. It causes incessant worries and troubles during the whole period of occupying this House, or when it passes through it again, unless benefic aspects from other planets are in operation at the same time. It causes loss of money, and unsatisfactory business transactions. It makes powerful enemies, merciless creditors, and is also a sign of ill-health and troubles of all kinds.

Seventh House

The Ascending Node (Dragon's Head) in this House is good for marriage, which it causes to be contracted on a lofty, sentimental and secure basis, provided Venus and the Moon are well situated in the horoscope. It is also very powerful in regard to partnerships and contracts, which it helps to make successful. It is also in this House that it is most favourably situated for lawsuits, which will be won through its support, thus bringing unexpected gains.

It is also a token of inheritance from grandparents, or an increase of wealth for the latter, by which the native will benefit.

The Descending Node (Dragon's Tail) in the First House

has a detrimental influence on the development of the native in the early period of his life. It upsets his health, and often his mind as well, inasmuch as he will be too analytical and will not always see things as a whole, but will become absorbed in small details. In regard to any special question put, it would signify a very bad beginning for the matter under consideration, as it always entails trouble and worry. This influence in a horoscope continues for a fairly long period, inasmuch as the Nodes being retrograde the Dragon's Tail passes from the First to the Twelfth House, which is also malefic.

Eighth House

In this House the Ascending Node (Dragon's Head) promises a peaceful and natural death, and a happy ending to the life. If the malefic planets (Saturn, Mars and Uranus) are free from affliction in the horoscope, and provided the Sun and Moon are powerfully situated, the length of life may exceed a hundred years. This position is also fortunate for inheritances and legacies. The native's inherited property from his parents will be considerably increased, and he will also have the chance of unexpected gains from lotteries or gifts.

In the Second House, the Descending Node (Dragon's Tail) is not fortunate for money matters. It is harmful to the native, or, more strictly speaking, his enterprises will be upset by circumstances over which he will have no control. This position may cause bankruptcy. Moreover, in regard to the affections, it will indicate deceit on the part of people in a low station of life. If the horoscope on the whole is not good, it denotes loss of position on account of a woman of loose morals.

Ninth House

This position is excellent for things of the mind. The native will constantly progress when the Dragon's Head occupies this House. His synthetic mind will enable him to undertake anything and succeed in everything, so long as the horoscope on the whole is favourable. In a woman's horoscope it indicates marriage with a man above her station in life, and the husband will be "somebody" from the pecuniary as well as the social standpoint. It is also fortunate for travelling, which will occur under comfortable and pleasant circumstances. For a man this position is fortunate for taking up politics, as it enables him to emerge victorious in oratorical controversies through his facility of speech (provided Mercury is free from affliction), and especially through his ever-present common-sense.

The Descending Node (Dragon's Tail) in the Third House causes serious disagreements with those around the native. With an evil aspect of Mars it signifies blows and wounds received during a dispute. This position is not good for the native's education, and compels him to associate with low-class people, which may be to his detriment. It is also a token of disharmony with the parents, brothers, or brothers-in-law, and is detrimental to the native's good repute, gossip, slander and calumny being the fruits of the Dragon's Tail in the Third House.

Tenth House

The Ascending Node (Dragon's Head) in this House gives full and complete success generally. There will always be progress towards better things, as the native is truly gifted from the time of his birth, and these gifts will develop, since the Dragon's Head passes (owing to its movement) into the Ninth House. It is a lucky position, and the native may undertake anything; he will succeed, and attain to a high position with honours, fame and riches.

The Descending Node (Dragon's Tail) in the Fourth House is not good for domestic life, which is founded upon exaggerated selfishness; the couple think about themselves in preference to their family, so that the inharmonious home is likely to be broken up, thus indicating separation and disagreements. It also means pecuniary losses, an inheritance wasted in order to gratify sometimes very unworthy desires.

Eleventh House

In this House the Ascending Node (Dragon's Head) gives many friends and supporters who will help the native to progress. It is a good position for associations, and also reveals the possibilities of becoming a leader, a Shining Light. Great social success is promised, inasmuch as the motion of the Node in the course of life cannot be otherwise than favourable for progress from the worldly as well as the mental standpoint. This position also indicates increased wealth for the Mother or the Wife, and this will benefit the native and his children, whose Father's name and fame will help them in their turn.

In the Fifth House the Descending Node (Dragon's Tail) is detrimental to happiness in general. It may incline to gambling or speculation, which will not be successful, and pecuniary losses are inevitable if the native indulges the tendency. It is also the cause of ill-health of the children, and anxiety on their account.

Twelfth House

This position of the Ascending Node (Dragon's Head) in the Twelfth House, though not very fortunate, nevertheless brings relief in trouble. It gives Faith, and enables the native to convince himself that all is not lost. He will have to struggle and defend himself; there will be difficult periods in his life; but he will conquer with the aid of the benefic planets, and more prosperous times will come in the course of the Revolutions of the Ascending Node.

In the Sixth House the Descending Node (Dragon's Tail) will cause serious disorders in health, countless difficulties with subordinates, some of whom will try to harm the native, and may even rob him or endeavour to deprive him of his position. It is also a sign of disagreements with uncles and aunts.

Important Note. The Houses being opposite each other, the position of the Moon's Nodes gives a contradictory significance. It is therefore necessary to ascertain and arrive at a conclusion as to whether it is the Dragon's Head or the Dragon's Tail that occupies the best position and receives the most powerful aspects, before forming a judgment.

In an ordinary draw of twelve cards, according as to whether the card is right or reversed, it will be taken as the Dragon's Head or the Dragon's Tail, and only one position will be interpreted.

The Moon's Nodes in the Signs

Aries

THE Dragon's Head in Aries enables the native to undertake daring deeds with every chance of success; and he should not hesitate to go forward. Fortune favours him. This position indicates rashness that is profitable. It is also lucky for love, but after much torment on this account. In a critical situation the Dragon's Head in Aries helps the native to extricate himself from trouble. It is similar to the Square in an unfortunate hand; it is the antidote to misfortune.

The Dragon's Tail in Aries prophesies lawsuits connected with material questions. It also means disputes in the home and danger of separation. It is not a good position for the spiritual evolution of the native, as it makes him practical (often too practical), which may lead to trouble with the law, or with those with whom he comes into contact. This position, especially in the Fifth House, shows anxiety on account of a child. Nevertheless if the Dragon's Tail is in 20 of Libra and is well aspected, it is sometimes an indication of material abundance and increase of possessions. But money does not always bring happiness, and the native will realise this.

Taurus

The Dragon's Head in Taurus brings great pleasure in regard to the affections; the native loves more with his heart and mind than his senses, and this may cause him to worry needlessly, as the position denotes a certain amount of jealousy which, though not exhibited outwardly, nevertheless causes suffering. It is also a sign of hesitation in most matters, which is a mistake on the part of the native, inasmuch as this position should encourage him to act, to look forward confidently to the future, and above all not to encourage wrong thinking, to which his natural disposition inclines him. Things on the whole cannot go otherwise than well, but the native must be prepared to help himself and to abandon pessimism. In 20 of Taurus it signifies a journey connected with business, or else a plan which will turn out fortunately.

The Dragon's Tail in Scorpio is very evil. It often denotes lack of moral and physical courage, which induces the native to seek more or less questionable methods of succeeding, apart from steady exertion; but they will only be trifling methods, and the results will not fulfil his desires. This position is also harmful for the health. There are evident signs of lymphatism. Danger of pecuniary loss through theft is also shown.

Gemini

The Dragon's Head is in its Exaltation in this sign, and is therefore very powerful. It indicates victory after much anxiety and trouble. It is a token of success, and luck which often comes only when everything seems lost. The friends who surround the native are reliable, and will help him to succeed. The native has a noble mind, which will always enable him to fight against the current, but Faith and Perseverance are also required. Courage is not wanting, and this position makes the native good and straightforward. He will know how to gain the sympathy of people who will help him: he may therefore look straight ahead, for the Dragon's Head in Gemini is always a sign of progress.

The Dragon's Tail in Sagittarius robs the native of some of the quietude upon which he might otherwise count. Frequently over-confidence in himself will be detrimental, and cause him to undertake things before due considerations, so that when it is too late he might regret what he has done. Countless difficulties will arise, but he will conquer them through exertion and courage, and by clear-sightedness and caution, not always thinking that everything he does is right. Perfection does not exist in this world.

Cancer

The Dragon's Head is favourably situated in the Moon's domicile. It brings light in the darkness which may surround the native, helps him to see clearly into his affairs, and to act judiciously without hesitating. If inimical people (or events) encompass him, he will soon discover their weak point, and thus conquer them. The position is a lucky one. It gives the opportunity of extricating oneself from trouble and of overcoming difficulties through one's own good management. It is a sure Protection, and a promise of Progress without strife or violence.

The Dragon's Tail in Capricorn is a very evil position. It brings with it sorrow, and a tendency to neurasthenia, which it is difficult to overcome. It gives the native a character or disposition which is subject to constant changes; it is also a sign of disappointment in love through the native's own fault, as he has not the gift of attracting love. It is not always detrimental to the worldly position, but the native will not know how to enjoy life; he is ever seeking trouble, and this does not help to create a cheerful atmosphere for those who come into contact with him.

Leo

The Dragon's Head in Leo helps the native to realise his desires, which are of a lofty nature. He has a fine ambition, and even if he is not an artist he is none the less a man of good taste, a lover of form and of everything that is fine and noble.

His fine imagination should enable him to discover or to invent new, pleasing and attractive things, which will profit him. His enquiring mind makes him continually desire to know and learn something new. This helps him to progress. The Dragon's Head in Leo enables the native to conquer the difficulties of life.

The Dragon's Tail in Aquarius causes the native to be easily deceived. He is inclined to be indolent. He does not react, nor know how to act wisely, and this is detrimental to him. People should be kind, but they should know how to discriminate, and this is not the case with the Dragon's Tail in Aquarius, as the native is too much inclined to listen to fine words. This position also indicates deceit over love matters; it is a sign of infidelity on the part of the native or his partner. It also upsets either the mental or physical balance.

Virgo

The Dragon's Head in Virgo gives fine aspirations. It is an ideal position for poets and writers, but not for business people, as it is too idealistic and not sufficiently practical. This position of the Dragon's Head is not good for marriage; physical love is non-existent, but on the other hand there may be much platonic or idealistic love. There is an entire absence of anything mean; the mind endeavours to free itself from matter, and this does not always benefit the pecuniary position. The native does not view life in its true perspective, and will therefore have to contend with the problems of existence. Success comes nevertheless after long delay. There may be a fortunate and wealthy marriage, which will turn out happily if helped by good aspects of Venus and the Moon. Failing this, the position often indicates celibacy.

The Dragon's Tail in Pisces is again a sign of deceit in love, and of infidelity. The native unconsciously indulges in gossip which is detrimental to him. The position also brings physical and moral sufferings, brought about through the native himself. A general indolence is indicated, which can be modified by a good aspect of Mars. Stability in matters connected with the affections will never exist.

Libra

The Dragon's Head in Libra is a sign of balance and harmony in the native's life as a whole. It also gives stability in regard to the affections; the gratification of noble desires is shown in all things. The native has a fine intellect as well as great courage. Progress will be rapid and wealth as well as honour will be acquired. The Dragon's Head in Libra is favourable for the children and for the family ties.

The Dragon's Tail in Aries is often a sign of lack of conscience, or, at all events, of inconsequence. The native acts too precipitately; what he has decided to do must be done forthwith, and this leads to want of due reflection, which is detrimental to his affairs. He may suffer material losses, or experience trouble in other directions, due to his lack of cautiousness. This position inclines to fits of anger, but also gives great physical courage, and if the horoscope generally is good the Dragon's Tail in Aries will not be so unfortunate.

Scorpio

The Dragon's Head in Scorpio gives activity, perseverance and subtlety, which will enable the native to succeed. It is also a sign of good health, or, more strictly speaking, of physical stamina. Success will not always be attained as quickly as may be desired, but will come after great difficulties; and the native's dearly-bought happiness will endure all the longer.

The Dragon's Tail in Taurus gives material instincts, the necessity for physical exertion and sensuous desires, which will often cause the commission of blunders. This position makes the native selfish; he likes his own comfort above everything else, and as he is not lazy or work-shy he will obtain what he wants. The Dragon's Tail in Taurus gives fits of energy followed by periods of unconquerable weariness and laziness.

Sagittarius

The Dragon's Head in Sagittarius is the surest sign of happiness and quietude, so long as the native knows how to be contented, which is usually the case, inasmuch as progress is fairly quick in this sign.

The close family ties, that is, the wife and children, live on good terms within a relatively restricted circle. It is the sort of happiness that does not proclaim itself. Success is somewhat slow in coming, but can be relied upon, as the ascent is gradual and teaches patience.

The Dragon's Tail in Gemini often causes inharmonious relations with those around the native, or with distant relatives. This may entail disputes over money matters which will be detrimental to the native, as many people may be jealous of him and put obstacles in his way. Nevertheless, he will know how to defend himself, especially with the help of a good aspect from Mars or Mercury. In the former case success will come through violence; in the latter, through cunning.

Capricorn

The Dragon's Head in Capricorn gives prudence, much reflectiveness, an even disposition inclined to sadness, love of solitude, but withal shrewdness and diplomacy. The disposition is more reflective than melancholy. This position may bring stability to the worldly position, but seldom gives wealth, which, moreover, the native does not desire, as he is not very ambitious. There is likelihood of gains through house property. The Dragon's Head in Capricorn gives robust healht and physical resistance; and if the Lord of Life is free from affliction, is a sure sign of longevity.

The Dragon's Tail in Cancer always gives fickleness in love; it is a sign of infidelity, and often shows a risk of separation after scandal. The position of the native or of those around him is not clearly defined; he is surrounded by many secret or mysterious circumstances. This position may cause an accident, or danger while travelling. It entails liver or stomach disorders. All this is mitigated by a good aspect of Venus or Jupiter.

A bad aspect of Mars to the Dragon's Tail may cause a wound, and is often a sign of hæmorrhage. With an unfortunate position of the Moon, and with Cancer in the Sixth House, there is serious risk of lung trouble—tuberculosis or, at all events, bronchial disorders.

The Dragon's Tail (as well as the Dragon's Head) must be carefully studied when it occurs in the Moon's domicile, and especially in regard to this planet and the aspects which it may receive from the malefics. If the Moon is in Cancer in conjunction with the Dragon's Tail, misfortunes will occur in connection with matters ruled by the House occupied by Cancer. On the other hand, if the Dragon's Head is in conjunction with the Moon in Cancer, good luck may be expected.

Aquarius

The Dragon's Head in Aquarius is fortunate for the native from the moral and emotional standpoint. He is benevolent, faithful, sincere and will be fortunate in his affections. Many friends will try to help him, and he may expect to progress. He may take up politics, or become the leader of a school, or the head of an association.

This position mitigates the evil influence which other planetary aspects may exert over marriage and the stability of wedlock. In 20 of Aquarius, especially, the lofty and noble sentiments of the native will procure for him universal esteem and love.

The Dragon's Tail in Leo gives rashness and fighting proclivities which may often bring trouble. The native is, however, endowed with courage, and will know how to defend himself; he is noble-hearted, and though quick-tempered, not vindictive.

Worries and troubles may be caused through gossip and

over-readiness to confide his plans, so that others may take advantage of them. There is also an instinctive tendency to meddle with other people's affairs and over-confidence, which lead to difficulties.

Pisces

The Dragon's Head in Pisces gives vitality, and is a fortunate position for the children, especially when it is situated in the Fifth or Eleventh House. It is not, however, a guarantee of fidelity. Nevertheless, in spite of deceit, the home will remain stable, as the native possesses the family instinct. The Dragon's Head in Pisces helps in unexpected acquisition, especially from foreigners. It is also a sure sign of long journeys undertaken when least expected.

The Dragon's Tail in Virgo is not favourable for things of the mind. It makes the native materialistic and unappreciative of beauty. He is inclined to analysis, which makes him judge everything according to its pecuniary value; everything is considered in terms of money; he may marry well, but it can hardly be other than a marriage of convenience. Progress will be difficult.

The Part of Fortune

THE Part of Fortune is the Good Genius of the Horoscope. It influences wealth and must therefore be studied more especially on this account.

Its place in the chart will be found as follows:

It occupies the point of the Zodiac which is the same number of degrees distant from the Ascendant as the Sun and Moon are distant from one another.

Add the longitude of the Ascendant to that of the Moon, then subtract from this total longitude of the Sun. The result will give the longitude of the Part of Fortune.

Example:

The Ascendant is in 10 of Taurus.
The Moon in 20 of Capricorn.
The Sun in Libra.
If we number the signs, starting from Aries, thus:

Aries . . .	sign 0	Libra . . .	sign 6
Taurus . . .	„ 1	Scorpio . . .	„ 7
Gemini . . .	„ 2	Sagittarius . .	„ 8
Cancer . . .	„ 3	Capricorn . .	„ 9
Leo . . .	„ 4	Aquarius . .	„ 10
Virgo . . .	„ 5	Pisces . . .	„ 11

we obtain

Longitude of the Moon	sign 9 plus 20°
Longitude of the Ascendant . . .	sign 1 plus 10°
Add together . . .	sign 10 plus 30°

or sign 11 (30 degrees equal 1 sign): subtract from sign 11

the longitude of the Sun, which is Libra, or the sixth sign. The part of Fortune will therefore be in the Fifth sign, which is Virgo.

Another example:

The Ascendant is in 20 of Aquarius.
The Moon in Gemini.
The Sun in 20 of Leo.

Longitude of the Ascendant . . is in	sign 10 plus 20°
Longitude of the Moon . . . is in	sign 2
Add together . . .	sign 12 plus 20°

Subtract the longitude of the Sun, which corresponds to sign 4 plus 20°, the result is: Part of Fortune in the Eighth sign, Sagittarius.

In an ordinary lay-out of 12 cards, if the card which represents the sign in which the Part of Fortune is not drawn, it must be found among the remaining cards, and placed in the correct position it should occupy in the Zodiac.

When calculating the Part of Fortune, it may happen that the longitude of the Sun is greater than the total of the Longitude of the Ascendant and of the Moon. In this case we add 12, so as to be able to make the subtraction, and the remainder will be the degree corresponding to the place occupied by the Part of Fortune.

If we use an ephemeris, the calculations will be made according to the longitudes indicated, and the degrees which remain will give the decanate which the Part of Fortune must occupy in the sign.

Example:

10 signs 27° correspond to 20° of Aquarius for the cards.
2 signs 17° correspond to 10° of Gemini for the cards.
11 signs 4° correspond to Pisces for the cards.
0 sign 12° correspond to 10° of Aries for the cards, and so on.

The Part of Fortune in the Houses

Part of Fortune in the First House

If the Part of Fortune is well aspected in this House, it signifies that the native will make his fortune through his own merit and efforts. If it is badly aspected, it indicates, on the contrary, that the native will lose his possessions through his own fault. The position is not very good for the sentimental and philosophical evolution of the native; his tastes are more materialistic than idealistic, he will be a business man rather than a poetic lover or an artist.

Part of Fortune in the Second House

This is a good position. It prophesies important pecuniary gains; wealth will accrue from a remunerative business, and will come quickly, provided no evil aspects contradict. If, on the other hand, it is afflicted, the Part of Fortune indicates failure, loss of position and persistent ill-luck. Well aspected, it indicates a wealthy marriage, if Venus is dignified and in good aspect with the Part of Fortune.

Part of Fortune in the Third House

This often means honour as well as money for a writer. It sometimes means wealth from the native's parents or from those around him. This is a good position for those who have to make many journeys, and causes them to be profitable. It inclines to selfishness and self-seeking.

Part of Fortune in the Fourth House

The native who has the Part of Fortune in the Fourth House should go in for building, or make others build; his wealth will be derived chiefly from house property. It is also a good position for dealing in products of the soil, and will procure rapid gains from undertakings connected therewith. The Part of Fortune in the Fourth House gives sedentary instincts, love of collecting, and an over-strong leaning towards economy, which, however, will benefit the children after their father's death.

Part of Fortune in the Fifth House

The Part of Fortune in this House, and well aspected, is beneficial for material things.

The native will be fond of good living, of food, of gratifying his senses. Love of form will predominate, and material comforts will come to him as a matter of course, provided the aspects are benefic. If the Part of Fortune is afflicted by Mars or Saturn, this position will show that the native wants to gratify his desires above everything else, and this may lead him to adopt a line of conduct that will not be above reproach. This position of the Part of Fortune also gives aptitude for managing an hotel, a theatre, or places of entertainment. It is good for the children.

Part of Fortune in the Sixth House

This position never makes a chief, but always procures a remunerative post under the leadership of others. It is a good position for the manager of an hotel, or restaurant, or other catering establishment. It also procures pecuniary benefit in small businesses, such as dealers in game, poultry, etc. If afflicted, it may cause a train of adversity—expenditure of money through illness of the native or his family.

Part of Fortune in the Seventh House

In this Angular House, and well aspected, the Part of Fortune is powerful, and will procure real benefits for the native: honours, profits derived from industrial or commercial associations, gains from lawsuits, material benefits through marriage. It indicates a large family of children.

When judging the Part of Fortune in a House, it is necessary to note the aspects which it receives from the planets. Thus in the Seventh House, if it is well aspected by Mercury and Mars, it will be fortunate for lawsuits; if the aspect is from Venus and Jupiter, and is benefic, it will influence marriage; if the Moon and Venus are in good aspect with the Part of

Fortune, there will be many children; while malefic aspects will signify the contrary, and an evil aspect of Mars and Saturn will totally nullify the fortunate influence.

Part of Fortune in the Eighth House

Fortune will come through a wealthy marriage, or will be strongly influenced by women, especially if the Moon is well placed. In this House the Part of Fortune is favourable for inheritances, especially for women; it prophesies a long and wealthy life. With a malefic aspect of Mars it may cause the untimely death of the Wife, or of the Mother, especially if the Moon is afflicted.

Part of Fortune in the Ninth House

This position is not good for idealistic matters; the native is materialistic. He is likely to succeed in the export business, or will acquire money from abroad. It is also an indication of long journeys, and if Venus and Mercury are favourably situated and well aspected, may mean marriage with a wealthy foreigner.

With bad aspects the Part of Fortune will, on the contrary, signify loss of money abroad, or of foreign securities, if Mercury casts a malefic ray.

Part of Fortune in the Tenth House

In this House the Part of Fortune often gives an official or public post, or some great responsibility. This position is always a sign of progress, and the Tenth House must be very unfavourably situated, or receive malefic aspects from the planets, for the Part of Fortune to fail in bringing material benefit at some period of the native's life.

Part of Fortune in the Eleventh House

In this House the Part of Fortune favours the native's luck. He receives unfailing support from everyone, and seldom has to rely upon himself; his associates work for him, and his friends defend or take an interest in him without his being aware of the fact.

This is also a good position from the political standpoint,

not because the native is exceptionally gifted, but because everything succeeds with him, and if a political party is in need of support, he will be chosen for the post.

If the Part of Fortune receives bad aspects from the malefic planets, this position causes loss of money through associates; friends will owe money to the native, and they will not refund it, or if they do, it will be difficult to regain.

Part of Fortune in the Twelfth House

In this not over-fortunate House the Part of Fortune will serve as a guarantee against the attacks of Fate. It often means money acquired easily. Merchants often have the Part of Fortune in the Twelfth House.

If it is afflicted by evil aspects, it indicates losses entailed through robbery or theft. It is unfavourable in regard to employees or subordinates, who will not be honest and who (as in the Sixth House) will try to usurp the position of their chief, or betray him to a competitor.

The Part of Fortune in the Signs

Part of Fortune in Aries

IN this sign it gives the possibility of acquiring wealth through the native's own creative mind; bold ideas will always help to extricate him from difficulties. Where money is money goes, and his fortune will continually increase. He will, however, often have to stint himself—especially in 20 of Aries, where he will frequently be on the verge of a catastrophe. He will not sink, however, but will sustain a severe shock, and have to go slow for a time, only to start off again more boldly than ever. It is a good position for a banker, who will succeed in this line provided the Fifth House is free from affliction, and the Moon does not receive evil aspects from Mars or Uranus.

Part of Fortune in Taurus

The Part of Fortune in this sign is a guarantee of material comfort, which the native desires first and foremost. He will often obtain this through marriage, feminine support being shown in material matters. There will be many changes in the native's life, and these will, generally speaking, be in the upward direction, provided the Part of Fortune is free from affliction. It also denotes infidelity, which is profitable, especially in a feminine horoscope. In 10 of Taurus it brings periods of trial, followed by periods of luck. With an evil aspect of Mars, especially in 20 of Taurus, it may cause needless expenditure, which may prove very detrimental. The native's fortune will either be unstable, or he will make a show of wealth which does not correspond to its real extent.

Part of Fortune in Gemini

In this sign, which is the domicile of Mercury, the Part of Fortune is favourably situated, and always procures success through the native's own merit, intelligence and efforts. He will make friends who will help him. It is a lucky position for a writer or barrister, and also for a politician. In 10 of Gemini Fortune will come more slowly, through the native lacking self-confidence, and being afraid of not succeeding. He should go ahead, and if the Eleventh House is favourable, success will surely come, and stay. In 20 of Gemini the position is even more favourable: progress in this case is bound to come.

Part of Fortune in Cancer

The part of Fortune in Cancer is a good position, as, over and above the luck which it brings of itself, it also benefits by the good fortune from the Moon, if the latter happens to be in good aspect. Should the Moon be in conjunction with the Part of Fortune in Cancer, and this sign occupy an Angular House, it is extremely lucky, and enables the native to undertake and succeed in anything. It is one of the most convincing signs of Wealth. The Part of Fortune in Cancer is always favourable for the Mother or Wife, and often means wealth derived from one or the other for the native.

In 10 of Cancer the Part of Fortune is favourable for travelling, or short journeys, and gives protection against difficulties which may arise. The same applies to 20 of Cancer, where it may rapidly procure wealth. It gives support or light during troubled times.

Part of Fortune in Leo

This is a favourable position for the native's progress, and he should occupy a prominent position in life. He is well fitted to become a leader, provided the benefic planets are well situated and favourably aspected. Progress will be helped by Luck, and this, especially if the position occurs in 20 of Leo, may create numerous enemies, antagonisms and quarrels, which the native will conquer, however, sometimes even through violence. In 10 of Leo the position procures gain through writings or spoken words; it is good for a barrister, an orator, a politician or a writer.

Part of Fortune in Virgo

This position indicates success, especially from the mental standpoint, in a position ruled by Mercury. It also means the acquisition of wealth through rigid economy. It may be a sign of riches, but never of philanthropy. Unless there are good aspects, it shows want of broadmindedness. Success will be achieved principally through small things and many undertakings on a small scale. Ready money will be the special lot of the native. The Part of Fortune in 10 of Virgo is not very fortunate for the worldly position, which will only be established after many delays and difficulties. In 20 of Virgo it may signify a wealthy marriage, provided the Moon and Venus are well situated.

Part of Fortune in Libra

In Libra the Part of Fortune is very well situated in regard to the Fortune and Success of the native. Unless evil aspects from the malefic planets spoil this lucky position, the native may expect great benefits from the material things of life; rapid promotion in position; a fortunate and happy marriage; and good health in general.

In 10 of Libra the benefits will be of an even more idealistic nature, as the mental faculties given by this decanate procure greater, nobler and finer pleasures. The Part of Fortune in this sign indicates honours and a prominent position.

In 20 of Libra it also means continual increase of wealth and general prosperity.

Part of Fortune in Scorpio

This is a favourable position for ambitious and self-seeking people, provided they are industrious. Fortune smiles upon them, but they will not hesitate to commit wrong deeds, or, at all events, to cause pain to those around them (unless good aspects of Venus, the Moon or Jupiter modify this). The part of Fortune in Scorpio gives success in undertakings and favours lawsuits.

In 10 of Scorpio it gives good health and physical resistance, which will be required, inasmuch as the native may have to make his fortune several times over.

If the Part of Fortune is in 20 of Scorpio and in evil aspect with Mars, it indicates loss of money through gambling or theft. In this decanate it may also signify that the native engages in enterprises which are not always quite aboveboard.

Part of Fortune in Sagittarius

In this sign the Part of Fortune indicates that fortune will be acquired slowly, without trouble and without drawbacks, through the native's perseverance, honesty, and especially through his good management. It is a position of security. It denotes the upper middle-class, officialdom in the broadest sense of the term; it represents respect for the rights of property, of capital, of the chief; it is the line of conduct followed by the father, who will guide his son along the same path.

In 10 of Sagittarius, a good aspect of Jupiter to the Part of Fortune is a sure sign of great and constantly accumulating riches.

In 20 of Sagittarius the Part of Fortune brings a fortune chiefly consisting in land and house property, and often inclines the native to be slightly avaricious, continually worrying about his possessions, and fearful of losing them. Nevertheless he is quite safe.

Part of Fortune in Capricorn

This position is not very favourable for the native, not because he lacks money, but because he does not know how to benefit by what he possesses. Wealth does not make him happier, he worries continually, and fears for the morrow. With this position, wealth will come through real estate. The native likes concrete, permanent things; he represents the peasant who does not place much reliance on bank-notes.

In 10 of Capricorn the position is not very favourable, especially when afflicted by Jupiter. The native invests his money at a high rate of interest; he gets good dividends for a certain time, but does not recover his capital. Favourable aspects of Jupiter and Mercury may procure pecuniary gains through usury.

In 20 of Capricorn the Part of Fortune brings greater security. The native will be well advised to invest his money in a life-annuity, for he will live to an advanced age if the Sun is well placed in the horoscope.

Part of Fortune in Aquarius

In this sign it gives great success in undertakings, especially those on a large scale. The native is of a naturally benevolent disposition and sympathetic, and this will promote his interests. He will be able to undertake big things with other people's money, which will benefit him without being detrimental to his associates.

In 10 of Aquarius the Part of Fortune may entail loss through the Mother or Wife. It also means expenditure of money.

In 20 of Aquarius the position is much improved. The native's ideas are broad, noble and lofty, and, with good aspects of the Sun and Jupiter, he should attain to an exalted position which will bring him riches, honour and fame.

Part of Fortune in Pisces

This is not always a sign of riches, but if the Part of Fortune is well aspected here, it prophesies a comfortable position, derived from small and unexpected gains. With a good aspect of the Moon, the position gives the possibility of frequent gain through lotteries, but never of large amounts.

As with the Part of Fortune in 20 of Capricorn, its position in 10 of Pisces should recommend the native to be cautious. He will live long, if the luminaries are well situated, and he must therefore provide for his old age, so that an annuity investment is advisable.

In 20 of Pisces the position is much improved. It means a steady accumulation of money, which will come quite naturally, especially if 20 of Pisces is in the First, Fourth, Seventh or Tenth House. It is also a good position for gains through gambling, provided Mars and the Fifth House are powerful.

SIGNS OF THE ZODIAC
INTERCEPTED SIGNS
ASPECTS
RULERS OF THE HOUSES

The Signs of the Zodiac in the Ascendant

Aries

WHEN this sign occupies the Ascendant, and is not intercepted, the native is fairly tall, with a muscular strongly built body, but with delicate joints. The eyes are small, but piercing, often of a light colour; the hair is dry, coarse and straight, red or brown. The face is freckled, nose aquiline. Baldness at the temples occurs at an early age, and the hair becomes prematurely white.

Aries in the Ascendant, from the standpoint of character, gives ambition, moral and physical courage and energy, which enables the native to succeed through his own efforts.

Taurus

The Ascendant occupied by this sign usually gives a somewhat short stature, with a thick-set body, inclined to stoutness, rugged features, full lips, a thick neck—giving on the whole a squat appearance. The native's hair will be of a dark colour, eyes rather round and inclined to be prominent and watery, long lashes, thick eyebrows. Hands and feet short and broad.

From the moral standpoint the influence is benefic. The native is steadfast, persevering, firm and yet gentle, unless his anger is aroused, when he may then become very violent. His ideals, though not specially noble, are not materialistic; he is a good listener and can keep his own counsel, so that even if his education is not superior, he can acquire a certain degree of veneer as he advances in years, thanks to his adaptability.

This position indicates progress in worldly matters through

the native's own efforts. He has a practical and organising mind, and is equally well suited for business as for the management of property, or for a political career.

Gemini

With the Ascendant in this sign the native is tall above the average, with well-developed muscles and long limbs; a highly coloured complexion, great vitality and physical stamina. His eyes will be brown or hazel. His hair dark; his skin fair. He will walk and move about quickly, and his voice will be clear and of a pleasant tone.

The intellect will be fine and synthetic, and very quick at grasping things. A certain precipitation in everything will enable the native to learn quickly. His visual memory is excellent, but he cannot remember names, unless the Moon occupies the sign. The defect of those born with Gemini in the Ascendant is that they are shy, lacking in self-confidence, and do not push themselves forward, in spite of their innate pride and ambition.

Success often comes through this sign, and the native progresses through his own merit, although luck, of which he knows how to avail himself in his own interests, often helps him. He is usually practical, without despising idealistic things. He is a man of refined tastes, and a lover of beautiful things, but he also appreciates the money which can procure them.

Cancer

The native of this sign is of medium stature, with delicate bones, a plump and well-rounded body and face. The veins show through the flesh and impart to it an attractive bluish tint. He has nice teeth of a chalky colour, and dull appearance, which will decay early in life because they are insufficiently protected by the enamel. His hands and feet are small and plump, forehead round and broad, and often high on account of the thin, sparse, prematurely falling hair. The eyes are grey or bluish, watery and prominent, nose small and short, the space between the nostrils and the lower lip inclined to be long.

In disposition he is changeable, fickle, fond of travel and novelty, although he does not dislike his domestic circle and his family, to whom he is greatly attached, until the day comes when he realises that his feelings are not reciprocated. He will then escape without hope of ever returning.

He is sociable, intellectual, poetical, inclined to be pessimistic and to worry about the future, and this will make him economical. Cancer is a lucky sign. It often enables its native to make a rich marriage and to gain several inheritances. For a man it often brings wealth through women.

Leo

With this sign in the Ascendant the native is of an average stature, with a broad chest, a clear complexion and a springy gait in youth. As the years advance the native becomes heavier owing to defective circulation.

His hair is light-coloured and sparse; eyes blue or pale grey, sometimes green; face full and round; muscles well developed, bony structure robust, joints delicate, hands and feet small in proportion to the stature.

The native goes straight ahead, his confidence in his strength and success enabling him to take a pleasant view of life. He is full of vitality. Capable of great exertion, and knowing exactly what he wants, he succeeds along his chosen path, providing that the Lord of this sign, the Sun, is well situated.

Leo in the Ascendant often means two marriages, denoting separation or divorce for the native or his parents. This prevents the period of youth from being exactly what he would like it to be. He will nevertheless attain to a higher position than his father.

Virgo

When Virgo occupies the Ascendant it gives height to the stature. The native is usually slim, his face and forehead are rounded, eyes light or else very dark, the complexion sallow and the hair matching the eyes.

The disposition is prudent, eloquent, industrious and quick, subtle and critical; the mental qualities are good, but over-analytical, so that the native is very methodical and a good organiser. A certain inclination toward pessimism makes him magnify the unpleasant facts of life. The period of youth is often unhappy, or does not come up to expectations.

The native's mental aptitude is good, but often not employed to the best advantage. In spite of organisation in details, there is a lack of ideas from the synthetic standpoint, so that, unless Mars, Uranus or Saturn are powerful in the horoscope, the native will have more chance to succeed with others than alone.

It is a good position for taking up science, medicine or occultism, and also gives great adaptability for commercial pursuits.

Libra

The Ascendant in this sign gives a slim form, a rounded and comely face, well-formed hips, a well-balanced gait, small nose, pink-and-white complexion, fair, chestnut or light hair, dark-blue or black, bright and compelling eyes, with long and silky lashes.

Towards the fortieth year the native with Libra in the Ascendant inclines to stoutness, and his pleasant and comely face becomes blotchy through faulty digestion, or kidney trouble.

Libra gives fine intellectual qualities, and a certain degree of ambition, especially in a feminine horoscope. The character is even, kindly, gentle, well-balanced, artistic, and the native will succeed without great difficulty.

This position inclines to early marriage. Libra does not usually give great physical courage, as the native can obtain what he wants without much exertion.

Scorpio

With this sign on the Ascendant the native is of average height, with a strong constitution, physical resistance, a muscular body, dark complexion, thick, curly (more often frizzy) hair, which may be dark or red; rather thick eyebrows, aquiline nose, short neck and a tendency to incline the head forward. The hands and feet are long, rather fleshy or dumpy, and the body on the whole inclined to premature stoutness.

From the moral standpoint the native is self-confident, brave, energetic and enduring. He knows what he wants and will do anything to get it. He has a critical mind, which immediately senses what others think. It is difficult to deceive him, for he is intuitive, or else observant.

This position gives the native fine possibilities of succeeding through his own industry, knowledge and skill. With Mercury on the cusp of the Ascendant he will be a remarkably good business man; while a good position of Mars will make him a banker or financier who will have to be reckoned with.

This position of the Ascendant is also fortunate for surgeons, occulists, and also for meat-dealers. The native will often lose his father or mother early in life, according to the aspects which Mars sends to the Sun or Moon.

Sagittarius

Sagittarius on the Ascendant makes the native tall, well built, but inclined to obesity at an early age, and also to baldness at the temples. The hair is brown or chestnut, nose large, face long, complexion clear but ruddy. There is an inclination to stoop.

This position gives fine moral qualities. The native is frank and loyal, and his word is as good as his bond. He is affectionate, devoted and generous, and knows how to win the love of those around him; he will be ready to risk his fortune and even his life, if he judges that those in whom he takes an interest are worth it. He is extremely logical, and his benevolence is self-conscious.

This position gives a taste for travelling, a love of philosophy, and enables its native to succeed as a Government official, or a director. His mind is essentially materialistic, but this does not prevent him from being interested in religion or philosophy in its practical aspect.

Capricorn

This sign gives a short, slight, bony figure. The native sometimes reaches an average stature, but will never be tall. The nose is long, the face sharp, neck thin with a very prominent Adam's apple; chin thin and long, hair straight, black and oily, the beard very thin.

The whole aspect is nervous, the chest thin and hollow, the shoulders will stoop should the native exceed the average height.

Morally Capricorn chiefly denotes an exaggerated sense of independence, craftiness, shrewdness in small matters, much patience and perseverance, often leading to a meagre result, especially in the initial period of life. Later on, if the horoscope on the whole is favourable, Capricorn on the Ascendant procures success in politics or business due to cunning.

Aquarius

This sign on the Ascendant gives a fine stature, a well-formed body, a ruddy complexion, brown eyes, an attractive oval-shaped face and light-coloured hair which soon becomes thin, especially on the temples. In women the hair is very abundant, and of a beautiful blonde colour.

From the moral standpoint Aquarius gives benevolence, cheerfulness and liveliness. The native is impulsive, energetic and enterprising; is gifted with fine intellectual and practical qualities, and has a strong personality. He knows exactly what he wants, his ideas are firmly established, and may incline him to be self-opinionated. He has good chances of success in politics, or in some prominent position. He may also have a taste for the fine Arts, and if the horoscope on the whole confirms it, may progress in this direction.

Marriage is usually fortunate, but he may be widowed. As regards family, the native suffers premature losses.

Pisces

With this sign on the Ascendant the stature is often below the average. The face is well-rounded and full, the body plump, nose small and round, the limbs small and short, hair black and abundant, the eyes lifeless or dreamy.

The disposition is gentle (even indolent), incapable of reacting. The native takes things as they come. He is good-natured, slightly selfish without being spiteful, and shows affection and a readiness to render service to others, provided this does not require too much physical exertion. He detests walking and anything that entails fatigue. His indolence is only equalled by his reserve and his self-centredness.

If the native has not inherited wealth, his position will be commonplace, but if he has means, this position makes a benevolent individual, who likes to help the weak. Pisces in the Ascendant is favourable for domestic life, which is peaceful and calm. It may conduce to a large family of children.

Intercepted Signs

It sometimes happens, when calculating a horoscope, that the cusps of two consecutive Houses are in the same sign, so that the next House and the one opposite to it will often intercept a whole sign.

This has a special meaning according to the House containing the intercepted sign.

Aries Intercepted in the Houses

I. This is an indication of injury to the head, neck or feet during childhood. It causes changeableness, a precarious position, or difficulties in creating it, independence, abruptness of character, which will cause the native to quarrel with those around him.

II. It gives feverish activity, great nervousness, lack of system, and hindrances in regard to marriage.

III. It brings difficulties with brothers and sisters or with the parents. It often means obstacles in regard to education in youth, and the risk of an accident while travelling.

IV. There are misfortunes in regard to women, and the native's wife in particular. It indicates that the father will die first.

V. It causes losses through speculations. For a woman it means danger of dishonour; sometimes a mystery connected with a child; an operation.

VI. This means countless disputes in the home, with the marriage partner, or with servants. Loss of the vital force and blood disorders.

VII. This is a bad position for partnerships. It causes disputes with the wife, danger of separation, or widowhood. Misfortune in business matters.

VIII. A violent death, often in a foreign country. With bad aspects, it indicates a suicidal tendency.

IX. The mind is troubled and pessimistic. The native is very argumentative. Disputes with brothers and sisters are indicated. There is danger while travelling.

X. There is little personal merit; luck alone will help to create a position. Few difficulties in life, but also few means of defence.

XI. Friends who will try to injure the native after a dispute. Risk of pecuniary loss for the mother or mother-in-law of the native.

XII. This mitigates the troubles and trials of life, or will procure the means of defence. Nevertheless the occupation is of a precarious nature, and there are numerous enemies.

Taurus Intercepted in the Houses

I. This position delays marriage, but causes many trifling love affairs. For women it means many love affairs, and inconsequent behaviour.

II. Protection and love of a wealthy person outside a legal marriage. Risk of a scandal on account of infidelity. An unhappy marriage.

III. Jealousy between brothers and sisters. A journey hindered for some sentimental reason.

IV. Danger of loss of position through a woman. For a man, loss of his wife. For a woman, danger of scandal or dishonour.

V. A disorderly life, exaggerated love of pleasure. Often childlessness, or premature death of children, or at all events danger of illness of the offspring.

VI. Trouble over love affairs. Possibility of miscarriage. Mars in bad aspect with Venus shows danger of death in connection with childbirth.

VII. Delays marriage, or causes a quick separation of the marriage partners. Infidelity.

VIII. Danger of widowhood. Premature death of the mother or wife. Sorrow connected with relatives or friends.

IX. Love troubles; mysterious love affairs which hinder marriage; often causes a hopeless love affair in youth.

X. Love of expenditure which entails loss of fortune. A difficult life for the mother; illness of the wife.

XI. Quarrel with friends about women; trouble connected with the affections coming from the children. Disputes with associates.

XII. Great trials in connection with love affairs. Illness affecting the generative system.

Gemini Intercepted in the Houses

I. Inclines to indiscreet chatter, which tendency causes the native to be constantly making trouble for himself with those around him. This position, moreover, makes him very highly strung.

II. Too much reflection prevents the native from doing things. He is afraid of what he undertakes to do, he hesitates, and thus misses opportunities for success.

III. Inclines to many journeys, and enables the native to win easily diplomas, scholarships and positions of preferment. It gives the support of learned people, and the possibility of travelling without expense.

IV. Gives the saving instinct; provokes quarrels with the family, especially with relatives through marriage.

V. Makes the native seek his own pleasure in love, and often his own interests. Favours a wealthy marriage, but not a love match.

VI. Numerous disputes with inferiors. The health is greatly influenced by the nerves. It often indicates difficulty in speech or pronunciation.

VII. Undesirable acquaintances. Disputes in the home regarding money; loss of a lawsuit or cancellation of a contract. Damages to be paid.

VII. Danger of food-poisoning; intestinal disorders. Loss of money or disappointment over inheritance.

IX. Sometimes gives peculiar ideas about philosophy or religion. May cause marriage with a foreigner, or else the native goes to live in a foreign country. Risk of pecuniary loss in connection with foreign goods.

X. Improvement in business affairs, or in an occupation ruled by Mercury. Gives fine artistic ability. The native spends money freely for his own pleasure.

XI. Brings troubles over love affairs. Causes fickleness in affection, and provokes quarrels with associates over money matters.

XII. Undesirable companions, who are detrimental to the native. Pecuniary loss. Trouble connected with the children, or with relatives younger than the native. Injury caused through domestic animals.

Cancer Intercepted in the Houses

I. Lack of due reflection. The pursuit of chimerical plans. Lack of practical sense. Delicate health in childhood; weakness of the chest.

II. Danger of loss through speculations or gambling. Typhoid or scarlet fever during childhood. Trouble through the mother, or on her account.

III. A large family, brothers and sisters. Many journeys on account of business, which do not procure the expected gains. Transitory love affairs.

IV. Confusion in family matters. Difficulties in the initial period of life. Accident due to water.

V. Dangerous or mysterious love affairs. Infidelity. Trouble with children, or childbirth. Love of pleasure and of food.

VI. Weakness of the kidneys. A gouty heredity. Usually a short life, unless the Luminaries are powerful. Danger of injury to the eyes.

VII. Infidelity in marriage. Risk of separation of the marriage partner. Partnerships of short duration. Unfaithful partners in business.

VIII. Premature death of the wife or mother. Many difficulties regarding inheritances. Annoyances following upon a death.

IX. Peculiar ideas; clairvoyance; mediumship. Risk of accident or injury to the head while travelling, which may result in loss of memory or of the mental faculties.

X. Good fortune in worldly matters; alternating ups and downs. Wealthy marriage. Help from the wife or mother.

XI. Many women friends. Vexations regarding girl-children. Family disputes caused through the mother-in-law or sisters-in-law.

XII. Ill-health; a languid or chronic illness, especially in a masculine horoscope; chest-weakness, kidney or bladder troubles. Tendency to cancer.

Leo Intercepted in the Houses

I. Ambition and pride which are detrimental to the native, causing many enmities of powerful people. Progress will be difficult, but assured.

II. Necessitates great expenditure of money to achieve

success. Progress is assured if the native is supported by his mother or wife.

III. Brings difficulties in the initial period of life. Progress come towards the thirty-eighth to fortieth year, and is due to the support of the parents or those around the native.

IV. An unhappy marriage brings trouble in the home. Often it is the parents who are divorced or separated. Gains through house property.

V. This position is bad for the children: they are good-looking and intelligent, but delicate in health, unless Venus and the Moon are well situated in the horoscope. Expenditure of money for the native's own pleasure in places of amusement.

VI. Disease or weakness of the heart. In a woman, weakness of the spinal fluid, pains in the back. A long life if the Sun is well placed.

VII. Divorce, separation, disputes with partners, loss of money through unfortunate contracts. Many enemies who try to injure the native. A long life.

VIII. Premature death of the husband or father; danger of death by violence if Mars is in bad aspect with the cusp of the Eighth House. Eye trouble.

IX. This gives mysterious occupations; makes the native interest himself in occultism; induces him to visit foreign countries. Death occurs far from the land of birth.

X. This often procures scandalous notoriety, or promotion following upon a mysterious event. If the Sun is well placed it means an exalted position which will be gained by the native himself.

XI. Powerful friends cause the native to be always inferior to the people with whom he associates. An unfortunate marriage makes the children live away from home.

XII. This is very detrimental to the worldly position, on account of powerful enemies. Risk of imprisonment, or else trouble with those administering the law. Danger of death through accident or violence.

Virgo Intercepted in the Houses

I. This gives an analytical mind, inclined to criticism, so that the native is continually arguing with others or with himself.

II. Selfishness; numerous small and unsuccessful enterprises. Not a fortunate position for marriage. Celibacy, or marriage late in life, which will not be happy.

III. Disputes with those around the native; either relatives or friends. Many journeys connected with business. Money gained through sale of land property. Great economy.

IV. A lonely and dreary home-life; loveless old-age. Inclines to a long life. Good intellectual faculties, ability to study the occult sciences.

V. Unfortunate for the children; a limited family. In a woman's horoscope: childlessness.

VI. Stomach disorders, defective assimilation, nervous illness. Danger of brain trouble.

VII. Very unfortunate for partnerships; makes celibates. Unfortunate for business undertakings if Mercury is afflicted in the horoscope.

VIII. Ear-trouble. A long life provided the Sun is powerful in the chart. Many losses through death. Premature death of the parents.

IX. A utopian mind; unprofitable philosophic discussions. An aspect of the Moon and Mercury inclines to dreams that come true.

X. Unfortunate for worldly affairs generally. Danger of loss of money, or bankruptcy, if Mars is in the Fifth House, or in aspect with its cusp.

XI. Not favourable for friendships with the opposite sex. Favours the acquisition of possessions through diplomacy, with helpful friends of a higher social status than the native's.

XII. Numerous political disputes; enemies who try to harm the native; unprofitable words or actions; loss of time, unprofitable use of the native's faculties.

Libra Intercepted in the Houses

I. This position makes the native somewhat selfish, but very lovable if it procures pleasure for himself. He readily attracts others.

II. Good business abilities; a well-balanced mind and body; money easily earned.

III. Makes the native a lover of form, of refined tastes; gives a good education in the Arts or Literature, but inclines to dangerous connections.

IV. Usually gives long life and good health, unless the Moon is afflicted. Premature death, or illness of native's sister.

V. Very favourable for the children if Venus is well situated in the chart. It means, however, fickleness in love, and an exaggerated desire for material pleasures. Many visits to places of entertainment at night.

VI. Kidney trouble, defective blood-circulation.

VII. A fortunate marriage, which is delayed on account of disagreement between the two families, especially of the father. Many, but profitable, lawsuits.

VIII. Marriage with a childless person. Widowhood; two unions with persons older than the native.

IX. Many journeys. Marriage abroad, or with a foreigner. Attraction for some one in a lower station of life than the native.

X. Rise in the worldly position, especially from the 35th year. Success in a luxury trade. Friendships with women of exalted station.

XI. Fine children if Venus is well placed in the horoscope, and the Fifth House well situated. There is often, however, a mystery connected with them; or it may mean children born out of wedlock.

XII. Disorders of the circulation. Unsatisfactory home conditions. Trouble in connection with the marriage partner's family.

Scorpio Intercepted in the Houses

I. Long journeys, or many short journeys, which delay marriage. Lack of mental stability; fickleness in love.

II. Much strife and many disputes on account of an inheritance coming from a woman. The mother will die first of a painful illness. Often means widowhood.

III. Promotion of the native through his own good management; he has a studious mind. Troubles over love affairs in youth. Jealousy on account of a brother or sister.

IV. Disputes with the wife on account of friends. Jealousy, a quarrel, separation or divorce. Illness of the mother or wife.

V. Trouble on account of the children. Emotional troubles. Gains from places of entertainment. Money gained after breaking off of some connection.

VI. Illness affecting the abdominal organs. Disputes in the home. Trouble with inferiors or employees.

VII. Delayed marriage. A frivolous mind; sordid and materialistic love nature. Shrewdness in business matters; gain through lawsuits.

VIII. Widowhood, or premature loss of a loved one in a higher social position than the native's, through which he benefits.

IX. A vindictive and quarrelsome, critical and disagreeable disposition, which entails many disputes with parents. Gains in a foreign country.

X. Rapid promotion through the native's own ability. Risk of loss of position towards the forty-fifth year through death of the wife, or separation from her.

XI. Many friendships with those of the opposite sex. Celibacy. Petty love affairs, jealousy and quarrels with associates on account of women.

XII. Many sorrows; serious and protracted illnesses. Death of children, or miscarriage for a woman.

Sagittarius Intercepted in the Houses

I. Difficulties in the early period of life. Long life, good fortune, fickleness. Troubles with employees or associates.

II. Family troubles in childhood; the native is not always brought up in his own family. Separation of the parents with consequent pecuniary loss.

III. Good for small undertakings, and procures the support of strangers. Frequent short journeys.

IV. Safeguards the native against the perils of life. A long life if Jupiter is well placed in a favourable House. Love of pleasure; selfishness.

V. The mind is more materialistic than idealistic; materialistic tastes, tendency to profligacy, fickleness in love, numerous and sometimes dangerous connections.

VI. Inimical influences surround the native in his home. Deceit on the part of some one younger than the native. Danger of loss of possessions.

VII. A good-natured disposition; the mentality of a commercial traveller; unprofitable gossip. Many undertakings which are unsuccessful because the native is too easily led to divulge his plans.

VIII. A hesitating mind. Tendency to neurasthenia; an imaginary invalid, or valetudinarian.

IX. Desire for knowledge, and to know and learn something new. Many and profitable journeys. Associations with cultured and learned people.

X. Protection in periods of difficulty. A comfortable, if not wealthy, worldly position, due to the native's own organising ability.

XI. A social circle of wealthy acquaintances who will help the native to progress. A calculating mind, which knows how to derive benefit from friends. Marriage for money.

XII. Harmful friends. Dishonest employees or servants who will hinder the native's progress. His position will remain precarious.

Capricorn Intercepted in the Houses

I. Gives an independent disposition, which does not bend easily. Few friends; a desire for solitude. An unhappy union.

II. Hinders or prevents any transaction connected with money, causes loss of inheritance. Often causes avarice through lack of means.

III. Makes the native, either the eldest, or the only son. Gives strong tendencies for the stúdy of abstract subjects. A philosophical and sometimes utopian mind.

IV. Early death of the father or husband. A rich marriage. Extensive real estate property built during the second half of the native's life. Danger from inundation.

V. Often makes marriage childless, or causes many short love affairs. Causes worries on account of the children.

VI. Ill-health; long, hereditary, or chronic illnesses; rheumatism, or disease leading to breaking-up of the body tissues.

VII. Not good for business partnerships. The native is not fitted for business. Ill-health during youth.

VIII. The first portion of life very sad; troubles on account of the mother or the wife. Unexpected pecuniary loss.

IX. Not very fortunate journeys. The native does not live in harmony with his brothers and sisters, as his character does not agree with theirs.

X. Difficulty in establishing the worldly position before the thirtieth year, but progress comes from this period onward, provided Saturn is dignified in the horoscope. This position is not fortunate for marriage, or else causes difficulties over family matters.

XI. Many vexations on account of the children. Mysterious, or detrimental friendships. Peculiar love affairs. Violent disputes with powerful people.

XII. Serious and protracted illnesses. A gouty or rheumatic heredity; kidney trouble, defective circulation. Danger of an operation.

Aquarius Intercepted in the Houses

I. Gives long life if the Sun is dignified in the horoscope. The health is delicate in the early period of life. The worldly position is difficult to establish. It is not fortunate for partnerships.

II. Makes the native very slow in everything he undertakes to do. Ill-health of the husband or father.

III. Not fortunate for travelling, which it makes risky. The native is sceptical, or over-credulous in regard to religion or occult powers.

IV. Gives an industrous, studious, thrifty and parsimonious disposition, which enables the native to gain a position in the world, which may, however, suffer a reverse if the aspects of Mars and Saturn are malefic.

V. An unhappy marriage, or celibacy. Does not favour the birth of children, or else they separate themselves from the native. This position spoils the joys of life.

VI. Causes numerous antagonisms with employees or subordinates. The home is ruined through theft or fire.

VII. Rise in position after many difficulties. It is not favourable for partnerships, which cannot endure. Lawsuits and difficulties with the sleeping-partner.

VIII. Disappointments, unless the Moon and Venus are well placed in the horoscope, in which case help will come from the mother or the wife. In a feminine horoscope, the Sun and Jupiter must be powerfully situated in order that the native may be fortunate.

IX. Delay in establishing the worldly position. An analytical mind which does not view things as they are in reality. Success comes towards the fortieth year through help from the parents.

X. Rise in the worldly position through real estate property. Not a favourable position for the native's marriage. Separation from his parents.

XI. Slow and gradual rise in worldly position. Trouble with the children on account of their health. Reliable friends.

XII. Usually a long life, but much moral and physical suffering.

Pisces Intercepted in the Houses

I. A fickle, ambitious and selfish disposition. The native is not fitted to marry. A tendency to laziness and inertia makes the position in life precarious.

II. Gains in some sort of industrial enterprise. A good organiser. Fortunate in material things, but many disappointments involving the affections. Bereavements and inheritances.

III. A good education, and a desire to acquire knowledge. Harmonious relations with parents and those around the native.

IV. Many changes of position; insecurity in material matters. A precarious position. Many children.

V. Selfishness; inordinate love of pleasure; luck and gains.

VI. Stagnation in business matters; gossip on the part of employees or servants, which is detrimental to the worldly position or peace of mind of the native.

VII. Fortune through partnerships, but numerous disputes with those around the native. Lack of self-confidence.

VIII. Makes the native marry a widow, or considerably delays marriage. If this takes place, the union is profitable, and necessary to enable the native to undertake big things, in which he will be successful.

IX. Numerous and profitable journeys. The position will be finally established in a foreign country, so that the native will be separated from his family.

X. A happy but lonely old age. Widowhood or celibacy.

XI. Numerous, but superficial friendships. Great success in the native's enterprises. Gains in the sale or purchase of foreign products.

XII. Illnesses caused through excess. An unhappy marriage, or deceit in love. Infidelity.

The Aspects

THE circle is divided into 360 degrees, and each sign therefore contains 30 degrees. Two planets are said to be in aspect with each other when their difference of longitude is equivalent to the distances given below.

In practice, we generally consider only aspects of 60, 90, 120, 180 and 0 degrees, i.e., the differences of 2 signs, 3 signs, 4 signs, 6 signs, or 0 sign between the planets, or the cusps of the Houses and the planets.

Two planets	0°	apart	are in	conjunction.
,,	30°	,,	,,	semi-sextile.
,,	45°	,,	,,	semi-square.
,,	60°	,,	,,	sextile.
,,	90°	,,	,,	square.
,,	120°	,,	,,	trine.
,,	135°	,,	,,	sesquiquadrate
,,	150°	,,	,,	quincunx.
,,	180°	,,	,,	opposition.

The conjunction is good or bad according to the planets aspecting each other.

The sextile is good.

The square is malefic.

The trine is benefic.

The opposition is malefic.

The planets move at different rates of speed. The quickest is the Moon, which applies to or encounters all the other planets; then come in their respective order: Mercury, Venus, Sun, Mars, Jupiter, Saturn and Neptune.

The planets have an orb of influence by which, even if they

are not exactly 60, 90, 120 or 180 degrees apart, they are nevertheless in aspect. The following are their respective orbs:

The Sun, total orb: 17°;
The Moon and Jupiter, total orb: 12°;
Neptune, Uranus and Saturn, total orb: 10°;
Venus, total orb: 8°;
Mars and Mercury, total orb: 7°.

The total orb only applies to the conjunction and opposition. For the sextile, we only allow one-third of the orb; for the square, one-half, and for the trine, two-thirds.

In practice, we ascertain if two planets are in aspect by adding their respective orbs, and divide the total by 2 for a conjunction or opposition; by 6 for a sextile; by 4 for a square; by 3 for a trine aspect.

The Ascendant has an orb of 10°; the cusps of the other Houses, about 4°; the fixed stars, about 5°, the Parallels of declination, 1°.

If Jupiter is at 20° Scorpio when Mars is at 10° 30′ in the same sign, the latter will start to apply to the conjunction of Jupiter, and the power of the aspect will increase the closer Mars approaches to Jupiter.

The Moon in Aspect with the other Planets

With the Sun.—When the Moon is in conjunction or good aspect with the Sun it indicates general harmony, good health, and success and benefits bearing upon matters ruled by the Houses occupied by the Luminaries.

In bad aspect, the Luminaries always cause weakness and difficulties that are not easily overcome. The Sun and Moon in opposition cause visual troubles; also separation of the marriage partners, or an ill-assorted couple.

With Mercury.—In good aspect the Moon is favourable for the mentality. Success is shown in all matters connected with the mind, but the success is not always material, on account of the mind being changeable. It is also good for travelling.

In bad aspect, it brings serious pecuniary troubles, and may cause failure in business. It entails mental disturbances owing to over-excitability. The native will be very intelligent, but will not be able to analyse his thoughts, which will be too prolific and too confused.

With Venus.—In good aspect with Venus the Moon is very fortunate for a wealthy union. Moreover, Venus gives more power of affection to the Moon, which, generally speaking, is cold. This position gives success in the Arts, Music, Painting, etc.

In bad aspect it is always a sign of scandal, or, at all events, of a mysterious love-affair, or of infidelity, or family disagreements, and does not favour harmonious associations.

With Mars.—The Moon in good aspect with Mars gives combative power, which enables the native to succeed, with the help of the Moon's lucky influence. Constant progress in life is indicated through the native's own merit, assisted by fortunate events.

In bad aspect with Mars, it gives activity to the imagination which is not always very desirable, and permits the realization of what the native has dreamed; but the result is not always satisfactory. This position intensifies the feelings, inclines to violence, gives unrealisable ambitions, and may cause the native to commit reprehensible deeds, through laziness or passion.

The conjunction of the Moon with Mars is malefic.

With Jupiter.—In good aspect, these two essentially benefic planets give a very benevolent, humane and sociable disposition. They promise success in a public career, if the Eleventh, Third and Ninth Houses are powerful.

This position favours a fortunate marriage, healthy children, a peaceful life, many friends and perfect happiness.

The Moon in bad aspect with Jupiter causes disagreements in the home; trouble on account of women or the mother; worry regarding journeys. It inclines to premature obesity, defective circulation, and liver complaints.

With Saturn.—In good aspect it gives patience, resignation sometimes, economy always. Fortune will smile upon the native as a result of his own efforts. He will enjoy good health; will acquire money through real estate property, and wealth will accrue through the sale and purchase of landed property.

The Moon in conjunction or bad aspect with Saturn causes scandals, involved family affairs, bereavements of women, widowhood, and often the untimely death of the mother. This is not a good position for children.

With Uranus.—This gives great erudition, and is favourable for the study of mysterious things. It gives originality and prudence, sometimes causes peculiarity, but always gives an uncommon personality.

In conjunction or bad aspect with Uranus, the Moon will cause mental disturbances, and an independence of character which will cause the native to live alone; there will be domestic troubles, and in case of marriage (which is unlikely) will entail separation after a short time.

With Neptune.—The Moon in good aspect with Neptune brings luck, and enables the native to succeed without great physical or mental exertion. It gives a large and intelligent family. It is a fortunate position for occultism, especially mediumship. It increases the imagination, and procures success in literature.

In bad aspect, the Moon causes danger while travelling; risks through women; scandal; gossip which will injure the native. It is not fortunate for marriage, which it delays, or causes the native to marry some one older than himself, or afflicted with some physical infirmity.

The Sun in Aspect with the other Planets

With Mercury.—The Sun can only form a conjunction with Mercury, from which it is never more than 28° apart. This position is good for the mind if it occurs within less than 4°, and exerts a benefic influence on business and the occupations ruled by Mercury.

With Venus.—The Sun only forms a conjunction or a semi-sextile with Venus, from which it is never more than 48° distant (the angle of 45° is a weak aspect). An aspect between Sun and Venus is favourable for pleasure, for a happy life, and enables the native to contract a wealthy marriage and progress rapidly.

With Mars.—The Sun in good aspect with Mars gives excellent health, vitality, courage, and self-confidence, which sometimes tends to recklessness, and causes the native to undertake things for which he does not appear to be fitted, but which are nevertheless successful. It gives a strong personality, which makes a leader, and also great physical and mental activity.

The Sun in conjunction or bad aspect with Mars gives the same physical and moral qualities, but the character is less harmonious, more hasty, more combative and despotic, and less cautious and reflective, so that the downfall, following upon the rise to a high position, will be catastrophic. It is not good for the parents on the masculine side: the father, husband or son. This aspect often presages heart-disease, and little happiness in the home circle.

With Jupiter.—The good aspects between the Sun and Jupiter cannot do otherwise than procure benefits for the native in matters ruled by the Houses which these two planets occupy. The health is good, and family and pecuniary affairs are satisfactory.

The bad aspects cause difficulties in the family, philosophical or religious trouble, numerous disputes with those surrounding the native, and ill-health through vitiated blood.

With Saturn.—The Sun in good aspect with Saturn gives a powerful personality, which makes the native a leader who knows how to control himself and to rule over others. It gives wealth in land and house property, and makes the native the richest and best esteemed member of his family.

In conjunction or bad aspect, it causes trouble of every kind for the native, in regard to health and family; it delays marriage or prevents it altogether, and causes the premature death of the father.

With Uranus.—The good aspects give a fine sense of independence, originality, ambition, and the possibility of success through the native's own merit. It is good for inventors and writers.

In conjunction or bad aspect, it is unfortunate for success, and causes numerous enmities, sudden reverses of position and ill-health through peculiar disorders.

With Neptune.—The good aspects give a love of everything that is beautiful and ancient, and thus enables the native to discover valuable things and to acquire money as an antique dealer.

The Sun in bad aspect with Neptune gives a desire to earn money too easily, which may be detrimental to the native's good repute. It also signifies troubles coming through women.

Mercury in Aspect with the other Planets

With Venus.—These two planets are never more than 78° apart, so that the aspects which concern us cannot be otherwise than benefic. They indicate kindness, a taste for the Beautiful, love of Form, of Music, of the Arts, of pleasure and of money, together with the possibility of obtaining everything that one desires, provided Venus and Mercury are free from affliction from the malefics.

With Mars.—Mercury in good aspect with Mars gives great mental activity, vivacity, cunning, quick repartee, liveliness. Success is promised in occupations requiring energy and initiative.

The bad aspects will cause quarrels, numerous disputes with brothers and sisters, and danger of accident while travelling.

The conjunction of Mars and Mercury is evil.

With Jupiter.—The good aspects give sound judgment and a love of truth in all things; often materialistic ideas. It is a good position for officials, and brings a peaceful, orderly and long life.

Mercury and Jupiter in bad aspect gives over-hastiness, sometimes envy and spitefulness. Married life is spoilt by quarrels with the marriage partner's family.

With Saturn.—The good aspects give system and method, gravity, prudence, and an analytical mind, which helps to succeed in a learned vocation. The native could be a professor or lawyer; he is faithful and honest.

Mercury in conjunction or bad aspect with Saturn makes the native jealous, lacking confidence in himself or others, malicious, seeing evil in everything. It causes divergences of opinion with those around him, false friends, unpopularity, and is unfavourable for the children or for relatives younger than the native.

With Uranus.—Mercury and Uranus in good aspect give fine mental qualities, originality, uncommon ideas, and promises success in scientific literature.

With the bad aspects, the qualities of mind remain the same, but the possibilities of material success are slight, and progress cannot be prophesied.

With Neptune.—Mercury in conjunction or good aspect with Neptune gives intuition, love of change, and is favourable for travelling. It is also a good position for the study of the occult sciences.

Mercury in bad aspect with Neptune makes the native incapable of defending himself in life; he is indolent, vacillating, fearful, dreamy, and lacking in will power, so that he will remain stagnant in the position which he occupies.

Venus in Aspect with the other Planets

With Jupiter.—Venus and Jupiter in good aspect cannot do otherwise than procure great benefits in matters ruled by the Houses which they occupy. They are fortunate for riches, for love, for the worldly position, and for the children.

The evil aspects incline the native, through his passionate nature, to licentiousness and infidelity. His benevolence diffuses itself; it extends to everyone, but is never sufficient to benefit anybody.

With Mars.—Venus in good aspect with Mars makes the native passionate and loving. It favours early marriage, and procures comforts and the gratification of self-love.

In bad aspect it often causes jealousy, infidelity, sentimental or affective troubles, the loss of friends, or false friends.

With Saturn.—In good aspect it is fortunate for pecuniary interests; it enables a woman to contract a wealthy marriage with an elderly man occupying a prominent position. It gives faithfulness and happiness in wedlock, and favours speculations.

In evil aspect it delays marriage, causes trouble with relatives older than the native, loss of money through unfortunate speculations, and makes the native squander his possessions on the wife's or other women's account.

With Uranus.—In good aspect it favours an early union, which may not be legal, but which will nevertheless be happy. It gives success in Art, Music or Literature.

In bad aspect it causes loss of affection, a broken engagement, sometimes a scandal before marriage, which is delayed or does not take place.

With Neptune.—Venus in good aspect with Neptune gives an amorous disposition, so that the native will have many love affairs in his youth. There will also be two marriages.

In bad aspect it causes pecuniary losses, and trouble on account of women; it is a sign of infidelity, scandal, and love caprices, for which the native pays dearly.

Mars in Aspect with the other Planets

With Jupiter.—Mars in good aspect with Jupiter prophesies honour in matters ruled by the Houses occupied by these two planets. It also gives generosity, good credit and important administrative posts, often in the army.

In bad aspect it gives over-impulsiveness and stubbornness. It is detrimental to the native's health, causing fevers and serious loss of vitality through excesses.

With Saturn.—Mars and Saturn in good aspect give prudence and perseverance; the Martial courage is tempered with reason so that the native exercises it in a good cause. It gives long life and good health.

The bad aspects cause grave disturbances in the native's life while they are in operation; they signify risk of serious injury or wounds, imprisonment, loss of money and widowhood.

The conjunction of Mars with another planet is always evil.

With Uranus.—Mars and Uranus in good aspect give great mental activity, with the possibility of success in a new system of religion or philosophy, or else to launch an invention.

In bad aspect they cause grave troubles in the family and in marriage. When Mars occupies the Twelfth House, or Uranus the Sixth House, there is danger of imprisonment, or of a serious illness in hospital.

With Neptune.—Mars in good aspect with Neptune gives great impulsiveness, violent reactions, spontaneity and generosity. It promises many journeys.

In bad aspect it signifies similar things, but with the additional risk of dangerous journeys, a scandalous union and wounds on account of infidelity.

Jupiter in Aspect with the other Planets

With Saturn.—The conjunction of Jupiter with any planet is fortunate. In good aspect with Saturn it prophesies a sure increase of the inherited property, many legacies or gifts, great gains through the exploitation of landed estates or buildings, together with sure and lasting benefits.

In bad aspect, it causes serious family troubles, especially with relatives of the male sex. The native's disposition is exaggeratedly selfish and materialistic.

With Uranus.—From the mental standpoint, the meaning of the aspects is the same as for Saturn, but from the material standpoint, when the aspects are evil, the troubles are more unexpected, more severe, and more lasting.

With Neptune.—In good aspect it gives to the native many occasions of luck in life; makes him gentle and kind, but somewhat effeminate; sincere, fond of home-life and of his personal comfort. It favours a marriage which is usually wealthy, and at all events happy.

In bad aspect it causes the native to allow himself to be easily duped by others. It is a sign of delicate health, of lymphatism, and also of domestic worries.

Saturn in Aspect with the other Planets

With Uranus.—Saturn in good aspect with Uranus has a good influence over matters ruled by the Houses occupied by the two planets; it gives a fine intellect, and enables the native to undertake anything he wishes.

The evil aspects between these two planets are very malefic. They cause pecuniary losses, loss of position, loss of loved ones, scandal, separation, widowhood.

With Neptune.—Saturn in good aspect with Neptune gives wealth and great mental culture, and causes the native to interest himself in occultism.

The bad aspects cause ill-health and hinder stability from the standpoint of money and the affections.

Uranus and Neptune in Aspect with the other Planets

The good aspects exert a strong influence over the moral character of the native, and make him original, eccentric and inclined towards the Mysterious.

The bad aspects may foreshadow disappointments in matters ruled by the Houses occupied by these two planets.

The Rulers of the Houses

We call Lord of the Ascendant, or planet which rules the First House, that which is domiciled in the Sign occupying the Ascendant.

When Aries is on the Ascendant, the Ruling Planet is Mars.

„	Taurus	„	„	„	„	Venus.
„	Gemini	„	„	„	„	Mercury.
„	Cancer	„	„	„	„	the Moon
„	Leo	„	„	„	„	the Sun.
„	Virgo	„	„	„	„	Mercury.
„	Libra	„	„	„	„	Venus.
„	Scorpio	„	„	„	„	Mars.
„	Sagittarius	„	„	„	„	Jupiter.
„	Capricorn	„	„	„	„	Saturn.
„	Aquarius	„	„	„	„	Saturn.
„	Pisces	„	„	„	„	Jupiter.

The same applies, of course, for all the other Houses, thus: when Aries is on the cusp of the Second House, the Ruler of this House is Mars, and so on.

The Ruler of the First House in the Houses

When the Ruler of the Ascendant is in the First House it signifies a long and fortunate life, usually filled with happiness, unless it is afflicted.

In the Second House.—Personal merit, ascent due to the native himself; commercial gains.

In the Third House.—Profitable journeys; harmonious relations with those around the native; good education, aptitude for study.

In the Fourth House.—A peaceful and happy home life; increase of the inheritance.

In the Fifth House.—Good for speculations, gambling, pleasure. Pleasure on account of the children.

In the Sixth House.—Not fortunate for the health; indicates unsatisfactory heredity, chronic disease.

In the Seventh House.—In opposition to the Ascendant, it signifies grave trouble coming through the wife, or through partners; obstacles, loss of position.

In the Eighth House.—A short life, or a violent death, according to the planet. A rich marriage.

In the Ninth House.—Long journeys; union with a foreigner; death in a foreign country.

In the Tenth House.—Very favourable for the worldly position.

In the Eleventh House.—Good for friendships.

In the Twelfth House.—Signifies grave troubles in the initial period of life, and a more prosperous ending.

The Ruler of the Second House in the Houses

It may denote:

In the First House.—Gains and success through the native's own merit.

In the Second House.—Easy and rapid acquisition of fortune; a wealthy marriage.

In the Third House.—The family helps the native to create his position; influential and helpful acquaintances.

In the Fourth House.—The father's name or his wealth will help the native to progress.

In the Fifth House.—Fortunate speculations. (Unless the Ruler should be Mars.)

In the Sixth House.—Inheritance from an uncle or aunt. Occupation carried on in the home.

In the Seventh House.—A wealthy marriage; a rich active or sleeping-partner.

In the Eighth House.—Fortune after a sentimentally inharmonious marriage.

In the Ninth House.—Import or Export business. Profitable voyages.

In the Tenth House.—A comfortable worldly position and rapidly acquired wealth.

In the Eleventh House.—Influential and numerous acquaintances. Support of powerful friends who help the native.

In the Twelfth House.—Numerous difficulties in establishing the position. If the Ruler of the Second House is dignified in this House: gains through farming or leases.

The Ruler of the Third House in the Houses

It indicates:

In the First House.—An investigating mind in search of knowledge. Success in an intellectual occupation.

In the Second House.—Fortunate undertakings with brothers and sisters. Profitable journeys.

In the Third House.—Harmonious relations with the native's environment.

In the Fourth House.—That the native will succeed to his father. Many journeys in connection with family matters.

In the Fifth House.—Many journeys for pleasure or business.

In the Sixth House.—A chronic illness necessitating treatment or a change of air.

In the Seventh House.—A lawsuit with the native's parents, or those around him regarding property in some place other than that which he inhabits.

In the Eighth House.—A journey for the purpose of gaining possession of an inheritance; or change of residence after a death.

In the Ninth House.—Change of residence towards middle age; travelling to acquire knowledge.

In the Tenth House.—Numerous journeys, or an occupation that necessitates travelling.

In the Eleventh House.—Many friends in different countries.

In the Twelfth House.—Legal trouble in connection with a written document; danger of accident while travelling; premature death of brothers or sisters.

The Ruler of the Fourth House in the Houses

This signifies:

In the First House.—Increase of the inherited property Gains through real estate transactions.

In the Second House.—Sale and purchase of landed estates; marriage with some one living in the country.

In the Third House.—Many changes of residence.

In the Fourth House.—Good fortune for the father. A good heredity.

In the Fifth House.—Squandering of the inherited property, through indulgence in pleasures, either by the father or his heirs. Losses through speculations.

In the Sixth House.—Unfortunate heredity. Hereditary disease.

In the Seventh House.—A wealthy and stable marriage.

In the Eighth House.—Progress in the worldly position through an inheritance.

In the Ninth House.—Property situated elsewhere than in the native's place of birth.

In the Tenth House.—An affluent position; frequently with influential people.

In the Eleventh House.—Lasting and reliable friendships.

In the Twelfth House.—A lonely position, or a position far distant from town.

The Ruler of the Fifth House in the Houses

In the First House.—Fortunate for the children and for the material things in life.

In the Second House.—Increase or decline in the worldly position through enterprises connected with luxuries or places of entertainment.

In the Third House.—Harmonious and pleasurable relations with those around the native.

In the Fourth House.—A happy and cheerful home-life.

In the Fifth House.—Fortunate for the children, and, unless the Ruler of the Fifth should be Mars, gains through speculations and games of chance.

In the Sixth House.—Ill-health through over-indulgence in pleasure.

In the Seventh House.—Lawsuits, or gaming debts. Disputes with the children.

In the Eighth House.—Anxiety on account of the children's health, or happiness jeopardised through a bereavement.

In the Ninth House.—Moral satisfaction brought about through the children. Intellectual pleasures.

In the Tenth House.—Good fortune, or trouble on account of the worldly position, according to the aspects. Fortunate or unfortunate speculations.

In the Eleventh House.—Pleasure and happiness caused through friends.

In the Twelfth House.—Loss of vitality; need for restraint in the indulgence of pleasure. Illness of a child.

The Ruler of the Sixth House in the Houses

In the First House.—Delicate health, or illness caused through excesses.

In the Second House.—Personal merit jeopardised through ill-health, or, illness caused through pecuniary troubles.

In the Third House.—Ill-health of those around the native; domestic troubles.

In the Fourth House.—Illness in the home, affecting either the native, his wife, or those with whom he lives.

In the Fifth House.—Temporary ill-health through excesses. Happiness jeopardised through ill-health. Illness of a child.

In the Sixth House.—Good health if the Ruler of this House is dignified; illness and domestic troubles, if it is afflicted.

In the Seventh House.—Troubles, lawsuits and worries caused by servants or employees.

In the Eighth House.—Serious illness affecting the native or some one dear to him, according to the aspects.

In the Ninth House.—Worries, a troubled state of mind; the native does not view things in their true perspective.

In the Tenth House.—The health is affected through business worries; over-work or unfortunate speculations.

In the Eleventh House.—Ill-health of a woman. Domestic troubles through an association.

In the Twelfth House.—Danger of an operation. Admission into a nursing home, or clinic.

The Ruler of the Seventh House in the Houses

In the First House.—If the Ruler of the Seventh is free from affliction in this house, it signifies a fortunate union.

In the Second House.—A fortunate marriage, if the Ruler is well aspected. Fluctuating position through a lawsuit.

In the Third House.—Disagreements and quarrels with those around the native. A successful, or unsuccessful lawsuit, according to the power or weakness of the Ruler.

In the Fourth House.—Harmony or disharmony in the home, according to the aspects between the Ruler of the Seventh and of the Fourth.

In the Fifth House.—Happiness in marriage or union; profitable speculations. If the Ruler is afflicted, it signifies quarrels with the children, or on their account.

In the Sixth House.—Domestic troubles. Lawsuit with employees or through them.

In the Seventh House.—Good fortune from the pecuniary and sentimental point of view, provided the Ruler of the Seventh is not afflicted by evil aspects of Jupiter or Mars.

In the Eighth House.—A wealthy union : dispute concerning an unexpected inheritance.

In the Ninth House.—Union with a foreigner, or marriage in a foreign country.

In the Tenth House.—Fortunate for everything, if the Ruler is well aspected.

In the Eleventh House.—Fortunate friendships, or, lawsuit with partners if Mars is Ruler of the Seventh.

In the Twelfth House.—Often means separation or divorce. Illness caused through an unsuccessful lawsuit. Loneliness.

The Ruler of the Eighth House in the Houses

In the First House.—Often means a sudden or quick, but not a premature death.

In the Second House.—Improvement in the position through an inheritance. A wealthy marriage.

In the Third House.—Danger of accident while travelling. Death of a brother or sister.

In the Fourth House.—The father will die first. Possibility of widowhood.

In the Fifth House.—Loss of a child. Death through over-indulgence in pleasure.

In the Sixth House.—Delicate health ; chronic illness.

In the Seventh House.—Sorrow in connection with the affections. Loss of a loved one, or illness on his (or her) account.

In the Eighth House.—Very fortunate, unless Scorpio occupies this House. A natural death. Happy ending to the life.

In the Ninth House.—Death abroad. If the Ruler is Mercury, adversely aspected it means an illness affecting the brain.

In the Tenth House.—Death through over-work, or following upon unfortunate undertakings. Death made public.

In the Eleventh House.—Death of the partner, which either jeopardises or else establishes the native's worldly position.

In the Twelfth House.—A lonely death. Ending of life in a clinic, hospital, or nursing home.

The Ruler of the Ninth House in the Houses

In the First House.—Very fortunate from the mental and moral standpoint.

In the Second House.—Personal merit, intellectuality, progress in the world.

In the Third House.—Gains in the exercise of a profession. Fame.

In the Fourth House.—Harmonious relations in the home; mental quietude.

In the Fifth House.—Refined pleasures, moral happiness. Learned and sensible children.

In the Sixth House.—Illness while travelling. Brain fatigue.

In the Seventh House.—Lawsuit connected with political or literary matters. An unhappy marriage.

In the Eighth House.—A moral inheritance. Rehabilitation of the memory of a loved one. Executor of a will.

In the Ninth House.—Remarkable mental faculties. Qualities of mind and heart. A refined occupation. Morally and materially profitable journeys.

In the Tenth House.—Fame sooner than money.

In the Eleventh House.—Friendships through mental collaboration.

In the Twelfth House.—Sorrow caused through vexatious matters. Illness incurred in a foreign country.

The Ruler of the Tenth House in the Houses

In the First House.—If the Ruler is well aspected: Continuous ascent. If afflicted: A life of toil and difficulty, finally successful, provided always that the native relies upon himself and not upon luck.

In the Second House.—Ascension due to the native's personal merit, and in connection with matters governed by the Ruler of the Second, and those governed by the Ruler of the Tenth.

In the Third House.—Help from relatives. A professional career.

In the Fourth House.—Increase of the patrimony. Possibility of gain through the exploitation of real estate property.

In the Fifth House.—Help from the children, who will be successful in life. If the Rulers of the Fifth and Tenth are Jupiter and Venus, or Moon and Sun, gains through speculations.

In the Sixth House.—Position jeopardised through the health.

Or, money earned through taking care of the health of others.

In the Seventh House.—Gains through business. Fortunate partnerships. A wealthy marriage.

In the Eighth House.—Improvement in the position through the wife, or through her influence. Inheritance or gift. A quick death, or a violent death if Mars occupies the Tenth.

In the Ninth House.—Business carried on in a foreign country or with foreigners. A prominent position.

In the Tenth House.—If the Ruler of the Tenth is benefic (Sun, Jupiter, Venus, Moon, Mercury or Neptune) it signifies a quick ascension, in which Luck is a factor, but the position may be ruined by aspects from the malefics. If Mars is the Ruler, progress will be slower; it will be achieved by the native himself, and be permanent. If Saturn is Ruler, progress will be still slower, but correspondingly more stable. Death, in the last two cases, will be violent.

In the Eleventh House.—Fortune through partnerships. Help from friends and acquaintances.

In the Twelfth House.—Free from affliction, it signifies difficulty in establishing a position. The Ruler of the Tenth, weak and afflicted in the Twelfth, always brings ruin or loss of credit.

The Ruler of the Eleventh House in the Houses

In the First House.—A sympathetic individual. Many helpful friends.

In the Second House.—Helpful acquaintances; profitable partnerships, which help the native to achieve success.

In the Third House.—Pleasant relations with those around the native and among his relatives.

In the Fourth House.—A friendly home life gives the domestic instinct.

In the Fifth House.—The children will help their parents: Fortunate speculations.

In the Sixth House.—Faithful and devoted employees. A happy domestic circle. Satisfactory health.

In the Seventh House.—Fortunate contracts. Harmonious relations between husband and wife, and with partners.

In the Eighth House.—Inheritance from friends. Sincere and enduring friendships.

In the Ninth House.—Intellectual acquaintances. Travelling with pleasant companions. Friendships in a foreign country, or with people of a different nationality from that of the native.

In the Tenth House.—Numerous friends and acquaintances on whom the native can rely.

In the Eleventh House.—General sympathy, harmony, quietude and joyfulness.

In the Twelfth House.—Worries and troubles through friends. Loss of dear ones, unfaithfulness. Dissolution of partnership.

The Ruler of the Twelfth House in the Houses

In the First House.—An unfortunate beginning of life. Loneliness. Troubles and sorrows through the family. Delicate childhood.

In the Second House.—Unfortunate enterprises. Many trials which are detrimental to the native's personal merit.

In the Third House.—Constraint in matters affecting the education; a misdirected line of training. Dispute or sorrow coming from those around the native.

In the Fourth House.—An inharmonious, poor or invalid home-life. Troubles due to the father, or marriage partner. Dispute connected with an inheritance.

In the Fifth House.—Unfortunate speculations. Sorrows. A delicate child.

In the Sixth House.—Theft by an employee. Illness necessitating an operation, if Mars is Ruler of the Twelfth.

In the Seventh House.—Domestic troubles. Danger of separation. Lawsuits; pecuniary difficulties through promissory notes, contracts, or agreements.

In the Eighth House.—A chronic or languid illness. A painful death.

In the Ninth House.—A disturbed state of mind; mistaken ideas; unsuccessful mental pursuits. A dangerous journey, or a journey that does not procure the expected results.

In the Tenth House.—Difficulties in establishing the position; alternating ups-and-downs. Many trials which the native will overcome if the Rulers are well placed.

In the Eleventh House.—Few reliable friends. Numerous jealousies.

In the Twelfth House.—If the Ruler is a benefic, it means many trials in life, over which the native will triumph. Mars, Saturn, Uranus, Moon or Neptune will cause disappointment after disappointment; sorrow and grief; worries and lack of success.

Symbolism of the Major Cards

I
I
ASCENDANT

The Ascendant

WITH the head and breast of a maiden; the claws of a lion, the body of a dog, the tail of a dragon, and wings, the Sphinx rules over the enigma of all life, whose course rises between his parted lips and follows the thread of Destiny according to its own rhythm.

This Card signifies the Commencement of everything in existence. It represents, in the pack, the Consultant.

NOEUD ASCENDANT
NOEUD DESCENDANT

The Moon's Nodes

THE Ascending Node (DRAGON'S HEAD). A young and lively maiden, the child of fancy, filled with life and potent loveliness. With a noble and gracious movement she raises aloft a torch, the bearer of sweet and pleasant things.

This Card, when turned towards the Dragon's Head, indicates happy and pleasant events which are about to occur, bringing joy and satisfaction. If often means the coming of a long-awaited child. It is a sign of fruitfulness in all things.

The Descending Node (DRAGON'S TAIL). In the greenish night, scarcely illuminated by the pale crescent of the waning moon, a shapeless monster of serpentine form sinks deeper and deeper in a slimy, unwholesome and miry substance.

This Card turned towards the Dragon's Tail indicates hidden and mysterious things from which escape is difficult. It represents worries and troubles of every kind. It is the sign of a chronic or languid illness, and is not fortunate for the emotions.

PARTIE
DE FORTUNE

The Part of Fortune

THE WINGED WHEEL, with beams of Gold, moves according to the sway of circumstances and of fancy, dispensing Good and Evil to Mankind. It is the blind and soulless instrument of Fate.

This is the Card of Change. It is fortunate or unfortunate (more often fortunate than otherwise). It brings material pleasures, and especially indicates an improvement in unpleasant matters.

SOLEIL
SOLEIL

The Sun

WITH flowing hair, his head wreathed with olive-leaves, in the pride of his youth, in a pose of nobly restrained triumph, APOLLO, the god of Light and of Fame, with his harmoniously formed body, captivating beauty, his gaze lost in Infinity, meditates serenely on a dream of Power, with which he is possessed.

The Day Luminary shines in the Heavens, and bathes the Earth in its benignant warmth.

This Card represents the Father. It promises enlightenment for everything which it approaches. It is an indication of stability, power, strength, ambition and success. It brings gold, and always compels the earning or spending of money.

It is a symbol of the Lord of Life. Weak or afflicted, it causes cardiac, visual, or pulmonary troubles.

LUNE
LUNE

The Moon

THE Goddess of Night, the Queen of Silence, according to Horatio, bears imprinted upon her countenance the memory of a painful or mysterious event. Deep is her sorrow; her laxity and freedom are equalled only by her melancholy and imagination.

In the nocturnal darkness of the Heavens, she daily pursues the mad course of her thoughts, while the heavenly canopy is illumined by the pale light of her crescent.

This Card represents the Mother, the Wife, and is the guide of good fortune. It prophesies mysterious events, and is often (like the guilty night which it represents) the sign of infidelity. It is fortunate for legacies and childbirth. It gives a fine imagination, with an exaggerated tendency to unreality.

Like the Sun, the Moon is Ruler of Life. When afflicted, it indicates paralysis, defective brain functions, kidney or bladder troubles, visual disorders, chest trouble.

MERCURE
MERCURE

Mercury

YOUTHFUL, of gracious mien, his shoulders girt with a cloak that scarcely conceals his form, his head surmounted by the winged petasus, carrying in his hand the caduceus, or magic wand, symbolising equilibrium, with his free and easy, tremulous and nimble demeanour, Mercury, the sly god, ambassador and messenger of Olympus, alert and quick, prepares himself to accomplish some piece of cunning work which will help him to fulfil a delicate or perilous mission.

This card represents a child or young person. It brings youth. It is the card of shrewdness, of creative intelligence, of nerve force, and of journeys. It is good or evil according to its position in the horoscope, but it always conveys the idea of something new, or of a change.

From the physical standpoint, if it is afflicted, it causes throat trouble, nervous diseases, loss of memory.

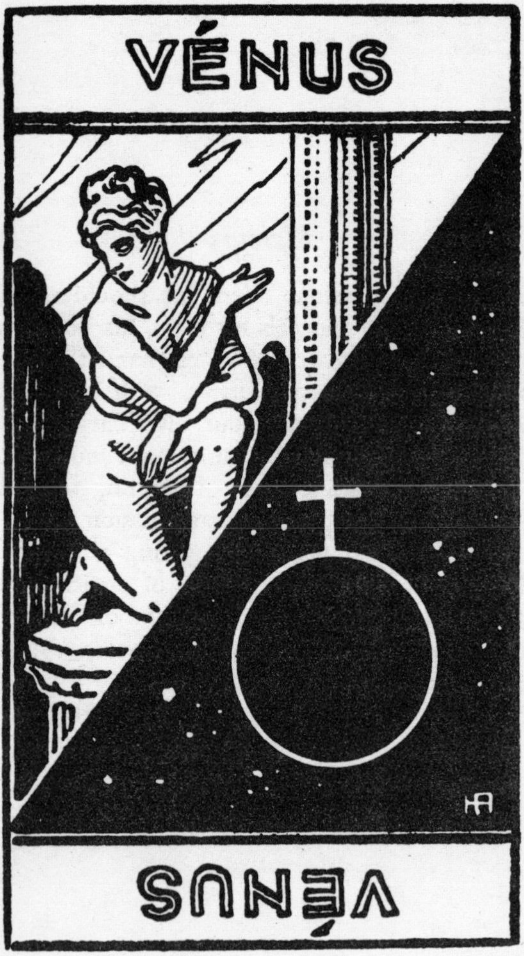
VÉNUS
VÉNUS

Venus

NUDE, with her soft, wavy golden hair, plump and lithe figure, the charming Goddess of the Graces, of Games and of Laughter, the mother of Love, of Beauty and of Pleasures, the goddess of caresses and voluptuousness, sometimes violent and awful in her vengeance, presents herself temptingly to the passionate admirers of her palpitating form, promising the pleasures of the flesh, with all the ruthlessness of her fickleness.

This card represents the Woman, the sweetheart. It denotes Harmony, Beauty, Love, but also profligacy. It is a fortunate card to draw, as it brings splendid good fortune, and success through help.

If afflicted, it causes abdominal, kidney, or bladder trouble and sexual complaints.

MARS
MARS

Mars

HELMETED, pike in hand and shield by his side, with his firm chin covered with a red beard, the chief's wand concealed, scarcely rested from his hard fighting, Mars, the God of War and of the Passions, is about to give himself up to the indulgence of Love and Voluptuousness. His activity and vitality will often lead him to guilty associations with Venus and the weak women whom Love possesses.

This card represents the Man, the Lover. It denotes anger, frankness, passion, strength. It brings success through industry and activity, and also through personal merit.

When afflicted, this card causes blood disorders, hæmorrhage, bronchial diseases, dementia, gall stones requiring surgical treatment.

JUPITER
HA
JUPITER

Jupiter

MAJESTIC, with flowing hair and Olympian beard, seated upon a throne of ivory, holding the Lightning, the Sacred Eagle at his feet, Zeus, Monarch and Father of the gods and of men, acquits himself of his duties and presides over the evolutions of worlds and of nations, protecting the innocent and chastising the wicked.

His work accomplished, he gives himself up to the pleasures of the table and of the flesh, loving the fair and the dusky, the goddesses and the humans alike.

This card represents the family, material things, comfort. It is fortunate in a lay-out as it prophesies protection. It may also be taken for the husband or protector.

This card gives ambition and the means of gratifying it.

Afflicted, it causes from the physical standpoint loss of vitality, plethora of the organs, liver trouble, asthma, impurity of the blood, gout and baldness.

SATURNE
SATURNE

Saturn

HE is the god who devours his children, just the same as insatiable Time absorbs the minutes, hours, months and centuries

This taciturn old man, holding the scythe and the hour-glass in his hand, bending under the weight of his years, the eternal Utopian, dreams of the Golden Age of the dwellers of the Latrum Hill over whom he formerly ruled.

This card represents the grandfather, old-age, Death, the end or recommencement of All Things.

It is a card of good counsel, and of prudence which procures moral support rather than pecuniary help in times of difficulty. It represents intellect, economy, real estate property and safe investments, which are the foundation and security of family life.

If often causes illnesses and infirmities : deafness, defective teeth, hæmorrhoids, intestinal disorders, cancer and diseases entailing decomposition of the body tissues.

URANUS
URANUS

Uranus

A SAD and impetuous old man meditates. Cruel and selfish, filled with ideas of strength and power, the father of Saturn reflects upon his lost virility, his wasted life, his moral and physical loneliness.

This card represents the old man, the selfish and cruel being, the despotic ruler who makes himself more feared than loved.

It often brings unexpected and evil things, as well as fortunate events, which are only transitory. Apart from its concrete significance, it gives intellect and knowledge.

It often brings disagreements in the family.

Physically, it causes sudden and violent illnesses : pleurisy, congestion of the lungs or brain, toxæmia.

NEPTUNE
NEPTUNE

Neptune

HOLDING the trident in his left hand, and a dolphin in his right hand, standing erect on the ocean waves, with a strange mien which inspires everyone with a sort of awe, Neptune, the god of the Ocean and of the watery element, suddenly and unexpectedly appears in his grand and superhuman simplicity.

It is the card of permanency and continuity. It represents in a lay-out the uncles or the brothers-in-law, and may be taken as signifying a widower or bachelor of attractive personality. It also means a friendship that has become a burden and which cannot be got rid of.

Physically, it causes boils, blood-poisoning, jaundice, dropsy, diabetes, rheumatism.

BELIER
FEU-DIURNE-MASCULIN
CHAUD ♂ MOBILE

Symbolism of the Minor Cards

Aries

THE card which symbolises this sign shows a landscape of rugged and uneven appearance. Its bare and barren peaks, its solid castle resting on a foundation of impregnable rock surely convey the idea of strength and of power.

Aries (the Ram) also gives an impression of energy, violence and blind will-power. It is easy to comprehend its battling spirit, which in a moment of fierce anger makes it charge straight ahead, without regard for obstacles, heedless of the possible consequences of its action, at the risk of fracturing the head.

The nervous paws enable him to move quickly, while his prominent muscles add to the general impression of strength.

Aries, the Ram, does not approve of resistance against him. He is not afraid of the obstacles in his path, he tackles them boldly.

Astrologically, it is a Fiery, masculine, dry, bitter, cardinal, diurnal sign. It is the day domicile of the planet Mars. The Sun is exalted in Aries, Saturn is in its fall therein, and Venus in its exile.

In a lay-out, Aries always retains its power, and must be taken as a cardinal card.

Its general meaning is: pride, rash action and imprudence. It gives little imagination but, on the other hand, much power of realisation. It is a sign of fickleness in love, gluttony, sometimes intemperance in drink, of shamelessness or immorality, should Venus or Saturn occupy Aries. It is usually fortunate for material things, giving success through activity and courage.

Physically it rules over the head and face. It causes ear-ache, tooth-ache, nasal disorders and abscesses in the face.

10 BELIER
EXALTATION AU 19°

10 *of Aries*

THIS card represents Andromeda on her rock. Deliciously feminine, and yet proud, this almost divine heroine, with her stern graciousness allied to her Beauty, chained to the rock by Evil Forces, at the mercy of a sea monster, is on the point of yielding, when the providential and unexpected rescuer comes in bold flight on a winged horse in the gold of the sky. It is intelligent and daring will-power, animating brave and active benevolence, which brings freedom and the compensating triumph of happy wedlock.

Its significance in the pack is that of victory after sacrifice. It promises fame and wealth after innumerable difficulties.

It conveys the idea of friendship, goodness and devotion. If Venus occupies 10 of Aries it may cause disappointments through exaggerated coquetry.

The Sun and Jupiter are sure indications of success. It is a card of preservation, showing protection at the most critical moment. It gives a taste for luxuries and the spending of money. It always indicates a difficulty regarding marriage or a delayed union, which will eventually succeed.

Saturn and Venus occupying 10 of Aries may be a sign of bereavement for a young girl connected with the consultant, or danger of an accident.

20 BELIER
♄
CHUTE AU 21°
♀
EN EXIL

20 of Aries

IN spite of his heavy appearance, this unfortunate mammal is gifted with extreme mobility, and this mobility is dangerous for everything that comes in its vicinity, for with a single and unconscious lash of his tail he will submerge the imprudent individual who would try to capture him. This mobile mastodon represents Fate.

The card presages danger of falls and wounds. It is the unexpected catastrophe, the effects of which are far-reaching.

It is detrimental to fruitfulness: it brings alternating losses and gains. The card being cardinal (or movable) it cannot be relied upon; it represents insecurity and entails ruin at the most unexpected moment.

It is a card of misfortune, disgrace and illness. It gives love of pleasure, and a fierce and selfish disposition.

TAUREAU
TERRE · NOCTURNE · FEMININ
FROID ♀ SEC

Taurus (The Bull)

COMING to a dead halt at the sight of a peacefully grazing heifer; his feet well dug into the tender grass which he loves and so ruthlessly tramples upon, with moist snout, round eyes, horns pointing to the wind, thick neck, powerful shoulders and swishing tail: such is the demeanour of the vain, fierce, trusting, but powerful and confiding Bull, full of animal instincts and desires and tremulous sensuousness.

It is a feminine, cold, dry, fixed, nocturnal card of the Earthy element.

It indicates concentration, timidity: it requires the goad to stir it into action. It shows greed for gain, indicates secret love affairs, and corresponds to the Line of Life joined to the Line of Head with a Girdle of Venus in a firm hand with a prominent and lined Mount of Venus.

It is not a good card for mental matters: it denotes exaggerated materialism, gives a tendency to immorality, and love of comfort with the possibility of acquiring it through one's own exertions.

Taurus governs the neck and throat: it causes laryngitis, and abscesses in the throat or neck.

10 TAUREAU
HA
♄ ☾ ♃
EXALTATION AU 3°

10 *of Taurus*

WITH his loathsome and repulsive face, his mane of live serpents, his eyes which petrify all that come under his gaze, this monster represents jealousy and hatred.

This card denotes over-confidence which results in wrong action and difficulties. It is unconscious onward progress up to the point where the consultant is brought to a dead stop, unable to go forward or step backward. It is stoppage, stagnation, deadlock.

It represents duality. It often indicates the spiteful and jealous rival, over whom the consultant can triumph if she acts wisely. It is the card of transformation into evil.

20 TAUREAU
EN CHUTE
EN EXIL

20 *of Taurus*

THESE are the seven light and ethereal spirits taking flight towards the sky dotted with pale gold spots. They are leaving this sorrowful earth for a higher sphere.

This card indicates excessive imagination, and is a sure sign that the consultant considers his wishes as being realities. It also signifies travelling, the journey usually being fortunate.

It is also an indication of moral and physical instability, pessimistic tendencies, and denotes worries and anxieties rather than real obstacles. It causes illnesses of the watery element: pleurisy, kidney trouble. When it occupies the Ascendant, it denotes eye trouble.

GEMEAUX
AIR . DIURNE . MASCULIN
CHAUD ☿ HUMIDE

Gemini (The Twins)

THIS represents two pretty little cherubim, harmoniously united in their charming duality. They are smilingly planning to do subtle and refined things, holding the shaft of sly irony, and the vibrating lyre of the Arts, while yet retaining the rod of intellectual and sacred science.

Gemini is masculine, warm, moist, neither cardinal nor fixed, convertible, fruitful, diurnal, of the Airy element.

It represents subtle intellect, refined taste, the Arts, love of Music; little constancy in the affections; success in business pursuits. It also gives harmonious relations between the brothers and sisters, which it represents.

This card governs the shoulders, and often causes nervous diseases or bilious disorders.

10 GEMEAUX
HA
EXALTATION AU 3°

10 *of Gemini*

THERE is something that is human in the face, which expresses concentration of mind, deep reflection, and fear, together with a look of sorrowful intelligence and dogged, nervous physical strength.

And yet the Goat, which suckled Jupiter and Almathea, need have no fear of Destiny. A horn of plenty, filled with delicious fruit, is within her reach. Will she not dare to grasp it?

This card represents disquiet, imaginary worry, fear of doing the wrong thing. Over-scrupulousness hinders success at the moment. Nevertheless the result will be favourable, and success assured, but protection is necessary, because this card in itself only gives shyness and pride, which prevent the consultant from asking for help, so that perseverance and sometimes stubbornness are the foundations of this card.

20 GEMEAUX
EN EXIL

20 of *Gemini*

SEATED close to Sirius, his faithful and docile Dog languidly stretched at his feet, Orion, the splendid huntsman, with his magnificent figure, his delicate and refined features, sun-kissed hair, and magnetic, compelling eyes, appears in the full power of his intelligence, his hardy manhood, his quiet success and his healthy pride; his virile stability of equilibrium and beauty.

He does not meditate upon future death nor the transformations that await him. He enjoys to their fullest extent the present moment and its activities.

This card represents activity and power, as well as Beauty. It stands for the Leader of big undertakings, with whom everything succeeds in the material sense. It is also the man of pleasure, the boon companion, the knight of the gentler sex, the lover of hunting, and of material comforts.

It is also the card of good-temper, of moral and physical courage. It may indicate a sudden ending. It denotes leadership, benevolence as well as pride.

CANCER
HA
EAU-NOCTURNE-FEMININ
FROIDE
MOBILE

Cancer

THE oval-shaped face of a Woman, with abundant, fair hair, greyish-blue eyes that reflect the dull sheen of water, filled with a gentle, absorbing, and even dangerous poetry that inclines to dreaminess, melancholy and sadness.

She holds in her hands a soft veil bearing the imprint of the sign of the Crab, the changeable and mobile crustacean of the sea, which subsists in the watery element without much physical exertion.

Cancer is moist, cold, lymphatic, feminine, cardinal, fruitful, nocturnal and belongs to the Watery element.

It represents inconstancy, which gives love of change. It is lacking in moral and physical courage, but gives success without great exertion. It always shows mysterious or hidden things, and may indicate infidelity.

Cancer rules over the lungs and breast, and also causes stomach disorders, tumours, languid diseases.

10 CANCER
♄ ♆
EN EXIL

10 *of Cancer*

IN the variegated blue of a serenely clear sky, heavy clouds, the forerunners of a coming storm, suddenly make their appearance. On a rock a handsome and noble youth is stricken in the full tide of his strength, ready to sink.

This card threatens grave danger, disagreements, or quarrels. It represents an unknown enemy who is acquainted with the consultant's affairs and who will do him harm.

It is the card of unfortunate journeys, of unexpected catastrophes, help arriving too late.

20 CANCER
♂
♅
CHUTE AU 28°
EN EXALTATION

20 *of Cancer*

TORCH in hand, breaking through the thickness of the clouds, he descends into the night, which he banishes with his virile strength, putting to flight the powers of darkness. A loving, loyal, but hasty friend, he rushes forward to the rescue.

This is the card of friendship, of help which can be relied upon in any circumstance. It carries light into the darkness of things, and brings joy to the heart. It is a card of protection, of sincerity, but also of violence.

It is fortunate for journeys.

LION
HR
FEU-DIURNE-MASCULIN
STERILE
FIXE

Leo (The Lion)

WHILE the flaming Sun glows on the horizon with a rosy hue, the noble and stately head of the King of Beasts, pulsating with life, proud splendour and ideal strength, emerges, alone, untamed, majestic in the power of its intellect.

Leo is warm, dry, masculine, fixed, barren, diurnal and of the Fiery element.

It is the card of cruelty, power, ambition and pride. It gives riches and power, but through violent methods.

It gives love of food and pleasures; and strengthens everything which it approaches: health, intellect and business.

It governs the heart and back. If it is unfortunately situated in a lay-out, it gives palpitations, pleurisy, convulsions.

10 LION
HA
♃ ♄ ♀

10 *of Leo*

SLEEK and faithful, with watchful ear and eye, nose pointing towards the wind, inquisitive, ready for the salacious enjoyments of his species, tenacious in his desires, the celestial dog advances, his head lowered at the scolding tones of his master, whom he is nevertheless ready to defend with his strength and love.

It is the card of fidelity, but also of rambling talk and gossip.

It gives power, strength, and great kindness beneath an uncouth outward appearance. It also causes an unhealthy inquisitiveness, which leads to meddling with other people's affairs, and, under unfortunate auspices, sets snares which turn out unsuccessfully.

It indicates tenacity, and may bring riches, but may also cause a downfall. It is a materialistic card that does not show much idealism.

20 LION
♅ ET ♄
EN EXIL

20 of *Leo*

IN a filthy, loathsome and pestilential pond, the vile, venomous and slimy hydra dwells, with its multiple and ever-renewed evil-looking heads.

This card represents difficulties that are well-nigh insurmountable, to conquer which perseverance, courage and continuity of purpose, combined with incessant toil are necessary.

Innumerable difficulties encompass the consultant and poison his life slowly but surely. He must change his environment, bestir himself, not allow his temperament to get the better of him, nor his petty ways or vices to master him : routine hinders his progress. He must react if he does not wish to be overthrown, but to conquer.

Unhealthy thoughts and actions are the foundation of this card. It is necessary for the consultant to rid himself quickly and without hesitation of the torpor or glamour which surrounds him.

VIERGE
TERRE-NOCTURNE-FEMININ
STERILE ☿ FROIDE

Virgo (The Virgin)

HOLDING the olive-branch of Peace in one hand, and the hexagram (representing perfect equilibrium) in the other, this wan, melancholy, lonely and sad-looking young woman suffers in silence through the thoughts of men, and defends herself against their weakness or their baseness.

Virgo is cold, dry, barren, feminine and Earthy. It is a sad and lonely, but withal straightforward and well-balanced influence. It brings enlightenment, good reasoning powers, and gives to everything which it approaches moral cleanliness and purity.

It governs the liver, intestines and abdomen. It may indicate appendicitis, or disorders affecting the generative organs.

10 VIERGE
EN EXIL ET
HA

10 *of Virgo*

BORNE over the tempestuous waves, overcoming obstacles, fighting the unchained elements and remorseless Destiny with the help of the gods, the vessel reaches port after innumerable difficulties, her sides ripped open, her masts broken, but still able to resist the onslaught of the waves.

This card represents difficult enterprises which may lead to successful results after many losses and incredible difficulties. It indicates disputes between partners, relatives, friends or marriage partners, but there will not be a rupture. It also signifies worries and troubles, but final success will ensue through courage and powerful help.

This card is not fortunate for journeys, and those which occur will cause many disappointments, and may even be dangerous.

20 VIERGE
EN CHUTE AU 27°

20 *of Virgo*

HER profile of great spirituality and loveliness, framed with hair powdered with stars, her expression wonderfully tender in its femininity, made yet softer by the pale gold of her fairy-like tresses, she presents the Kiss of Love, idealistic and supreme, full of charm and grace.

This card is fortunate for love affairs, for luck and for business; but there is little personal merit, which does not enter into the question. The consultant depends upon the gifts with which nature has endowed her.

It represents a pretty and flattered woman, who offers the gift of her mind, or her bodily charms.

It promises fortunate love affairs, a wealthy and influential marriage. It is not fortunate for children, with whom disputes may occur. It sometimes also denotes disputes with relatives by marriage.

BALANCE
AIR — DIURNE — MASCULIN
CHAUD ♀ MOBILE.

Libra (The Scales)

THE Scales are tending towards Equilibrium. They are held by a firm hand—the hand of Justice, of Sincerity, of Truth and Right.

Libra is full-blooded, gentle, moist, masculine, diurnal, cardinal and of the Airy element.

It is above everything the card of Justice and of Equilibrium. It gives fidelity, sincerity, and tends to equality in all things.

It represents kindness combined with justice. It is favourable for the imagination and for artistic tastes, imparting intellectuality to all things which it approaches.

It governs especially the kidneys, bladder and hips.

10 BALANCE
EN CHUTE AU 19°

10 *of Libra*

A SAGE, enamoured of Science, is bending over an old parchment, from which he is seeking to extract the beneficent sap and juice through the Keys of Knowledge.

In his tangled mane of hair the blossoms of intellectuality and the pure imaginations of triumphant spirituality are being made fluid.

This is the card of Science, which brings light to all things, discovers all things. It signifies faith in Spirituality and detachment from matter.

It brings success through knowledge, and the understanding of All, which is the key to happiness.

It provides the kindling spark which helps to solve the most intricate problems of life. It is the thread which can be followed along the path that leads to success and the realisation of one's desires.

20 BALANCE
EN EXIL
EN EXALTATION AU 21°

20 of Libra

THIS is the ever-growing ear of golden corn, symbolising fruitful Nature's Gifts.

The strong tree, bearing its abundance of ripe fruit, represents the recompense of man's well-directed efforts.

This is the card of abundance gained through effort and skill. It gives the possibility of success in agricultural occupations, and love of rural life. It may grant power and dominion. It is, however, a card of anxiety in regard to the children.

It represents the kind and hard-working man, fond of comfort, of good food and good wine.

It also signifies the end of some thing or event, and the commencement of another.

SCORPION
EAU-NOCTURNE-FEMININ-
FROID ♂ FIXE

Scorpio (The Scorpion)

CLOSE to a pool of stagnant water, this essentially terrestrial creature creeps stealthily along, apparently harmless and slowly overcoming or circumventing its obstacles, while searching for the victim (however powerful and strong) whom it will attack without fear, knowing that its diminutive size will enable it to conceal itself easily and without risk, its faculties of dissimulation constituting its strongest weapon.

Scorpio is moist, cold, fixed, nocturnal, feminine, and of the Watery element.

It is an intellectual card, which makes it possible to succeed through trickery, or, at all events, through cunning. It gives ambition and a tendency to sarcasm, and often represents a false friend. The consultant knows what he wants, and possesses the ability of obtaining it, if not through violence, then through his shrewdness, exertion and skill, which will be the factors in his success.

It governs the generative system. It causes hæmorrhoids, and tumours in the groin.

10 SCORPION
♄ ☾ ♂
EN CHUTE AU 3°

10 *of Scorpio*

THE Head of a Serpent joined to its Tail, thus completes the Circle and constitutes the Sacred Gnostic Symbol of that which is without beginning and without end, and of which the High Priests of the Supreme Initiations only speak with awe and in secret.

It is the card of eloquence, of prudence, of cunning and also of falsehood.

It is the ending and the recommencement of some event or thing: it is eternity. It denotes health and physical resistance.

20 SCORPION
EN EXIL

20 *of Scorpio*

IN the silvery light of the pale moon, the slender and muscular silhouette of a wolf is outlined. He is uttering his fearful death-cry before hurling himself against the defenceless beings whom he will ferociously attack, or else run away like a coward on the least sign of danger.

This card often causes the consultant to undertake heavier tasks than he is able to accomplish. It is a sign of fierceness and cowardice. It represents trickery, and even theft. It gives good organisation, but also denotes meanness and spitefulness.

SAGITTAIRE
FEU-DIURNE-MASCULIN
CHAUD
SEC

Sagittarius

A KINDLY, intelligent and urbane-looking Centaur is treading with cautious hoofs the mountain-side in search of a few simples, and to gaze upon the stars from its summit. He carries an arrow which he will skilfully shoot at any evil-doer.

Sagittarius is warm, dry, masculine and of the Fiery element.

It is the card of peace, pacifism, quietude, of desire for upward progress, and gives every possibility of achieving it through skill and prudence.

It also represents intellectuality, and fruitful thoughts.

It governs the thighs and pelvis, and causes gout, sciatica and rheumatism.

10 SAGITTAIRE
☿ ☊ ♂
EN CHUTE AU 3°

10 *of Sagittarius*

A VIGOROUS and brawny Colossus demonstrates his strength and power by opening the Lion's mouth. Great must be his physical resistance and his tenacity so that he may withstand the reaction of the untamed beast.

This is the card of dominion, of courage, of strength, but also of anger. It is a Martial card of the highest value : it gives success through effort and personal merit, bringing esteem and renown, but it is also surrounded by enemies who must be repulsed before success can be attained, and violence will often have to be employed.

It is a card which always gives renown and promotion.

20 SAGITTAIRE
EN EXIL

20 *of Sagittarius*

THIS mythical and fabulous Beast, with his Ophidian tail, his demoniac wings, his flaming tongue, and leonine claws, was formerly consecrated to Minerva, the Goddess of Wisdom. He watches ceaselessly, sleeplessly, over the threshold which he guards.

This is the card of clairvoyance. It signifies the need for ceaseless caution and watchfulness, security being non-existent. It is necessary to carry out one's plan to its final ending, nothing ever giving tangible results unless it is carried through patiently.

It is a card that warns the consultant to be careful, not on account of threatened danger, but in order to show his enemies that he is well able to defend himself.

CAPRICORNE
TERRE-NOCTURNE-FEMININ
STERILE ♑ MOBILE

Capricorn (The Goat)

THE head of a he-goat and the body of a she-goat, terminating with the tail of a fish.

The expression of the face betrays disquieting instincts, the smile is sardonic and bitter, reflecting the sad and evil thoughts of the mind.

Capricorn is cold, dry, acid, nocturnal, feminine, barren, cardinal, and belongs to the Earthy element.

It causes deep and unreasoning melancholy, which is not always well-balanced. It seeks or causes disagreements. It is capable of destroying everything of Beauty and Joy with which it comes into contact.

It governs the knees and nerves, and may also cause grave disorders of the lungs or brain.

10 CAPRICORNE
EN CHUTE AU 15°
EN EXIL

10 *of Capricorn*

A BIRD of prey is watching from the summit of an inaccessible rock. He searches the valley with his piercing and scrutinising eyes, in quest of the carrion with which to appease his loathsome hunger: the easy victims of his greed and cowardice.

This is the card of Death, but also of perspicacity and shrewdness. It also denotes, in some cases, dealings in shady matters, and cowardice.

It is the attack against which there is no chance of defence. It also indicates an evil influence which surrounds the consultant: Fate only waits for a moment of weakness on his part to strike her blow. It sometimes represents the adversary or competitor who is looking for the weak spot in the consultant's armour, or for momentary negligence on his part, so that he can attack him.

20 CAPRICORNE
EXALTATION AU 28°

20 *of Capricorn*

SOARING alone in the inaccessible heights, the Eagle suddenly swoops down like Lightning upon the man on whom Fate has set his Seal; and like Fate, he gives neither mercy nor quarter, but pursues his victim to the bitter end.

This card represents proud solitude, strength, independence, daring, and faithfulness towards the loved ones.

It indicates, however, approaching danger, and accidents while travelling.

It denotes set purpose, narrow-mindedness; gives courage but not mercy; and often prevents the discernment of friends from enemies.

VERSEAU
AIR — DIURNE — MASCULIN
CHAUD ♄ FIXE

Aquarius (The Water-bearer)

SECLUDED from the world, this sea-shell, with its graceful and well-modulated curves, pours out the clear, cool water which carries to all things the benign virtues of its fructifying and thirst-quenching effects, which men may sometimes abuse for their own sordid and selfish ends.

Aquarius is warm, moist, mild, full-blooded, masculine, fixed diurnal, and belongs to the Airy element.

It is an excellent card, and represents goodness, fidelity, reason, honesty. This combination of virtues may often cause the consultant to be tricked and even overcome by evilly-disposed people.

It is also a sign of loneliness. It governs the thighs and legs, and often causes varicose ulcers or phlebitis.

10 VERSEAU
HA
EN EXIL

10 *of Aquarius*

THIS aquatic mammalian, which has often been immortalised in sculpture, glides softly with his lithe body over the bitter waters, with his gaze fixed in an oblique direction. He is dangerous on account of his hypocritical and deceptive behaviour.

This is the card of double-dealing, which lulls suspicion with fine stories. It represents a hypocritical and soft-mannered person, who smiles upon you, but who slanders you behind your back, or acts spitefully towards you.

In some cases it represents simply the artist who charms with his music or with his voice, and plunges you in a world of dreams. More frequently this card denotes some one who knows the consultant's plans or weak points and knows how to take advantage of them.

20 VERSEAU
♂ ♅ ♃
EN JOIE

20 *of Aquarius*

A THOROUGHBRED steed is pawing the ground and snorting in the heat of his idealistic enthusiasm. He is preparing to take his flight towards the Elysian fields, there to place at the service of those Wise Ones who have sacred and useful missions to accomplish his virility, his ardour and his energy.

This card gives the perception of the Great and the Beautiful. It denotes dreaminess and imagination, but also the desire of acquiring knowledge, of learning something new every day.

It is a card of protection and help in emergencies. It is fortunate and helpful when placed near to a well-aspected Mars or Jupiter.

POISSONS
EAU · NOCTURNE · FEMININ
FECOND ♃ FROID

Pisces (The Fishes)

ON a field of green and turbid water, two Fishes appear to be confiding to one another. Their words are as murky as the element in which they dwell.

Pisces is moist, cold, feminine, nocturnal, fruitful, and belongs to the Watery element.

It represents trickery, deceit, slander and shamelessness in wrong-doing. This card revels in evil, and will always come out in connection with misfortune.

It governs the feet, causes defective circulation, and coryza.

10 POISSONS
☿ CHUTE AU 15°

10 *of Pisces*

STATELY, and with beguiling eye, the Swan glides carelessly along towards the object of his amorous desire, but this will last scarcely longer than the trail of his passage over the lake which he is crossing.

This is a card of instability and fickleness in love. It represents double-dealing, and love for the sake of gain. In illness, however, it denotes vitality and enables the sick person to stem the tide.

It often indicates pleasant things or events, but these are of short duration.

20 POISSONS
EN EXALTATION
AU 27° EN JOIE
HA

20 *of Pisces*

THIS apparently motionless but powerful figure represents a river which is slowly but surely leaving its bed, while destroying everything which it encounters. Nothing can arrest it before the appointed time arrives. Then a period of rest intervenes, as calm and normal as that of the overflow.

This card represents self-confidence, inertia, but also Fate, whether good or evil—the remorseless Force against which nothing avails.

It counsels to wait for better days to come. The Consultant must not give up hope; there is no reason why he should not carry on; he must allow his best friend, Time, to do its work.

A Few Methods of Laying out the Cards

I

SEPARATE the Minor cards from the Major cards (the Planets, the Ascendant, the Part of Fortune and the Moon's Nodes).

Take twelve cards from the Minor ones and cover these with the twelve Major cards.

The Minor card which is covered by the Ascendant will be the starting-point of the horoscope. The Second House will be given by the next Decanate, the Third House by the following Decanate, and so on. Below we give the Decanates in their right order, and with their corresponding degrees.

0	ARIES.	120	LEO.	240	SAGITTARIUS.
10	10 of Aries	130	10 of Leo.	250	10 of Sagittarius.
20	20 of Aries.	140	20 of Leo.	260	20 of Sagittarius.
30	TAURUS.	150	VIRGO.	270	CAPRICORN
40	10 of Taurus.	160	10 of Virgo.	280	10 of Capricorn.
50	20 of Taurus.	170	20 of Virgo.	290	20 of Capricorn.
60	GEMINI.	180	LIBRA.	300	AQUARIUS.
70	10 of Gemini	190	10 of Libra.	310	10 of Aquarius.
80	20 of Gemini.	200	20 of Libra.	320	20 of Aquarius.
90	CANCER.	210	SCORPIO.	330	PISCES.
100	10 of Cancer.	220	10 of Scorpio.	340	10 of Pisces.
110	20 of Cancer.	230	20 of Scorpio.	350	20 of Pisces.

Next, place each Planet close to the Minor card on which it was situated at the commencement of the lay-out.

Example

We have drawn twelve Minor cards in the following order:

1. 10 of Scorpio.
2. GEMINI.
3. 10 of Aquarius.
4. ARIES.
5. VIRGO.
6. 10 of Libra.
7. PISCES.
8. SAGITTARIUS.
9. 20 of Virgo.
10. 20 of Gemini.
11. 20 of Libra.
12. 20 of Pisces.

These cards are covered respectively by:

1. Venus.
2. Sun.
3. Ascendant.
4. Mercury.
5. Moon.
6. Mars.
7. Neptune.
8. Dragon's Head (Ascending Node).
9. Saturn.
10. Jupiter.
11. Part of Fortune.
12. Uranus.

The Ascendant is on 10 of Aquarius;
The Second House: Pisces;
Third House: 20 of Pisces;
Fourth House: ARIES;
Fifth House: GEMINI;
Sixth House: 20 of Gemini;
Seventh House: VIRGO;
Eighth House: 20 of Virgo;
Ninth House: 10 of Libra;
Tenth House: 20 of Libra;
Eleventh House: 10 of Scorpio;
Twelfth House: SAGITTARIUS.

This gives the following lay-out:

First House:	10 of Aquarius.	Ascendant.
Second House:	PISCES.	Neptune.
Third House:	20 of Pisces.	Uranus.
Fourth House:	ARIES.	Mercury.
Fifth House:	GEMINI.	Sun.
Sixth House:	20 of Gemini.	Jupiter.
Seventh House:	VIRGO.	Moon.
Eighth House:	20 of Virgo.	Saturn.
Ninth House:	10 of Libra.	Mars.
Tenth House:	20 of Libra.	Part of Fortune.
Eleventh House:	10 of Scorpio.	Venus.
Twelfth House:	SAGITTARIUS.	Nodes.

Commence the interpretation by taking the Planets in the Signs, then in their Houses, and noting their aspects; then the Ruler of each House in the House which it occupies.

In regard to the aspects, we proceed thus:

Starting with Neptune, which is in Pisces, corresponding to 330° in the table of the order of Decanates, we find that:

330−60=270, which is the position of Capricorn. There are no aspects.

330+60=390, or 30, which is the position of Taurus. There are no aspects.

330+90=420−360, or 60, which is the position of Gemini, in which we find the Sun. Neptune is therefore in square aspect with the Sun.

330−90=240 corresponds to SAGITARIUS, in which we find the Nodes. Neptune is therefore also in square aspect with this card.

330+120=450−360=90, which corresponds to Cancer. There are no aspects.

330−120=210, which corresponds to Scorpio. No aspects.

We then take the next planet: Uranus, which is in 20 of Pisces, whose position is at 350°, and we find:

350−60=290, which corresponds to 20 of Capricorn. No aspects.

350+60=410=50, which corresponds to 20 of Taurus. No aspects.

350−90=260, which corresponds to 20 of Sagittarius. No aspects.

350+90=440=80, which corresponds to 20 of Gemini, in

which we find Jupiter Uranus is therefore in square aspect with Jupiter.

350+120=470−360=110, which corresponds to 20 of Cancer. No aspects.

350−120=230, which corresponds to 20 of Scorpio. No aspects.

We proceed in the same way for all the planets.

II

1. Separate the Minor from the Major cards.

2. Set out the Minor cards in the order of the Decanates: Aries; 10 of Aries; 20 of Aries. Taurus, 10 of Taurus, etc.

3. Take the Ephemeris for the year of birth; find the sidereal time for the date of birth and add to it the hour when this occurs at any time between noon and midnight; or, subtract from the sidereal time on the date of birth the difference between the hour of birth and noon, if the birth occurs at any time between midnight and noon. (See footnote, page 12).

For a birth at 3 p.m. we get the sidereal time given in the Ephemeris, plus 3 hours.

For a birth at 3 a.m. we get the sidereal time, minus the difference between the time in the morning and noon: in this case, 12 hours, less 3 hours, which gives 9 *hours,* which we subtract from the sidereal time given in the Ephemeris.

It is sometimes necessary to add 24 hours to the sidereal time when the subtraction cannot be made.

4. Having ascertained the sidereal time at birth, we consult a table of Houses for the latitude of the place of birth.

5. Note the cusps of the Houses when taking the Decanate, which corresponds to the one indicated by the tables for the corresponding sidereal time.

We will thus obtain the Tenth, Eleventh, Twelfth, First, Second and Third Houses, which we set out thus:

I.	X.
II.	XI.
III.	XII.

The Fourth, Fifth and Sixth Houses will be placed opposite the Tenth, Eleventh and Twelfth Houses, and we therefore take from the pack the Decanates opposite to those that have already been drawn. The Seventh, Eighth and Ninth Houses are situated opposite to the First, Second and Third Houses, so we again draw out the Decanates opposite to those of the First, Second and Third Houses.

The Cusps of the Houses will therefore appear thus :

I.	IV.	VII.	X.
II.	V.	VIII.	XI.
III.	VI.	IX.	XII.

Note.—In order to readily understand what follows, the pack of Astrological Tarot Cards should be *held in the hands,* and the method of procedure actually carried out *while reading the directions given.*

In practice, when the Minor cards have been placed in the order of the Decanates, we proceed as follows in order to obtain the Cusps of the Houses :

In the Table of Houses we find that the Tenth House is at 10° *of Sagittarius :*

We find this card, and cut the pack there, putting the bottom cards on the top, so that the 10 of Sagittarius is uppermost. We next draw out 18 cards which we place on the right-hand side, leaving 18 cards for the left-hand side. The Cusp of the Tenth House will be given by 10 of Sagittarius, and the Cusp of the Fourth House by the uppermost card on the left-hand side, which is 10 of Gemini.

We therefore draw out these two cards.

The Eleventh House is at 25° of Sagittarius, which corresponds to 20 of Sagittarius. This is the first top card on the right-hand side, and the Fifth House will be provided by the first top card on the left-hand side, which is 20 of Gemini.

We therefore draw out these two cards, which we place respectively on the right-hand side and left-hand side underneath the two other cards.

The Twelfth House is at 11° of Capricorn, which corresponds to 10 of Capricorn. This is the second card from the right-hand pack, and we place it underneath the two other cards on the right-hand side, putting the Capricorn card (which we do not require at present) to the right of the right-hand side pack.

The Sixth House is provided by the second card from the left-hand side pack. This is 10 of Cancer, and we place it underneath the two cards on the left-hand side, putting the Cancer card (which we do not require at present) to the left of the left-hand side pack.

The First House is at 5° of Aquarius. We therefore find Aquarius in the right-hand side pack. This is the second card which we place on the left-hand side of the first card drawn from the left-hand side pack, and we put the 20 of Capricorn (which we do not require for the moment) on the right of the right-hand side pack, on the Capricorn card.

The Seventh House will be given by the second card from the left-hand side pack. This is Leo, and we place it to the left of the first card drawn from the right-hand side pack, and we put the 20 of Cancer (which we do not require for the moment) on the left of the left-hand side pack, on the Cancer card.

The Second House is at 15° of Aries. We take one card after another from the pack on the right-hand side, and place each one in succession on the 20 of Capricorn, until we find the 10 of Aries, which corresponds to the Cusp of the Second House. This is the seventh card, and we place it to the left of the Aquarius card.

The Cusp of the Eighth House will be given by the seventh card from the pack on the left-hand side, and we lay the six cards which we are not using on the 20 of Cancer. This seventh card corresponds to the 10 of Libra, which we place on the right under the Leo card.

The Third House is at 20° of Taurus. We take away the cards from the pack on the right-hand side, and lay them over the Aries card, until we have found the 20 of Taurus, which corresponds to the cusp of the Third House. This is the fourth card, and we put it to the left of the 10 of Aries.

The Cusp of the Tenth House will be given by the fourth card in the pack on the left-hand side, and we put the three cards which we do not require on the Libra card. This fourth card corresponds to 20 of Scorpio, and we place it to the right of the 10 of Libra.

We have thus obtained the Cusps of the Twelve Houses. We now put the remaining cards from the left-hand side and right-hand side packs on their respective packs of cards which have not been used.

We again take the Ephemeris and calculate the positions of the planets. These are given for noon, and we therefore calculate the exact hour of birth for the place of birth. (See pages 12 onwards.)

For example: we find that the Sun is at 8° 32′ of Sagittarius. As this decanate has not come out, we now draw it from the pack and lay it on the 20 of Scorpio, in the Ninth House, with the Sun, which we draw from the pack of Major cards.

The Moon is at 24° of Libra, which corresponds to 20 of Libra. This decanate has not come out either, so we now draw it and place it on 10 of Libra in the Eighth House, with the Moon, which we draw from the pack of Major cards.

Neptune is at 27° of Leo, or 20 of Leo. This card has not come out, so we draw it also, and place it over Leo in the Seventh House, with the Neptune card from the Major pack.

Uranus is at 25° of Pisces. We draw out 20 of Pisces, and lay it on the Aquarius card, in the First House, with the Uranus card.

Saturn is at 29° of Scorpio. 20 of Scorpio is in the Ninth House, which contains the Sun in Sagittarius. We therefore place Saturn between the 20 of Scorpio and the Sagittarius cards.

Jupiter is at 20 of Aquarius, which has not yet been drawn from the pack. The Cusp of the First House is in Aquarius. We therefore get the 20 of Aquarius card and lay it on Aquarius, and then the Jupiter card, which will be placed between the 20 of Aquarius and the 20 of Pisces cards.

Mars is at 4° of Taurus. 20 of Taurus is in the Third House, so that the Taurus card must occupy the Second House, on the Cusp of which is 10 of Aries. We therefore lay Taurus over this card, and then the Mars card.

Venus is at 11° of Sagittarius. The 10 of Sagittarius is in the Tenth House, so we lay Venus over this card.

Mercury is at 26° of Scorpio. 20 of Scorpio occupies the Cusp of the Ninth House, which also contains Saturn in 29° of Scorpio, so we place the Mercury card between the 20 of Scorpio and the Saturn cards.

We also find in the Ephemeris that the Moon's Ascending Node (Dragon's Head) is at 8° of Cancer, while the Sixth House is occupied by 10 of Cancer. Cancer has not been drawn, so we now find it and lay it over 20 of Gemini in the Fifth House, with the Ascending Node card, bearing in mind that the Descending Node (Dragon's Tail) should occupy the opposite House, viz. the Eleventh House in Capricorn, and we therefore draw the Capricorn card and place it in the Eleventh House.

We have now only to ascertain the position of the Part of Fortune, which is found thus:

The Ascendant is in Aquarius, or 300°;

The Moon is in 20 of Libra, or 200°.

These added together give a total of 500°. We subtract the position of the Sun, which is in Sagittarius, or 240°, and this leaves 260° which corresponds to 20 of Sagittarius. This card is on the Cusp of the Eleventh House, on which we place the Part of Fortune.

III

Take twelve cards haphazard, and set them out as shown below. Supposing that the cards are those which we indicate :

I.	V.	IX.
10 of Scorpio.	Sagittarius.	Capricorn.
II.	VI.	X.
Part of Fortune.	Uranus.	20 of Libra.
III.	VII.	XI.
20 of Taurus.	10 of Taurus.	Ascendant.
IV.	VIII.	XII.
20 of Capricorn.	20 of Gemini.	Jupiter.

For the interpretation, we refer back to the symbolism of the cards, and we find that 10 of Scorpio indicates the commencement of something, and is a sign of health and physical resistance.

The Part of Fortune is in the Second House, where it shows pecuniary gains, a remunerative transaction.

20 of Taurus is in the Third House, which governs short journeys. It clearly denotes a journey, since the card itself promises a journey.

20 of Capricorn in the Fifth House gives loneliness in the home, an independent disposition, so that the domestic circle is not altogether harmonious.

Sagittarius in the Fifth House gives quietude and pleasure in this House of happiness. It also brings joy on the children's account.

We take each card in the same way and study it in relation to the Houses, and the lay-out as a whole will appear fortunate or unfortunate. The Major cards that come out will, of course, be dignified. If the Ascendant is drawn it is a sign of success in regard to what is desired, and the realisation of the desire will be achieved through help corresponding with the House occupied by the Ascendant. In the foregoing example the Ascendant occupied the Eleventh House, which presages that the expected result will come through friendships or through friends.

IV.

Take twelve cards at random and set them out as for method III., but instead of basing yourself on the Houses, study the *planets*, when the cards drawn convey the idea of a Major card. In the order in which they are drawn they indicate:

I.	The Ascendant.	VII.	Jupiter.
II.	The Moon.	VIII.	Saturn.
III.	The Sun.	IX.	Uranus.
IV.	Mercury.	X.	Neptune.
V.	Venus.	XI.	Part of Fortune.
VI.	Mars.	XII.	The Nodes.

We will suppose that we have drawn:

10 of Capricorn.	Ascendant.
20 of Aquarius.	20 of Gemini.
The Sun.	Part of Fortune.
20 of Cancer.	Mars.
The Nodes.	Libra.
10 of Cancer.	Jupiter.

In the interpretation we find that the Ascendant (I.) is in Capricorn, and we ascertain, moreover, the meaning of 10 of Capricorn.

The Moon (II.) is in 20 of Aquarius;

The Sun (III.) is on the Sun, and we consider that the Sun is occupying Leo, which is its own domicile.

Mercury (IV.) is in 20 of Cancer.

Venus (V.) is on the Moon's Nodes.

Mars (VI.) is in 20 of Cancer.

Jupiter (VII.) occupies the Ascendant.

Saturn (VIII.) is in 20 of Gemini.

Uranus (IX.) is in conjunction with the Part of Fortune.

Neptune (X.) is in conjunction with Mars, which is situated in Pisces, this sign being the Joy of Neptune.

The Part of Fortune (XI.) is in Libra.

The Moon's Nodes (XII.) are close to Jupiter, which is taken as occupying Sagittarius, the place of Exaltation of one of the Nodes (Gemini being the sign which we should have taken had Mercury been drawn instead of Jupiter).

For this method of laying out the cards we must study:

1. Any card that comes out in its normal order, viz. the Ascendant first; the Moon second; the Sun third; and so on, must be taken as dignified and powerful and having great influence in the lay-out.

2. Any card which comes out in some order different from its own must be taken as in conjunction with the card which occupies its place (when it is represented by a planet) and in the latter's most fortunate domicile. For example: if Jupiter comes out fourth, it will be in conjunction with Mercury, and in Gemini. If Uranus comes out fifth, it will be in conjunction with Venus in Libra.

3. If the first card drawn is a planet, it must be taken as occupying the Ascendant, and dignified.

4. A planet that comes out eleventh is in conjunction with the Part of Fortune, and must be specially studied in regard to money matters. Thus, Mercury or Jupiter are fortunate if they come out eleventh, whereas Uranus and Saturn are not so fortunate.

5. Any planet that comes out twelfth will occupy the place of exaltation of one of the Nodes, either Sagittarius or Gemini.

6. When the Ascendant comes out, it indicates the First House wherever it is situated. Thus, in the foregoing example, the Ascendant having come out seventh, the First House is situated there, and the next House, which contains Saturn, is the Second House; the Third House is occupied by the Part of Fortune; the Fourth House by Mars, and so on.

7. The aspects between the planets that have actually come out must be studied. Thus, in the example we find that the Sun is in Leo (120°) and Jupiter is in Sagittarius (240°). These two planets are therefore in trine aspect to each other. The Ascendant and Jupiter are in conjunction, both occupying Sagittarius, so that the Sun is also in trine aspect with the Ascendant.

Note.—By studying only the symbolism of the cards, the Astrological Tarot may be used for every method of laying-out: by 5, by 7, by 21, according to the name, or by the cross, or any other method.

The Interpretation

IN order to judge an astrological lay-out of the cards, it is necessary to sum it up as a whole: nothing should be judged in its details, but must be taken in its entirety.

This is how we proceed when the chart is drawn up on paper or by means of the cards:

1. Find the highest dignified planet in the horoscope.

This will be the planet that occupies its own domicile. Should there be several planets thus situated, the most powerful will be the most positive, or that which occupies an Angular House, and in the following order of dignity: The First, the Tenth, the Seventh, the Fourth House.

If there is no planet in its own domicile, the most powerful will be the one which is in the sign of its exaltation.

2. Find the weakest planet.

This will be the planet which is in exile or in its fall. When several planets are thus placed, the most unfortunate will be the most malefic, and that which occupies the Sixth, Twelfth or Eighth House.

3. Find the Ruler of Life (hyleg).

For this we must carefully study the position of the Sun and its aspects, as it is the Sun which, together with the Moon, gives Life to everything that exists.

It is all the more powerful when it is oriental; i.e., when it occupies one of the signs situated between Leo and Capricorn and is in one of the following Houses: First, Tenth, Eleventh, Seventh or Ninth.

If the Sun is weak and unfavourably placed in the chart, the Moon must be taken as Hyleg. It will be all the more powerful if it occupies one of the signs included between Aquarius and Cancer.

4. Find the Ruler of Death.

Several significators may be taken:

(*a*) The Ruler of the Eighth House;

(*b*) The planets occupying the Eighth House ;

(*c*) Any malefic planet that is in conjunction with the benefic Ruler of the Eighth House.

(*d*) Any malefic planet that is in bad aspect with the Cusp of the Eighth House.

A benefic planet may be Ruler of Death, but all things being equal, we may take Mars, Uranus or Saturn.

5. Find the Ruler of the Ascendant.

See the House which it occupies, its aspects with any planets that may be situated in the First House, and study these planets also, and the Houses which they rule. It is evident that a planet which occupies the First House and is Ruler of the Sixth or the Twelfth House will have a marked influence on the native's health.

6. Study the power of the Angles (I., IV., VII., X.)

See their Rulers and the aspects which they receive.

All this will provide a key by which it will be possible to obtain a synthetic idea of the native's Destiny.

It will afterwards be possible to study the chart in its details and to answer any questions which may be of special interest.

Health

(*a*) Study the condition of the Sun and Moon and of the First House, and the aspects which it receives.

(*b*) Study also the Sixth House and its Ruler, and the aspects to the Cusp of this House.

(*c*) See whether Saturn, Mars and Uranus are more elevated than the Sun and Moon. Should this be the case, health will not be as good as if these planets had been placed below the luminaries.

(*d*) A malefic planet on the Cusp of the Sixth House or of the Twelfth always signifies some physical imperfection corresponding to the sign occupied by that House.

Marriage

In order to make a sound judgment regarding a marriage that should take place, it would be necessary to study the horoscopes of the future couple to ascertain whether the significators of marriage in the woman's chart are in good aspect with the marriage significators in the man's horoscope.

The marriage significators for a man are :

Venus (the wife), Moon (the Mother) ;

The seventh House and the planets situated therein.

The marriage significators for a woman are:

Mars (the husband), Sun (the Father);

The Seventh House and the planets which it occupies.

In both cases, for a man as well as for a woman, it is necessary to pay special attention to the Ruler of the Seventh House.

If the significators are in good aspect with one another, with the Cusps of the First House, of the Fifth House (Children), of the Eleventh House (Friends), and of the Fourth House (the Home), the marriage has every chance of being happy.

It is well to judge the importance of the aspects of Jupiter.

When the marriage significators are more elevated than the Sun, they presage a premature marriage, or marriage with some one younger than the consultant. When the marriage significators are situated below the Sun, or in the Second, Third, Eighth or Ninth House, marriage takes place after the thirtieth year, or with some one older than the consultant.

The Lord of the Seventh House, and the planets situated therein, describe fairly accurately the character, health and temperament of the marriage partner.

As we have already said, the husband is represented by the Sun, the wife by the Moon; therefore the benefic or malefic aspects received by the two luminaries will also help to describe them.

The Sun for a woman, and the Moon for a man, in double signs (Gemini, Pisces and the first 15 degrees of Sagittarius), applying to one or more planets before the end of a sign, indicate more than one union. Divorce is likely if Uranus or Saturn in the Seventh House is in bad aspect with the luminary that signifies marriage.

Children

The fruitful signs are Cancer, Scorpio and Pisces; the barren signs are Gemini, Leo and Virgo.

The significators of children are:

(*a*) The fruitful planets: Moon, Venus, Jupiter;

(*b*) The Fifth House, and its opposite, the Eleventh House.

There will certainly be children if:

A fruitful planet occupies the Fifth House, or is Ruler of the Fifth; or, if the Cusp of the Fifth, in a fruitful sign, receives a good aspect from a fruitful planet.

Saturn kills children; Uranus, Mars and Sun are not favourable to them, so that the malefic aspects of these planets to the significators of children are dangerous. The same applies when a barren planet is powerfully situated in the Fifth House.

Parents and Relatives

The Father: Sun and Fourth House;

The Mother: Moon and Tenth House;

Brothers and sisters: the Third House, Mars for the brothers, and Venus for the sisters.

The Rulers of the Fourth, Tenth and Third House will also have to be studied, with the aspects which they may send to the Cusps of these Houses, or to the planets which signify the parents and relatives.

Subordinates

The significators of subordinates are:

(*a*) Mercury;

(*b*) The Sixth House and its Ruler, and the planets occupying that House. Mars indicates the male employees and Venus the female employees.

(*c*) The Aspects received by the Cusp of the Ascendant, of the Tenth House, and also of the Second House.

The Seventh House must also receive attention, as it concerns lawsuits. Also the Third House (those around the consultant) and the Eleventh House (friendship and loyalty).

Friends

The significators of Friends are first of all Jupiter and Venus; next, the planets occupying or ruling the Eleventh House.

Also note the aspects of the planets involved to the Cusps of the Fifth, Tenth and Second House.

Money and Position

There are several significators of Wealth, so that if the horoscope as a whole is fortunate, this matter will be satisfactory for the Consultant. It may be quickly judged by:

(*a*) The Second House: acquired wealth;

(*b*) The Fourth House: inherited wealth;

(*c*) The Tenth House: honours and worldly position.

In regard to acquired wealth, study the Second House, its ruler and any planets that may be situated therein; also the Part of Fortune, and the aspects, position and influence of Jupiter, which is the great dispenser of possessions.

For inherited wealth, study the Fourth House and its Ruler; also Saturn and the position which it occupies in the chart. Neither should it be forgotten that the Sun represents the Father and the Moon the Mother.

Jupiter must also be considered as, without help from this planet, there is no possibility of money.

In regard to honours, in addition to the Tenth House and its Ruler, note also the planets that may be situated in this House, the aspects to its Cusp, the position and influence of Jupiter; and, last and most important, the Sun, which governs honours. The position of the luminary will be most favourable if it is close to the Cusp of the Ascendant or of the Tenth House.

It is evident that in regard to wealth, everything must be taken into consideration, and the possibilities of success in life will be all the greater if the mental faculties are brilliant, while the consultant's moral character will also need to be carefully studied.

In this respect, the Moon gives imagination and Mercury reasoning powers, so that these two planets must be studied, as well as the First House, the Third House (education) and the Ninth House (mind, knowledge).

The profession or employment is shown by the planet governing the First House and the Tenth House, as well as the planets that may be situated in these Houses.

Journeys

The significators of travel are:

(*a*) Mercury and the Moon;

(*b*) The Third House (short journeys) and the Ninth House (long journeys).

(*c*) The Cardinal signs (Aries, Cancer, Libra and Capricorn).